T0316390

Dialectics of 9/11 and the War on Terror
Educational Responses

"In the post-9/11 United States, classrooms have too often become spaces of paranoia and hostility against Muslim American youth. This powerful book proposes an original dialectical pedagogy that can work past misrepresentations and caricatures in curriculum and the media to include the voices of students. Elbih grounds her urgent practical recommendations for educators in her own empirical investigation, as well as in a crucial political and historical contextualization of Islamophobia that has been missing until now in the field of education. Theoretically astute and comprehensively researched, *Dialectics of 9/11 and the War on Terror* is necessary reading for all teachers, scholars, and cultural workers committed to supporting Muslim American students in these difficult times."

—*Noah De Lissovoy, Associate Professor of Cultural Studies in Education, University of Texas at Austin*

"This book provides timely qualitative research on how the impact of 9/11 and the ongoing 'War on Terror' has affected schooling in America. This is a thorough and engaging study of the dialectics produced by the circumstances following the 9/11 tragedy through the narratives of stakeholders—students and teachers—as well as through examining curricular bias. This is a much-needed educational intervention that will help raise awareness of the educational stakes involved in countering Islamophobia in times of war and terror."

—*Jasmin Zine, Professor of Sociology, Wilfrid Laurier University*

"In a time of growing global White Supremacy and mounting hostility against Muslims and other minorities, it is crucial to rethink Paulo Freire's emancipatory pedagogy. This book builds on *Pedagogy of the Oppressed* and introduces an original dialectical framework to help teachers unlock the secrets behind the damaging dialectic and improve their curriculum and instruction of 9/11, the War on Terror, and Muslims. The book is easy to read and will engage teachers, scholars, and curriculum developers in an empirical and intellectual journey."

—*Ricky Lee Allen, Associate Professor of Language, Literacy & Sociocultural Studies, University of New Mexico*

Dialectics of 9/11 and the War on Terror

Studies in Criticality

Shirley R. Steinberg
General Editor

Vol. 360

The Counterpoints series is part of the Peter Lang Education list.
Every volume is peer reviewed and meets
the highest quality standards for content and production.

PETER LANG
New York • Bern • Frankfurt • Berlin
Brussels • Vienna • Oxford • Warsaw

Randa Elbih

Dialectics of 9/11 and the War on Terror

Educational Responses

PETER LANG
New York • Bern • Frankfurt • Berlin
Brussels • Vienna • Oxford • Warsaw

Library of Congress Cataloging-in-Publication Data

Name: Elbih, Randa, author.
Title: Dialectics of 9/11 and the war on terror: educational responses / Randa Elbih.
Description: New York: Peter Lang, 2018.
Series: Counterpoints; v. 360 | ISSN 1058-1634
Includes bibliographical references and index.
Identifiers: LCCN 2015047994 | ISBN 978-1-4331-4865-1 (hardcover: alk. paper)
ISBN 978-1-4331-3105-9 (pbk.: alk. paper) | ISBN 978-1-4539-1810-4 (ebook pdf)
ISBN 978-1-4331-4863-7 (epub) | ISBN 978-1-4331-4864-4 (mobi)
Subjects: LCSH: Educational sociology—United States.
Social sciences—Study and teaching—United States. | Muslim students—
United States. | September 11 Terrorist Attacks, 2001—Influence.
Classification: LCC LC191.4.E53 | DDC 306.430973—dc23
LC record available at http://lccn.loc.gov/2015047994
DOI 10.3726/978-1-4539-1810-4

Bibliographic information published by **Die Deutsche Nationalbibliothek**.
Die Deutsche Nationalbibliothek lists this publication in the "Deutsche
Nationalbibliografie"; detailed bibliographic data are available
on the Internet at http://dnb.d-nb.de/.

The paper in this book meets the guidelines for permanence and durability
of the Committee on Production Guidelines for Book Longevity
of the Council of Library Resources.

© 2018 Peter Lang Publishing, Inc., New York
29 Broadway, 18th floor, New York, NY 10006
www.peterlang.com

Printed in the United States of America

For all the teachers, curriculum developers, and critical pedagogues who work hard to support critical thinking, social justice, and democracy.

Authentic thinking that is concerned about reality and derives meaning and generates action upon the world takes place only with true communication.

—Paulo Freire, *Pedagogy of The Oppressed*, 1970

TABLE OF CONTENTS

PREFACE

When I first moved from Egypt to the United States to pursue my graduate work, it was in a post-9/11 world. As a Muslim woman who wore hijab, I could not believe the way people treated me, and treated others who shared a similar physical profile. I began my career as an Art and Math middle school teacher, but quickly saw a need for more discussion on the treatment of 9/11 in the classroom, and for more awareness of the psychological and emotional impact of how 9/11 is taught on Muslim and Arab American students. I decided to pursue a doctoral degree unraveling why and how these misperceptions about Muslims grow, and what I, as a teacher, could do about them.

Most scholarly research on the implications of the War on Terror in school environments has centered upon the experience of Muslim American youth. My contribution to this field is a greater understanding of the role and experience of the educator, addressing specifically what teachers can do to improve their pedagogy and curriculum in regards to current events such as 9/11 and the War on Terror, as well as how they teach and talk about Islam. I saw a need for greater investigation of the connection between neoliberalism, terrorism, and education as it impacts textbooks, students, and teachers.

Unique about my research and this book is the triangulation of empirical data collected from teachers, students, and textbooks. This triangulation not only provides authenticity to the data and my interpretations, but also provides multiple perspectives to fully hone in on the question. By exploring these resources side by side, the reader will be able to connect the pieces of seemingly isolated events and people, and will achieve a holistic understanding of the War on Terror and its educational implications.

My research demonstrates the importance of rebuilding teachers' social studies curriculum to educate students (and teachers) about who Muslims are, and to create greater nuance and depth in the understanding of the War on Terror. This is critical for the personal and professional development of Muslim Americans in the classroom, as well as instrumental in fostering critical thinking and empathy among all students. It is only through better education that we can combat cultural stereotypes and strengthen democratic values.

The book investigates the following questions: How do American teachers teach about current events such as 9/11 and the War on Terror? To what extent are teachers' pedagogies, curriculum, and resources influenced by the current political context? What is the effect of this pedagogy and curriculum on Muslim American students? How can teachers prevent racism and xenophobia from spreading from the television into their classrooms and beyond? To answer these questions, I gathered empirical data through research conducted in 2010 and 2011 in Albuquerque, New Mexico. Specifically, I interviewed nine Muslim American students and five high school teachers about their experiences discussing current events such as 9/11 and the War on Terror within the school system. I also conducted textual analysis of seven high school social studies textbooks commonly used in New Mexico. More details on the methods are presented in Chapters 3, 4, and 5, including how and where I conducted the study, how I selected the students and teachers interviewed, which textbooks I selected for analysis and why, and how I evaluated the data I collected.

Ultimately, my goals with this book are simple. I want to demonstrate that it is both urgent and possible for teachers to teach against oppression. One of the great injustices of our time is the way that innocent Muslims, especially those in high school, are pegged as dangerous and undesirable "others." The psychological scars of this kind of isolation and disrespect are severe for them, yet also damaging for others who are taught that treating others in this manner is acceptable. In order to develop true democratic ideals of liberty and justice for all, we must re-evaluate how we teachers teach about current events, especially as they relate to 9/11 and the War on Terror.

ACKNOWLEDGMENTS

It takes a lot of time and effort to write a book. This project would not have been possible without the many individuals and institutions that helped me along the way. This project grew out of my previous work at the University of New Mexico (UNM) and was made possible by the generous funding I received from Helen and Wilson Howard Ivins.

A special thanks goes out to Jasmin Zine. She is a great mentor and was the first person to encourage me to consider publishing my research, and for this, and her friendship, I am eternally grateful. I would also like to thank Rickey Lee Allen who first introduced me to critical pedagogy, Ruth Galvan Trinidad for carefully reading earlier writings of the material, and to Glenabah Martinez, Diane Torres-Velasquez, and my friend Daniel Sanford who provided insightful comments and resources that helped the project in its earlier stages.

My sincere gratitude goes to the Edit Prose team and especially my editor, Kathryn Curtis, for her patient support and valuable feedback that made this book shine. Also, many thanks to Jeannie Ballew, Senior Editor at Edit Prose, for her constructive comments along the way. I am also so pleased to showcase this book with such a highly regarded publishing company, Peter Lang, and a distinguished scholar and series editor, Shirley R. Steinberg. I am grateful to Jennifer Beszley (Production Editor), Sarah Bode (Acquisitions Editor), and

Sara McBride (Editorial Assistant) at Peter Lang for guiding the manuscript through the production process.

I'd also like to extend my appreciation to University of Saint Joseph, Connecticut (USJ), where I continue to hone my teaching on these critical issues. Watching my students grow is such a blessing, and I am forever grateful to USJ's commitment to social justice.

To my husband, Wesley Mueller; my daughters, Nour Osman & Maryam Mueller, and step-son, Dietrich Mueller: thank you for your support and understanding through my project. I could not have finished this without you by my side. Many thanks to my parents, Nabil Elbih, and Omneia Seoudi and my aunt, Ebtisam Wilkins for their continuous support and celebration of my accomplishments.

To Paulo Freire, a man I would have liked to meet, and to all critical pedagogues' including Henry Giroux, Peter McLaren, Michael Apple, Noah DeLissovoy, Joe L. Kincheloe, and Shirley R. Steinberg. Your intellectual frameworks for critical pedagogy have helped shape the ideas of this book. Thank you all for your efforts towards developing a pedagogy that is intelligent and just.

Finally, I am indebted to the teachers and Muslim students who participated in this study, despite the challenges and pressures they faced. Their stories and experiences are the driving force behind this book.

· 1 ·

UNCOVERING THE LOPSIDED DIALECTIC OF 9/11 AND THE WAR ON TERROR

September 11, 2001 shocked the United States to its very core. New York City, a historic beacon of safety and an emblem for America's grit and strength, was brought to her knees when two errant planes crashed into the Twin Towers. In the hours, days, and months that followed, the country struggled to make sense of what had happened and how to prevent it from ever happening again. However, in the wake of these horrific atrocities, the United States sacrificed the unalienable rights of her people out of fear. Espionage, torture, and discrimination against Muslim- and Arab-American citizens have left lasting effects on our media, culture, and school system. In a day and age where there are now videos games with the specific goal to kill all Muslims, it is unsurprising that most Muslim- and Arab-American high school students face daily harassment and a heightened incidence of suicide.

Statistics show increasing discrimination against Muslims at American schools, resulting in greater emotional and psychological stress. For instance, a 2014 Council on American–Islamic Relations (CAIR) study found that among the 621 Muslim students surveyed between the ages of 11 and 18 in California public schools, 55% reported being bullied. Because of this, it is probably unsurprising that around 83% do not feel safe enough in school to reveal their Muslim identity. Some students even reported receiving death threats, and almost one in five students experienced discrimination by a school staff member. All these factors combined lead to emotional and psychological stress among students. In worst-case scenarios, it might even lead to suicide. Focus News reports that the rate of Muslims committing suicide in Orange County and Los Angeles alone between 2006 and 2008 was 15.5 times higher than the rate in the previous ten years (Mogahed, 2009). Indeed, discrimination leads to emotional and psychological stresses among Muslim youth that have dire consequences including suicide.

These discriminatory acts are not limited to schools but extend out into society. Muslims are surrounded by offensive messages everywhere they go; on the street, at work, at the airport, and even at their places of worship. Here are just a few recent examples. In 2015, a Muslim woman, Darlene Hider, was yelled at for wearing her hijab on board a Delta Air Lines flight. The woman who harassed her yelled, "This is America!" Hider complained that Delta staff failed to defend her (Kuruvilla, 2015). Additionally, according to the federal Equal Employment Opportunity Commission, Muslims filing complaints related to work discrimination have increased up nearly 60% from 2005 till 2009. In 2009 alone, Muslim workers filed 803 claims—445 of which were due to discharge, 291 due to harassment, and 185 were about terms and conditions of work (Greenhouse, 2010). One of the complaints mentioned in a New York Times article was by a Pakistani immigrant called Mohammad Kaleemuddin who worked for a construction company in Houston and got discharged after he complained about his supervisor and co-workers called him "Osama, al Qaeda, Taliban, and terrorist" (Greenhouse, 2010, para. 14). Hate crimes against Muslims specifically increased after the San Bernardino, California shooting by a Muslim couple that killed 14 people and injured 21 on December 2, 2015. During the same month following the events, 63 incidents of vandalism at mosques across the United States occurred, which tripled the number of incidents of 2014. Even congressman, Rep. André Carson, D-Indiana, received a death threat for being Muslim (Burke, 2015). These are only a few examples that expose a heightened discrimination against Muslims post 9/11.

But this discrimination is not limited to Muslims. The anti-Muslim fervor is so strong and so vitriolic that it extends to those who resemble them. For example, many studies show that Sikh students experience discrimination because they wear turbans and therefore are mistakenly perceived to be Muslims. A 2014 survey by the Sikh Coalition shows that 56% of Sikh students experience bullying and harassments, tied to the misperception of their peers. Often even Hindus are misperceived as Muslims and mistreated because of it. For instance, Bernie Sanders, the Democratic Party Presidential candidate, misperceived a Hindu man for a Muslim during MSNBC's town hall on March 15, 2016 (Gabbay, 2016). Even Christian Arabs are often conflated with Muslims, and the consequences are grave. In August 2016, a Christian Arab in Oklahoma was murdered based on the assumption that he was a Muslim (CBN, 2016). Frequently, individuals who stereotypically resemble Muslims face discriminatory consequences.

Confusing Muslims, Hindus, and Sikhs, as well as blaming an entire population for the actions of a few, points to a significant problem—ignorance. Most of the surveyed students in the Council on American–Islamic Relations (CAIR) study complained that their teachers failed to provide proper instruction about 9/11, and failed to address harassment against Muslim students by their peers. In the 2014 study of the Sikhs Coalition, 43% of participants believed that teachers and school administrations did not handle incidents of discrimination effectively. Is the reason ignorance, willful miseducation, or both? When all Muslims, Arabs, Sikhs, or Hindus are considered guilty by association for terroristic acts they did not commit, it is worth asking why and how these stereotypes—and their horrific consequences—exist?

It is not fair, of course, to blame the ills of society on only one of its sectors. That is not the aim of this book. However, it is worth understanding how certain sectors of society—such as education—may be complicit in perpetuating misunderstanding, and indirectly condoning violence against a denigrated people. For, truth be told, within the school system many students are not free to speak against these discriminatory narratives about Muslims. Students are often boxed in by an educational system that already provides all the "correct" answers for them. These answers so often foment the culture-clash mentality, with little encouragement for students to dig beneath the surface.

America's reaction to the tragedy of 9/11 stigmatized all Muslims and Arabs, and any who resemble the newly constructed image of the hateful terrorist are guilty by association. The attention turned to Muslims and Arabs by media, textbooks, and the culture, in general, is responsible for constructing an environment wherein Muslim American students become undesirable and dangerous others. What is the role of the teacher in all of this?

Educators must understand the damaging impact certain narratives have on youth. These young people are American citizens, rejected by the society in which they legally belong. As a growing population of America's future, teachers must understand what has been done to them, in order to prevent this unfair treatment from continuing in perpetuity. Teachers must learn to recognize the permeability between school and society so that instead of becoming tools of an unjust system, they can speak back to the one-sided perspective. This biased view creates a lopsided dialectic about Muslims, 9/11, and the War on Terror. It is this uneven dialogue that makes it easy to hate Muslims. As a teacher, it is critical to not only help students learn spelling and arithmetic but also to provide them the tools they will actually need to live their lives as global citizens. Teachers must consider how the rampant hatred of Muslims might impact their students, and how their students might then affect society.

The book suggests that ignorance and miseducation are as a result of a lopsided dialectic about 9/11 and the War on Terror in the media, textbooks, and society. If we consider a whole dialectic a sphere, a lopsided one is one with missing parts. The unbalanced discussion is one in which patriotism and militarism are exaggerated, and discussions of imperialism and Muslims sufferings are swept under the rug. The result of this uneven discourse is ignorance, intolerance, and discrimination. The problem is that this unidimensional conversation is contagious and affects Americans at educational institutions and in society in a complementary manner. The book examines how the crooked analysis is sustained and spread by a covert global financial and socio-political system that exists beyond the school borders yet controls and shapes teachers' pedagogies, school and society. The book chapters unlock the secrets behind the lopsided dialectic one after the other in sequence. By the time the reader reaches Chapter 8, they will understand the severity of the problem, and be ready for the solutions.

Chapter 2 will focus on the problem, which is the influence of the lopsided dialectic on teachers' pedagogies, leading to uncritical education. Specifically, the chapter begins by unpacking the modern history of the philosophy of education and the influence of the sociocultural and economic context on the role of schools and curriculum. Then the chapter takes a deep dive into critical pedagogy theory. Chapter 3 introduces the reader to the five teachers interviewed, illuminating the themes that arose from how they describe their pedagogical methods for teaching about the War on Terror. I also invite the reader to reflect on and evaluate the ability of the teachers to teach in a critical way and combat the skewed and pervasive perspective about 9/11 and the War on Terror. Chapter 4 discusses the results of this disproportionate dialectic—social and psychological trauma experienced by Muslim American youth. I listened to the stories of Muslim students in regards to their educational and social experiences, weaving together their responses in sub-categories that represent common themes that arose from the interview sessions. Chapter 5 presents one of the main causes of the problem—uncritical textbooks and curriculum in general. I walk the reader through a journey of analysis that shows the role of textbooks in universalizing and normalizing a lopsided discourse. Through analyzing how the War on Terror and other themes in seven social studies textbooks currently in use are represented, it is clear to see the level of thinking that it likely triggers among students. In Chapter 6, I discuss another cause of the problem which is the role of public pedagogy on the reproduction of Islamaphobia in the culture, politics, and media and its impact on instruction and teacher–student interactions. Chapter 7, brings to the attention of the reader what Islamophobia hides from us—neoliberal imperialism. The chapter highlights the role of terrorism in neoliberal imperialism and demonstrates the impact of neoliberal policies on education and democracy. Chapter 8 suggests that the solution lies in what I call "Critical Dialectical Pedagogy," or CDP. As a former teacher myself, I understand that it is a labor of love to run an effective classroom and that there are never enough hours in the day. Because of this, Chapter 9 provides a launching pad for lesson plans, resources, and discussion points for teachers to use in their classrooms. In Chapter 10, I suggest the next steps for CDP, critical pedagogy, and the future of democracy. Finally, Chapter 11 puts the puzzle pieces together and demonstrates to the reader how all the factors explained in each chapter contribute to the uneven discussion of current events such as 9/11 and the War on Terror.

Deeply rooted in critical pedagogy theory, the book is easy-to-read and directed towards teachers, scholars, and curriculum developers. The book includes actionable suggestions for teaching these topics in ways to diversify the dialectics of 9/11 and the War on Terror, and help educators self-reflect to improve their methodologies. The ultimate goal of the book is to grow Critical Dialectical Pedagogy (CDP), a new introduction to the field, to nurture the future of America's democracy.

Critical pedagogues have expressed their concerns about the role of uncritical education in the downfall of a democratic society. I join their efforts by writing this book. The hope is to empirically demonstrate the urgency for changing the way teachers perceive and educate about current events such as 9/11 and the War on Terror into a critical dialectical approach. It is so important for teachers to develop their critical dialectical pedagogy skills so that they can rectify the irregular dialectic of these current events to change society for the better. Imagine if all teachers take up the call to action of this book—I truly believe we would see the beginnings of a rational and accepting environment, the backbone of a true democracy. By reading this book, know that you are taking a step towards social liberation.

References

Burke, D. (2015, December 11). Threats, harassment, vandalism at mosques reach record high. *CNN*. Retrieved September 14, 2016 from http://www.nytimes.com/2010/09/24/business/24muslim.html?pagewanted=all&_r=0

Christian Arab murdered in Oklahoma after mistaken as Muslim. (2016, August 24). *CBN News: The Christian Perspective*. Retrieved September 20, 2016 from http://www1.cbn.com/cbnnews/cwn/2016/august/christian-arab-murdered-in-oklahoma-after-mistaken-as-muslim

Gabbay, T. (2016, March 15). They all look the same: Bernie mistakes Hindu man for Muslim. *Truth Revolt*. Retrieved September 14, 2016 from http://www.truthrevolt.org/news/they-all-look-same-bernie-mistakes-hindu-man-muslim

Go Home Terrorist: A report on bulling against Sikh American school children. (2014). *The Sikh Coalition*. Retrieved September 14, 2016 from http://www.sikhcoalition.org/documents/pdf/go-home-terrorist.pdf

Greenhouse, S. (2010, September 23). Muslims report rising discrimination at work. *The New York Times*. Retrieved September 14, 2016 from http://www.nytimes.com/2010/09/24/business/24muslim.html?pagewanted=all&_r=2

Kuruvilla, C. (2015, February 5). Muslim mom to woman who harassed her on a delta flight: I forgive you. *The Huffington Post*. Retrieved September 14, 2016 from http://www.huffingtonpost.com/2015/02/05/muslim-woman-hijab-delta_n_6616806.html

Mislabeled: The impact of school bullying and discrimination on California Muslim students. (2014). *CAIR California*. Retrieved September 14, 2016 from https://ca.cair.com/sfba/wp-content/uploads/2015/10/CAIR-CA-2015-Bullying-Report-Web.pdf

Mogahed, Y. (2009, April 1). Suicidal thoughts: Suicide rate among Southern Calif. Muslims increases. *InFocus News*. Retrieved September 14, 2016 from http://muslimobserver.com/suicidal-thoughts-suicide-rate-among-southern-calif-muslims-increases-2/

· 2 ·

HOW TEACHING CAN CHANGE THE WORLD?

Teachers can change the world. Not only can teachers change it, they also must. These are the images and experiences American students are steeped in: a Muslim woman set on fire in the streets of New York for wearing the *hijab*, an elderly man spat on for praying in public, insults hurled at a 5 year old Muslim girl that she barely understands in her school's play-ground. These images and experiences are a reality, and they are unacceptable. But in order for them to stop, teachers must work to educate their students about the urgency of change, and give their students the skills and abilities necessary to make those changes themselves.

Many teachers shy away, however, from teaching about these controversial topics. It is understandable and unsurprising why. For one, there are many unanswered questions about 9/11 and the War on Terror. What is terrorism? Who are terrorists? Why did these attacks happen, and when will the wars come to an end? But besides the general confusion about the topic there are other concerns for teachers. Namely, should I be fearful because of any backlash if I teach critically about the topic?

Despite the challenges, teaching about 9/11 and the War on Terror is crucial because of the events' historical significance and the emergence of consequential social and political policies that influence students' lives. The War on Terror and 9/11 resulted in social and political policies that affect life, in and out of the school, on a daily basis. Some of these policies take away freedoms in travel, immigration, and privacy, among others. Therefore, it is only logical that teachers would address the topics in the classroom so that students would be able to make sense of the contemporary social and political context.

In addition, many scholars strongly suggest discussing controversial issues such as 9/11 and the War on Terror in the classroom because they often lead to enhancing learners' critical skills and democratic values. Still, only a few students get this chance, and even those who do are likely to receive an education that is lopsided. Power structures that exist beyond the school gates influence the purpose and role of schools and hence, dictate what is to be taught as true in the curriculum. Exposing students to the controversial nature of 9/11 and the War on Terror, as well as unraveling how a few elites may be benefiting from the sustained military action abroad and systematic discrimination domestically, will help students decide for themselves what to believe, and how to act based on their opinions.

The best method for teaching against the discriminatory and violent rhetoric, personal experiences, and public policies now leveraged against Muslims in the U.S. and abroad is a philosophy of education that seeks to develop true critical thinking skills among pupils. But before delving into the potential remedies, it is important to understand what is at stake and how urgent the situation currently is.

How 9/11 Changed the United States

Imagine how much the events of 9/11 and the War on Terror remarkably changed and continue to shape society in the United States. September 11 and the War on Terror affected how society experiences transportation, immigration, and religion, among many other things. For example, the Aviation and Transportation Security Act, put into effect on November 19, 2001, transferred the responsibility of airport check-in security from airport authorities and commercial airlines to the federal government. Although the Act was issued to ensure safety of passengers, many experience these security checks as a long, arduous and frustrating process. For individuals of Arabic or Muslim heritage, there may be additional experiences of ethnic profiling. Another example of how 9/11 and the War on Terror has changed the United States is through a revision and tightening in the immigration process. Often this can lead to the separating and isolating of family members, between American citizens and their relatives who are from elsewhere, especially if that elsewhere happens to be in a predominantly Muslim country. Finally, the way Muslims are perceived and portrayed has changed drastically since 9/11. Often images of terrorists are mapped onto how we see Muslims and Arabs in general. This leads to a significant amount of, as it has euphemistically been called, "collateral damage," or accidental citizen casualties, among Afghanis and Iraqis. However, another collateral impact is how this fearful perspective has corroded and perverted core American values of human rights and justice. For example, the Senate Intelligence Committee's report on the CIA's torture of terrorist suspects demonstrated a high level of incompetency and disregard of Muslim and Arab life among high-level government officials (Collinson & Perez, 2014). This disrespect is also systematically applied to Muslim and Arab American citizens through controversial public policies such as the Patriot Act. Perhaps most disturbing, however, is that negative images of Islam and the Arab world coupled with ignorance reinforces this disrespect within the American public school system among impressionable youth. Teaching about 9/11 and the War on Terror, however, can provide some answers and insight for students struggling to understand the social and political context in which they live.

Why It Is Challenging to Teach About 9/11—And Why You Should Do It Anyway

There are many reasons why teaching about 9/11 is a significant challenge for educators. Diana Hess, dean of the University of Wisconsin-Madison School of Education, and Jeremy Stoddard, associate professor of education at William & Mary who have published extensively since 2003 on the representation of 9/11 in textbooks and state standards argued that, 9/11 "is not behind us" like other historical events and therefore schools struggle "to teach 'what happened' when so little time has passed that this information is still unclear relative to many events routinely taught as settled stories in history classes" (Hess, Stoddard, & Murto, 2008, p. 193). Many teachers struggle with questions such as: Who are the perpetrators of 9/11? Why did the terrorists attack the World Trade Center? Why has the government decided to attack Iraq and Afghanistan? Why is there a discussion about attacking Saudi Arabia now 15 years after the attack? One of the major challenges for teachers, clearly, is how confusing and nebulous the facts are.

Additional complications for teaching about 9/11 stem from the impact of the event on public policy and public life. The "powerful differences of opinion about the wisdom of many of the policies enacted immediately after 9/11 (such as the Patriot Act) and about what policies are necessary now" leads to controversy inside and outside the classroom (Hess et al., 2008, p. 193). Teachers may feel hesitant to bring these issues up, because they do not want to influence or appear as though they are indoctrinating their students, and may believe that they will somehow do so if they encourage discussion or evaluation of these issues (Wilson, Haas, Laughlin, & Sunal, 2002). But the decision to avoid these topics is often not a personal decision on behalf of the teacher. As "many social studies teachers neglect teaching controversial issues through discussion and interaction because of school and district policy" (Byford, Lennon, & Russell, 2009, p. 166). In their study of high school teachers' teaching of controversial issues, Byford et al. (2009) reported that "93% of the [teacher] respondents felt the need to protect themselves from administration" (p. 166). The overall sources of concern for teachers involved in this particular study were summarized as "student-related disruptions and conflict, as well as controversies that could implicate or be detrimental to a teacher and his or her career" (Byford et al., 2009, p. 169). It may come as no surprise that when selecting current events to teach in the classroom, teachers tend to choose events "which are not ideological and away from violence" (Deveci, 2007, p. 448). The controversial nature of the topics, in addition to the confusing nature of the subject matter, might make teachers hesitate to instruct the topics of 9/11 and the War on Terror.

Despite these challenges it cannot be stressed enough that it is urgent for teachers to teach critically about these topics. Both liberal and conservatives agree on the importance of teaching the topics. As Chester Finn of the conservative Thomas B. Fordham Foundation (2002) puts it, "it's right to teach about September 11th because it was one of the defining events of our age, of our nation's history and of these children's lives" (p. 4). Levesque (2003) reported that students "want and urgently need—to know more about the history (causes, development, changes) and politics of terrorism" (p. 192). Similarly, Kuthe (2011) stated that among the reasons why he personally teaches about 9/11 and its aftermath is that: "the post–9/11 world is the only one that [students] know" and teaching about it allows students to see those events as "a shift in our collective history" (p. 160). Hess (2009) believed that teaching students *how* to engage in political discussions can help resolve the lack of talk about controversial political issues within society. Though, one could argue there is already plenty of talk; what is actually missing is effective discussion. For Muslims, it is urgent to teach about 9/11 and the War on Terror so that they and their non-Muslim peers understand where current Islamophobic sentiment comes from. Teaching about 9/11 and its aftermath can strengthen students' ability to understand the social and political world around them within a historical context.

In addition to feeding students' eagerness to learn about 9/11 and the War on Terror, many scholars claim that students acquire democratic skills when teachers teach about controversial current events. For instance, Merryfield and Wilson (2005) emphasized that "our students' future depends on their ability to understand current issues, raise the right questions about problems, and find solutions ... the discussion of such issues, including those that are controversial, in the classroom engages young people in subjects that will frame the world they live in" (p. 414). Likewise, Graseck (2008) supported this view saying "if our students are to become competent analysts of world affairs and problem solvers tomorrow, we must engage them in informed deliberation on the uncertainties of history and the challenges of the present" (p. 371). When students share differing viewpoints, it prepares them for the realities of civic and democratic engagement (Hess, 2009). Hess (2009) explained that "participating in political discussion can have two powerful effects: it makes people more politically tolerant and it causes them to learn more about important issues" (p. 12). Learning about current events related to 9/11 and the War on Terror often leads to students gaining skills such as critical thinking, analysis, and problem solving abilities and prepares them to engage in a democratic society.

Why So Few Students Study Controversial Current Events

Unfortunately, despite the obvious benefits of studying controversial current events such as 9/11 and the War on Terror in a formal way, few students get the chance to do so. Or, if they do, the story they hear may be somewhat warped. Why? As mentioned previously, many teachers feel pressured by school administrations, parents, and students themselves to not teach certain controversial topics, or to teach these topics in a certain way. But these pressures exist because of much larger forces. Much of it has to do with the significant connection between school and society. There are many different forces of power at play within society, and the push and pull of those forces of power are evident within schools. Indeed, the late Joe Lyons Kincheloe, professor, and research chair at the Faculty of Education, McGill University in Montreal, Quebec, Canada and Shirley Steinberg, professor of critical pedagogy and cultural studies at University of Calgary, described schools as "contested public spaces shared by diverse forces of power" (2004, p. 2). Few students actually study controversial current events because of the powerful forces that influence the school environment.

Many of those forces of power demand that schools not be places where students critically evaluate current events, and rather spaces where students develop practical skills and abilities that will prepare them to be useful and contributing citizens in the industrial or technological economy. This push and pull between critical thinking and practical skill set has existed for many years and is well-represented through the contrasting views of Franklin Bobbit and John Dewey, two philosophers who both lived in the same era and represent the transition from the industrial period to modernism. For Franklin Bobbit (1918), one of the first Americans to suggest a standardized curriculum, schools were agents of social adaptation to conform students into the status quo, and equip them with professional and scientific knowledge to prepare them to take their role in industry. Conversely, John Dewey (1938), psychologist and leader of the progressive movement in education, considered the school an integral part of community life and a space for social reform. Bobbit believed that curricular work, like work in industry, should focus on maximizing profit and eliminating waste. In Bobbit's model, the teachers were given a curriculum designed by curriculum developers. Dewey recommended teachers themselves develop the curriculum, which in his mind should enhance students' social and psychological well-being through activities that examine existing social problems. In sum, Bobbit thought the aim of schools was to match individuals with the existing social and economic order. According to Dewey, however, the main goal of schools was to help students realize their potential so that they might contribute to the improvement of their communities. Dewey called his model Democratic Education, and Bobbit called his model the Scientific Method in Curriculum-Making. Growing opposition to Bobbit's theories, which influenced schools to become more autocratic and supervisory, gave rise to greater popularity for more democratic methods as espoused by Dewey. However, the push and pull between these two foundational perspectives on the philosophy of education has continued ever since, and these competing ideologies have left their mark on the school system. Perhaps now we are witnessing a rise in the belief that schools should not trouble themselves debating controversial current events, when there are valuable science, technology, engineering, and math (STEM) courses and programs that demand time and attention during the day.

The contrast between Bobbit and Dewey's models demonstrate how schools and school curriculum reflect and serve particular dominant ideologies of any era. As the socio-political context and ideological agendas of the time and place evolve, the aims of schools and curriculums also subsequently change. The influence of society and socio-political goals on the role of schools is evident in the United States' recent history. For example, during the Cold War, James Conant (1959), former president of Harvard, recommended that high schools work together to provide specialized courses to enhance academic advancement of gifted students in order to catch up to the Soviet Union (as cited in Flinders & Thornton, 2013). Seen as directly relevant for national defense, curriculum development projects focusing on Mathematics, Science, and Foreign Languages received remarkable federal and private financial support to transform U.S. school programs to serve national interests (Flinders & Thornton, 2013). In the postmodern era, theorists such as Samuel Bowles and Herbert Gintis made a direct connection between school and the economy in their book *Schooling in Capitalist America* (1976), arguing that the organization of schools mirror the hierarchical organization of the capitalist workforce in its structures, norms, and values. They also argued that schools mirror economic institutions in their ability to select individuals for certain professional roles. In regards to the curriculum about 9/11 and the War on Terror, this, too, is greatly influenced by ideology—socio-political, and economic. Present conservative nationalistic ideologies impede critical instruction about 9/11 and the War on Terror.

Curriculum Influences: Socio-Political Ideologies

One factor which influences the way teachers teach about 9/11 and the War on Terror has to do with dominant socio-political ideologies. For example, Kincheloe and Steinberg (2004) pointed out how the Thomas B. Fordham Foundation and Chester Finn (2002) argued that loyal teachers to America should not instruct about the history of Afghanistan, or Iraq's relationship with the United States, because doing so "blames America" for global wrongdoings. The Fordham Foundation is a conservative research group populated with former officials of the Reagan and Bush Administrations, Chester Finn among them. Kincheloe and Steinberg critiqued this style of naive thinking (which labels the global roots of terrorism as simply evil), as a fear of democracy. Foundations of this sort hold sway in the standard setting and curriculum development of schools across the United States, and are responsible for filtering their particular ideologies through schools through what the novel-ist and critique Raymond Williams originally called the "selective tradition" (1961). Selective tradition is the process by which certain knowledge and ideas are codified in the curriculum and textbook, while other elements of knowledge and ideas are dismissed. Michael Apple, professor of curriculum and instruction and educational policy studies, at the University of Wisconsin–Madison School of Education argued that this selective tradition often serves the interest of the upper class of society, or the dominant socio-political order, often reproducing social and educational inequality (Apple, 2004). Another example of selective tradition would be the treatment of Christopher Colum-bus within the classroom. Even recent textbooks, such as the 2005 edition of *A History of the United States* by Daniel Boorstin, describes Columbus as a hero and ignores the fact that he stole Native land and murdered Native people. This particular school textbook even represents the Natives in negative ways, stating that they had no signs of civilization and referencing their nakedness as an example (Loewen, 2007). The Eurocentric story represents the selec-tive tradition, and the untold story of the Native Americans represents the forsaken indigenous knowledge about the same topic. These sorts of represen-tations legitimize and normalize certain perspectives of history and ways of life, while disregarding diversity of opinion and thought. Lesson plans, text-books, and even modes of teacher behavior become what Apple (2004) called a hegemonic curriculum, which in the American context celebrates Western capitalist modes of thinking and disregards or makes invisible any serious con-sideration of opinions or ways of life that are different. These socio-political factors are evident in the construction of historical curriculum, and they are also evident today, in the construction of curriculum surrounding 9/11 and the War on Terror.

Curriculum Influences: Economic Ideologies

However, socio-political ideologies evident and filtered through the educa-tional system may also serve as a cover for economic ones. For example, the massacre of the Native Americans in the previous example of selective tradi-tion was excused through their lack of civilization, however this served as a cover for the economic pillage of land and resources that was truly the main motive for subduing, and then attempting to eradicate, the natives.

When it comes to the curriculum of the War on Terror and 9/11, eco-nomic ideologies may be just as strong, if not stronger, of an influence on how teachers teach these subjects than the socio-political ideologies. Now the United States and the world has entered a new economic era, one in which schools are especially influenced by what theorists call *neoliberalism*. A founding theorist of critical pedagogy, and the director of the McMaster Centre for Research, Henry Giroux described neoliberalism as an ideology that "construes profit making as the essence of democracy, consuming as the only operable form of citizenship, and upholds the irrational belief that the market cannot only solve all problems but serve as a model for structuring all social relations" (Harper, 2014, para. 3). The War on Terror has actually led to the United States becoming more entrenched in neoliberalism than ever before, and its effect is evident in the classroom.

Today, neoliberalism is the new face of capitalism (Fairclough, 2003). Historically in the United States, people were politically free if they were economically free. For example, only property-owning white males were allowed to cast a vote in the early days of the Republic (Crews, 2007). This excluded those who were economically dependent, such as women, children, and minorities, who were all considered property (Apple, 2006). Many movements emerged to contest this conflation of political freedom with economics. Over time women and minorities earned the right to vote, but the impact and role of economics on whose vote really matters has only grown over time. Now, freedom is often used by political figures and big business owners to describe the benefits of capitalism. Karl Marx, on the other hand, would describe the oppressive results of capitalism, in which a few elites accumulate wealth at the expense of the poor majority (Felluga, 2011). This process was and is accomplished through the creation and reinforcement of distinctions among people based on race, sex, ethnic origin, social class and hierarchical status as well as the support of a repressive state apparatus that operated under the leadership of said elites through ideology, violence and the law. In other words, rule by a small elite class can only function if within the society there are distinctions between more privileged and less privileged individuals. Scapegoating Muslims for their anachronistic culture and religion is another way of pointing to the natives and saying, "We killed them because they were uncivilized," when what is truly meant is, "There was some economic gain in all of this effort."

However, the economic gain to be made now at the expense of Muslim societies abroad and Muslim communities in the United States in a neoliberal world is far greater than the land and resources stolen during capitalism. What separates and distinguishes neoliberalism from capitalism is the preference for less state involvement, according to Keynesian economists. The idea for neoliberalism took root in the 1970s at the Chicago School of Economics. Its advocates supported privatization, government deregulation, and free trade. Reminiscent of Adam Smith's "invisible hand theory," which suggests a hidden power that regulates and stabilizes the market, the idea was that the market and the market alone should regulate itself, thereby leading to the most efficiency and economic growth. Central to the fundamental beliefs of neoliberalism is the use of the term freedom. Milton Friedman, the pulpit-pounding preacher of neoliberalism, famously wrote in his seminal work, *Capitalism and Freedom*, "Underlying most arguments against the free market is a lack of belief in freedom itself" (2002, p. 16). However, even former International Monetary Fund (IMF) and World Bank economist Joseph Stiglitz believed neoliberal policies led to greater economic inequity and sluggish growth (Stiglitz, 2004, para. 15). In fact, Milton Friedman's economic ideologies, when applied for the first time in Chile and Argentina in the 1960s–1980s, could only be enforced down the barrel of a gun. The implementation of these disastrous free-market policies could only be administered through military dictatorships, and ultimately led to the "disappearing," or death, of hundreds of thousands of Chileans and Argentines who fought back. The official stance of the military government in both of these instances was that these individuals were "disappeared" because they were political terrorists. In actuality, these "political terrorists" were teachers, social workers, journalists, and pregnant mothers. They were individuals who did not believe flooding their national market with cheap international goods (predominantly from the U.S.) was a good thing for their country. It was a good thing, however, for the United States and for their military dictator allies, and for a very long time the U.S. stood idly by as hundreds of thousands of people were rounded up and killed for a dubious crime of political terrorism. In a post-capitalistic world, where there are few natural resources and pieces of land for the taking, neoliberalism allows elites to make profits through the forced opening of foreign markets previously closed to them, historically in places like Argentina and Chile, and presently in the Middle East.

While neoliberalism has led to astronomical profits, i.e. immense freedom for some, it has also irrevocably plunged regular people in the United States and many other parts of the world into the most drastic income inequality seen in modern times. The leaders of this process are global elites "who float above national boundaries, laws, regulations, and oversight," and whose ultimate "task is to transform all nation-states into instruments to enrich their wealth and power" (Giroux, 2016, pp. 19–20). As such, "neoliberal societies, in general, exist in a perpetual state of war—a war waged by the financial and political elites against low-income groups, the elderly, minorities of color, the unemployed, the homeless, immigrants, and any others whom the ruling class considers disposable" (Giroux, 2016, p. 21). Instead of empowering a government that would be beholden to voters, neoliberalist policies empower the private sector, which is beholden to stakeholders and the bottom line. The greater good cannot win over greater profits. The net result is people who are without work and disenfranchised from their governments, along with an overall erosion of democracy.

As mentioned previously, the War on Terror served as an opportunity for neoliberalist policies to take hold in the Middle East, just as they took hold in South America many years ago, and allowed a global elite to benefit immensely while others, including Americans, lost out on countless freedoms. These neoliberal policies in the War on Terror have resulted in immense profits for some, and crushing debt for others, including the U.S. government on the whole. As the first war to be "paid for entirely on credit" (Stiglitz, 2011, para. 4), Stiglitz ties the spike in national unemployment rates and the mounting deficit to the wars on Afghanistan and Iraq, demonstrating how these macroeconomic weaknesses negatively impact American national security. But some made a killing in these wars, and not in terms of lives lost. Naomi Klein, Canadian journalist and author of the international bestseller, *The Shock Doctrine: The Rise of Disaster Capitalism* (2007), explained how the War in Iraq was the most comprehensive and full-scale example of what she called "disaster capitalism." Disaster capitalism leverages natural or man-made crises (of which war or the fear of terrorist attacks would be examples) for sweeping political, social and economic changes. On *The Rachel Maddow Show*, Klein claimed that "crises are handy because you can say 'we have no choice.' You don't have to win the argument anymore. You just have to say the sky is falling" (Maddow, Benen, & Katko, 2011). The goals of disaster capitalism, according to Klein, are to consolidate power and create opportunities for private enterprise under the guise of a crisis situation. September 11 did just that. The horrific event "would take an unpopular president and hand him an opportunity to launch a massive privatization initiative," which led to "the privatization of security, warfare, and reconstruction" (Klein, 2007, p. 174). Defense contractors and debt collectors certainly benefited from the expensive and ongoing War on Terror. In fact, Donald Rumsfeld, the secretary of defense, told the entire Pentagon that he would wage war on bureaucracy (Rumsfeld, 2001). In Klein's words, Rumsfeld believed "that the job of government is not to govern but to subcontract the task to the more efficient and generally superior private sector" (2007, p. 363).

During the 80s and 90s much of the government had already been privatized—water, electricity, highway management, garbage collection. However, the core of government had remained. Now even that core—the military, police, fire departments, prisons, border controls, and even public school systems came under fire. Companies such as Blackwater and Halliburton were written blank checks by the government, which upped defense spending year after year. And this war against terrorism was a new kind of war. According to the initial Department of Homeland Security documents, "Terrorists today can strike at any place, at any time, and with virtually any weapon" (Bush, 2002, p. 8). In other words, we must be prepared for anything and everything. This fear and forced patriotism essentially shrouded the truth that corporations made billions through taxpayer dollars to wage an undefined and potentially unending war (Klein, 2007). Michael Steed, a director of a homeland security firm named Paladin told *Wired* that he had "never seen a sustained deal flow like this" (Ratliff, 2005, para. 21). And the dollars just keep flowing.

The net effect on education of the rise of neoliberalism through the War on Terror was the erosion of public high schools and universities—many of which rely upon federal dollars. Unfortunately for public utilities, such as schools, while defense contractors and debt collectors benefitted, wartime expenses ate away at federal coffers. National debt ballooned from $6 trillion in 2001 to $10 trillion in 2008 as the Bush Administration slashed taxes on the wealthy, and Congress continued to hand the military blank checks. At a Pentagon Press conference on September 18, 2001, Donald H. Rumsfeld, who was at the time Defense Secretary, admitted that the Unite States had "either to change the way we live, which is unacceptable, or to change the way that they live, and we chose the latter." Instead, the expensive idea was to "transform the Middle East and the broader world of Islam generally," according to a May 2004 memo written by chief Pentagon strategist Douglas J. Feith (Bacevich, 2008, para. 9). Unfortunately, this decision would also greatly impact the lived realities of Muslim Americans within the United States, as well as countless other citizens, and students who attended public schools. It would also lead to militarization and forced patriotism within the schools, as well as significantly smaller budgets. According to a 2011 Congressional Budget Report, the total spending on the wars in Iraq and Afghanistan are $921 billion during Bush administration and $857 billion during Obama's adding nearly $1.8 trillion to the already $19 trillion U.S. debt (Amadeo, 2016). Increasing the money spent on defense raises not only the national debt but also Americans' worries about their children's education. Recent years have seen massive reductions in federal money dedicated to education. According to a US News report, Congress has cut federal funding for K-12 education since 2011 by 9.4% (Bidwell, 2015). These reductions mostly hit programs that were geared to assist homeless and minority children including their education and well-being as well as affect teachers' employment (Bidwell, 2015). Wars do benefit corporations financially but hurt Americans.

Therefore, many scholars point to the fact that neoliberalism and the War on Terror worked hand-in-hand to shape educational policies and school culture. Neoliberalism, vis-a-vis the War on Terror, impacted education by using the schools as a legitimizing site for greater repression, militarism, and forced patriotism. The French sociologist and philosopher, Pierre Bourdieu (1998) maintained that schools in general help universalize neoliberal ideology and reproduce subjects who conform to a neoliberal lifestyle. Seeing neoliberalism as "part of a broader project that aims to restore the total control of capital and class power" (2016, p. 18), Giroux argued that neoliberal policies are a "political, economic, and educative project" which "involves changing the way people think" through the use of "a particular brand of ideology, mode of governance, policymaking, and form of public pedagogy" (2016, p. 18). Public pedagogy refers to sources of information beyond the school borders (Giroux, 2004). This public pedagogy can lead to exaggerated individualism, destruction of social obligation, and authoritarianism (Giroux, 2016). Describing how schools mirror society, Leo, Giroux, McClennen, and Saltman (2013) wrote that the coming together of neoliberalism, terrorism and education resulted in "increased militarization, rampant xenophobia, a culture of fear, and massive national debt" (p. 1). De Lissovoy, assistant professor of cultural studies in education at the University of Texas–Austin echoed that the rise in militarism in society leads to schools that are becoming "both hardened and emptied" literally and figuratively as "the metal detectors and security personnel are outward manifestations of a broader repressive turn that also inflects pedagogical relationships, just as the inner vacuity of a test-based curriculum has its corollary in the literal emptying of students from schools" (De Lissovoy, 2008, pp. 3–4). In a post-9/11 context, Leo et al. (2013), the militarization of public education is demonstrated through values and traits such as blind patriotism, obedience to authority, a culture of fear, anti-dialogue, denial of politics, rigidity, intolerance, and fighting as a means of resolving problems (p. 16). In their words:

> Neoliberal education is education as enforcement, rather than education as access to engagement with a democratic public sphere. Dialogue and debate are forsaken in favor of the acquisition of "neutral" facts and the skills of data analysis. In these ways,

the discourse of market and corporeal discipline converge in a neoliberal perspective, and the student and teacher must be forced to accept the right knowledge. (Leo et al., 2013, p. 15)

In light of all of this, it should come as no surprise that, according to Giroux, the War on Terrorism is not about protecting the American people, but protecting the socio-political and economic interests of an elite. In his words, in the War on Terror, the "real enemy is not terrorism at all, but democracy itself" (Giroux, 2016, p. 45). The school curriculum is influenced by many factors, but in regards to instruction about the War on Terror and 9/11, the main influences are socio-political and economic. With a long history of using socio-political reasons for economic gain, it may be unsurprising to hear many scholars declare that many of the reasons behind the way the War on Terror is taught are, in fact, related to not only maintaining the interests of a financial elite.

Teaching Back: What Teachers Can Do to Change Society

It has been demonstrated that the sociopolitical order of society impacts schools and its aims, however, what is the role of schools in influencing society? We need a pedagogy now more than ever that fights to restore democratic values within the classroom and within society. Is it possible? Can schools actually transform society? September 11 spurred a great reorganization of external forces including economic, legislative, and cultural, as well as internal reorganization such as the subtle enforcement of certain belief systems (Leo et al., 2013). These external forces led to an impact on internal reorganization of belief, especially through schools. Clearly the political context in society impacts the role of schools significantly. However, what is not evident yet through this discussion is the influence of schools in shaping society. However, since education is political, it can either reproduce or resist dominant ideologies and has the potential to transform society (Apple, 2013). That being said, if students are not taught in the classroom to question the dominant narratives about 9/11, the War on Terror, and Muslims, it is less likely that in the future they will be cognitively prepared to question much of anything that is spread by the media and the culture. The foundation of democracy hinges on this ability. Schools are where future citizens are prepared to inherit their country, and their level or preparedness often falls along a spectrum that spans from passive obedience to active transformation.

Critical Pedagogy: One of the Best Ways to Teach Back

Fortunately for educators who care about social justice, there is much evidence that points to the fact that schools can influence society, just as society clearly impacts schools. The term pedagogy was originally derived from the Greek word *paidagōgia*, which means to guide and transform—certainly, the derivative understanding of pedagogy, of teaching, is one of transformation of the self and society. However, not all pedagogies are made equal. Many scholars in the field believe that the best method for this kind of transformation is *critical pedagogy*. Critical pedagogy is a philosophy of education inspired by Marxist critical theory. Critical pedagogy helps students understand and question oppression and challenge dominant ideologies that sustain inequalities.

Critical pedagogy allows questioning and critiquing given information, which are the foundations of a real democracy, and therefore critical pedagogy would be a helpful philosophy when teaching about 9/11 and terrorism to restore democracy. Teachers can use critical pedagogy to make sure that schools are sites for the development of democratic ideals and the skills students need in order to function within a complex and globalized world. Critical pedagogy is unique among other pedagogies in that it merges philosophy of education with political economy and social justice. Among its leading figures are Peter McLaren, Henry Giroux, Michael Apple, Joe L. Kincheloe, Shirley Steinberg, and, the founding father, the late Paulo Freire.

Paulo Freire was a Brazilian educator and philosopher who wrote the seminal work, *Pedagogy of the Oppressed*, considered one of the foundational texts of the critical pedagogy movement. Freire was influenced by the writings of John Dewey, Frantz Fanon, Karl Marx, Antonio Gramsci, Georg Wilhelm Friedrich Hegel, and Jean-Paul Sartre. Freire originally developed critical pedagogy to counter traditional education in Brazil and provide a philosophical blue-print for adult educators who wanted to help their illiterate peers learn to read in a humble and empowering way. Critical pedagogy centers on the interrogation of systems of domination and inequality to help people realize their position and oppression within that system. Critical pedagogy sees oppression as temporary and transformable. On the other hand, Freire (1970) argued that uncritical education indoctrinates students to the point that they no longer recognize oppression, and in fact begin to accept and sometimes even welcome it as an inevitable and integral part of their lives. In his words, "education as the exercise of domination stimulates the credulity of students, with ideological intent (often not perceived by educators) of indoctrinating them to adapt to the world of oppression" (p. 78). Freire's central idea of critical pedagogy is to "analyze the role of *conscientização*" which he described as the ability to be conscious of the "social, political, and economic contradictions and to take action against the oppressive element of reality" (Freire, 1970, p. 35). In the case of uncritical education, the result is often obedience rather than civic engagement. According to Giroux (2011), critical pedagogy takes its adherents beyond political and ethical analysis to provide tools that "unsettle commonsense assumptions, theorize matters of self and social agency, and engage the ever-changing demands and promises of a democratic polity" (p. 3). Critical pedagogy provides students with a sense of agency and the intellectual means with which to recognize oppression within society and take action to make improvements.

Freire described two approaches to education: "problem-posing" or "banking," terms he coined in the *Pedagogy of the Oppressed* (1970) to define the teacher-student relationship. The problem-posing concept of education refers to pedagogies that emphasize critical thinking, which leads to true liberation. The banking concept of education, on the other hand, is what Freire considers the traditional method of education, which perpetuates a culture of silence and prevents people from confronting and dismantling their own oppression. There are five elements that can help to parse out whether the pedagogue is using one or the other: (a) the degree to which the teachers and students untangle reality, (b) the presence of hierarchy within the teacher-student relationship, (c) dialogue, (d) the development of *praxis* (which Freire defines as action plus reflection), and (e) the encouragement of pupils to be agents of history rather than mere observers of it. Thus, critical pedagogy not only focuses on unveiling oppression within society, but also emphasizes the role of schools to counter such systems of oppression.

Problem-posing education is, of course, radical. Many teachers may be repelled by this, and claim that they will use the banking model for the time being, until the political and social climate allows for more progressive educational reform. Freire disagreed. Freire urged teachers not to use banking education as a pedagogy out of convenience, instead to take control by employing the problem-posing education and "be revolutionary—that is to say, dialogical—from the outset" (p. 86). In the following chapters, I will demonstrate how this is possible.

Conclusion

In many ways, American schools follow the example of society. Through ideology, selective tradition, and hegemony in textbooks and classrooms, a school mimics the United States' socio-political and economic hegemony in the way it processes individuals into future citizens and professionals. Therefore, information in textbooks about 9/11 and the War on Terror typically mirrors the culture which surrounds it. The selective traditions in textbooks and the public pedagogy within the culture are often regurgitated by the teacher in the classroom without critical analysis or a second thought. Teachers must know that without employing critical pedagogy, someone benefits and someone is disadvantaged as a result of whatever they teach.

In the current context of a growing and global neoliberal economic system, a handful of elites benefit financially over the expense of hundreds or thousands of people, including regular Americans, and these drastic financial changes seriously affect the educational system, including how controversial current events are taught. With the deregulation of the global market, millions across the globe are considered disposable. Global neoliberalist elites who are more powerful than nation-states make social, political, and economic changes in other countries and gather increasing fortunes at the expense of the most vulnerable populations among us. The War on Terror has served as a great vehicle through which to expand neoliberalism. In this instance, the most vulnerable population are Muslims, whose death tolls have skyrocketed in Afghanistan and Iraq and other places, breaking their families apart as their most revered historical and cultural institutions and infrastructure crumble around them in the wake of the explosions of missiles and drones. Muslim Americans are not immune either. Asked to leave airplanes because they make other customers nervous, held for weeks and months illegally without explanation for what they have done wrong, and verbal and physical abuse at work, school, and on the street—this is the lived experience of Muslim Americans in the wake of 9/11, an event which transformed into a lucrative business for some, and a traumatizing experience of racism for others. However, the damage of the war is not limited to Muslims. The war has corroded American democracy and taken away American freedoms, including intellectual freedom within schools.

The educational system is victim to and also complicit in this process. It has become a site of consent and reproduction of socio-political and economic hegemony. Heightened militarization and security in society are mirrored by the schools. Fear, intolerance, blind patriotism, and a vacuous curriculum influence school relations and classroom pedagogy.

Within such a toxic environment, are schools able to transform society? Is there a second chance for democracy, and can schools contribute to making this change? Many critical pedagogues would argue that education is political and certainly can change society. By adopting a critical pedagogy that resists mainstream narratives and questions the dominant discourse on 9/11, the War on Terror, and Muslims, students learn the foundations of democracy within the classroom and society. By urging problem-posing education, and rejecting banking education, critical pedagogy not only resists indoctrination and fatalistic acceptance of oppression, but it empowers the learners to look for alternatives to their unjust situations. Critical pedagogy relies on the learner to develop consciousness through a teacher who eliminates hierarchy, upholds dialogue, encourages praxis, unveils reality, and demonstrates to their students that they can become agents of change. Despite the challenges ahead, critical pedagogy and critical pedagogues have built a clear path forward.

The following chapter will appraise the pedagogies of five teachers in New Mexico for their capacity to teach about 9/11 and the War on Terror in a critical way. The goal of interviewing these teachers is so that you, reader, can see yourself in the successes and failures of your peers, and recognize that you are not alone in the process of professional improvement. Hopefully, it will become apparent where and how teachers are working to repair the lopsided dialectic, and what can be improved upon in their pedagogy, and in yours, in order to effectively do so. In reference to 9/11 and the War on Terror, the lopsided dialectic highlights some aspects of the conversation and ignores others, thus deceiving the listener. Therefore, critical pedagogy theorists, such as Freire, demonstrated theoretically how teachers either work to challenge injustice through deep analysis of reality, or discourage independent thought through acceptance of the status quo. Accordingly, current events related to the War on Terror are both an opportunity and a test for evaluation of critical teacher pedagogy.

Building upon the work of Paulo Freire and other critical pedagogues, I recommend a methodological approach called Critical Dialectical Pedagogy (CDP). CDP recognizes that technical and cognitive development go through a process towards achieving an end goal. Therefore, it is acceptable for teachers to be in the middle zone if they are working towards progress. Dialectics is the central part to CDP, and it is defined as a quest in search of the truth about an issue through investigating multiple angles. Critical Dialectical Pedagogy will be discussed at greater length in Chapter 8.

Teachers can and must change the world. Through accepting the status quo as it stands is to relinquish democracy and invite oppression of levels we may not yet be able to conceive. This is not a viable option. Despite the odds, there are already many teachers out there working diligently to make a difference. The following chapter will introduce you to a few of them.

References

Amadeo, K. (2016, September 8). War on terror facts, costs and timeline whose wars are more expensive? Bush or Obama? *U.S. Economy.* Retrieved September 21, 2016 from https://www.thebalance.com/war-on-terror-facts-costs-timeline-3306300

Apple, M. (2004). *Ideology and curriculum.* New York, NY: Routledge Flamer.

Apple, M. (2006). *Educating the right way: Markets, standards, god, and inequality.* New York, NY: Routledge.

Apple, M. (2013). *Can education change society?* New York, NY: Routledge.

Bacevich, A. (2008, October 5). He told us to go shopping. Now the bill is due. *The Washington Post.* Retrieved September 21, 2016 from http://www.washingtonpost.com/wp-dyn/content/article/2008/10/03/AR2008100301977.html

Bidwell, A. (2015). Report: Federal education funding plummeting congress has cut spending for K-12 education by nearly 20 percent since 2011, a new report says. *U.S. News and World Report.* Retrieved September 21, 2016 from http://www.usnews.com/news/blogs/data-mine/2015/06/24/report-federal-education-funding-cut-by-5-times-more-than-all-spending

Bobbit, F. (1918). *The curriculum.* New York, NY: Cornell University Library.

Bourdieu, P. (1998, December). Utopia of endless exploitation: The essence of neoliberalism. What is neoliberalism? A program for destroying collective structures which may impede the pure market logic. *Le Monde Diplomatique.* Retrieved March 25, 2012 from http://mondediplo.com/1998/12/08bourdieu

Bowles, S., & Gintis, H. (1976). *Schooling in capitalist America: Educational reform and the contradictions of economic life.* New York, NY: Basic Books.

Bush, G. W. (2002, June). *Department of homeland security.* Retrieved September 21, 2016 from https://www.dhs.gov/xlibrary/assets/book.pdf

Byford, J., Lennon, S., & Russell, W. B. (2009). Teaching controversial issues in the social studies: A research study of high school teachers. *Clearing House: A Journal of Educational Strategies, Issues, and Ideas, 82*(4), 165–170.

Collinson, S., & Perez, E. (2014, December 9). Senate report: CIA misled public on torture. *CNN.* Retrieved September 13, 2016 from http://www.cnn.com/2014/12/09/politics/cia-torture-report/

Crews, E. (2007, Spring). Voting in early America. *Colonial Williamsburg Journal.* Retrieved September 21, 2016 from http://www.history.org/Foundation/journal/spring07/elections.cfm

De Lissovoy, N. (2008). *Power, crisis, and education for liberation: Rethinking critical pedagogy.* New York, NY: Palgrave Macmillan.

Deveci, H. (2007). Teachers' views on teaching current events in social studies. *Educational Sciences: Theory & Practice, 7*(1), 446–451.

Dewey, J. (1938). *Experience and education.* New York, NY: Macmillan.

Fairclough, N. (2003). *Analyzing discourse: Textual analysis for social research.* New York, NY: Routledge.

Felluga, D. (2011, January 31). Modules on Marx: On ideology. *Introductory Guide to Critical Theory*. Retrieved September 13, 2016 from http://www.purdue.edu/guidetotheory/marxism/modules/marxideology.html

Finn, C. (2002, September). September 11: What our children need to know. *Thomas B. Fordham Foundation*. Retrieved September 21, 2016 from http://www.edexcellence.net

Flinders, D. J., & Thornton, S. J. (2013). *The curriculum studies reader*. New York, NY: Routledge.

Freire, P. (1970). *Pedagogy of the oppressed*. New York, NY: Herder & Herder.

Friedman, M. (2002). *Capitalism and freedom*. Chicago, IL: The University of Chicago Press.

Giroux, H. (2004, March). Cultural studies, public pedagogy, and the responsibility of intellectuals. *Communication and Critical/Cultural Studies, 1*(1), 59–79.

Giroux, H. (2011). *On critical pedagogy*. New York, NY: Bloomsbury Academic.

Giroux, H. (2016). *America's addiction to terrorism*. New York, NY: Monthly Review Press.

Graseck, S. (2008). Explore the past to understand the present and shape the future. *Social Education, 72*(7), 367–370.

Harper, V. (2014, April 22). Henry A. Giroux: Neoliberalism, democracy and the university as a public sphere. *TruthOut: Interview*. Retrieved September 21, 2016 from http://www.truth-out.org/opinion/item/23156-henry-a-giroux-neoliberalism-democracy-and-the-university-as-a-public-sphere

Hess, D. (2009). *Controversy in the classroom: The democratic power of discussion*. New York, NY: Routledge.

Hess, D., Stoddard, J., & Murto, S. (2008). Examining the treatment of 9/11 and terrorism in high school textbooks. *Educating Democratic Citizens in Troubled Times: Qualitative Studies of Current Efforts*, 192–225.

Kincheloe, J. L., & Steinberg, S. R. (2004). *The miseducation of the west: How schools and the media distort our understanding of the Islamic world*. Westport, CT: Praeger Publishers.

Klein, N. (2007). *The shock doctrine: The rise of disaster capitalism*. New York, NY: Henry Holt & Company.

Kuthe, A. (2011). Teaching the war on terror: Tackling controversial issues in a New York City public high school. *The Social Studies, 102*(4), 160–163.

Leo, J. R., Giroux, H. A., McClennen, S. A., & Saltman, K. J. (2013). *Neoliberalism, education, and terrorism: Contemporary dialogues*. London: Paradigm Publishers.

Levesque, S. (2003). "Bin Laden is responsible; It was shown on tape": Canadian High School Students' historical understanding of terrorism. *Theory and Research in Social Education, 31*(2), 174–202.

Loewen, J. (2007). *Lies across America: What our historic sites get wrong*. New York, NY: Simon & Schuster.

Maddow, R. (Host), Benen, S. (Producer), & Katko, R. (Director). (2011, March 9). Naomi Klein on the Rachel Maddow Show. *MSNBC*. Retrieved March 16, 2016 from https://www.youtube.com/watch?v=Ks3VhMLbtNU

Merryfield, M. M., & Wilson, A. (2005). *Social studies and the world: Teaching global perspectives*. Silver Springs, MD: National Council for the Social Studies.

Ratliff, E. (2005, December 1). Fear, Inc. *Wired*. Retrieved September 28, 2016 from http://www.wired.com/2005/12/homeland/

Rumsfeld, D. (2001, September 10). Donald Rumsfeld speech about bureaucratic waste. *A Government of the People*. Retrieved September 14, 2016 from https://agovernmentofthepeople. com/2001/09/10/donald-rumsfeld-speech-about-bureaucratic-waste/

Stiglitz, J. (2004, March 5). Criticism of neoliberalism: Interview with Joseph Stiglitz. *Portland Independent Media Center*. Retrieved September 16, 2016 from http://portland.indymedia. org/en/2004/03/282123.shtml

Stiglitz, J. (2011, September 1). The true cost of 9/11. *Slate*. Retrieved October 11, 2016 from http://www.slate.com/articles/business/project_syndicate/2011/09/the_true_cost_of_911. html

Williams, R. (1961). *The long revolution*. New York, NY: Columbia University Press.

Wilson, E. K., Haas, M. E., Laughlin, M. A., & Sunal, C. S. (2002). Teachers' perspectives on incorporating current controversial issues into the social studies curriculum. *The International Social Studies Forum, 2*(1), 31–45.

· 3 ·

MEET THE TEACHERS

This chapter will evaluate the ability of teachers to teach in a critical way and combat the lopsided yet pervasive dialectic about 9/11 and the War on Terror. If we conceive of the whole dialectic as a sphere, and representative of holistic and diverse perspectives on an event, a lopsided dialectic would be a sphere cut in halves, or fourths, or with chunks of it removed. In regard to 9/11 and the War on Terror, the lopsided dialectic is one in which American media, culture, and textbooks are the main voices heard. These voices often encourage patriotism and militarism. These voices rarely point out evidence of American wrongdoing in other countries targeted by their military force, or discriminatory and unconstitutional policies that affect Muslims domestically. What is missing in this lopsided dialectic are, predominantly, Muslim voices: from Arab and Muslim newspapers and media, voices of Muslims living in Afghanistan and Iraq, and voices of Muslim youth in America. Whether teachers mean to or not, the absence of these voices deflates the dialectic and actually impedes the possibility of true critical thought. Teachers contribute, often unwittingly, to this lopsided dialectic.

But teachers can be a source for change. It could also be argued that teachers' voices are often missing as well from this lopsided dialectic, as well. In order to help teachers and others in the field of critical pedagogy reflect on how to reorient this lopsided dialectic in regards to 9/11 and the War on Terror, I invite the reader to evaluate interview transcripts from five teachers in New Mexico who all discuss their efforts to teach about these controversial, yet important, topics.

It can be useful for researchers, teachers, and educators to reflect on these stories through the lens of the main aspects of Freire's theory of critical pedagogy as a tool for developing better critical pedagogy in their own classrooms. As such, the main question to keep in mind as you read the teacher transcripts is: to what degree are teachers supporting intellectual liberation within their classroom?

Before Osama bin Laden Died: A Few Conversations with Teachers

To investigate the teacher's role in either maintaining or questioning the lopsided dialectic, I conducted teacher interviews in New Mexico where I lived, studied and worked in 2010–2011. At the time of our interviews, the United States' was at an interesting and critical turning point in the War on Terror. In 2009, a year prior to beginning these interviews, the rebel group Boko Haram had begun to lead a bloody insurgency against the government of Nigeria in the name of Islam. The War on Terror seemed to be spreading to East and West Africa, as well as South East Asia. In 2010, the Obama administration announced their intention to increase troop numbers in Afghanistan by 30,000, bringing the total number of U.S. troops deployed there up to 100,000. Then on May 2, 2011, the unbelievable happened. Early in the morning, as most people in Abbottabad, Pakistan were still in bed, asleep, a small group of U.S. Forces raided a large compound where they believed Osama bin Laden, al-Qaeda leader and 9/11 mastermind, to be hiding. In the ensuing firefight, he was shot and killed, and his body was tossed into the ocean. But bin Laden's death came after my conversations with the teachers. At the time of our interviews, the United States was still in hot pursuit of bin Laden, and actively seeking to destroy terrorism wherever it might have been across the world.

Though I selected New Mexico out of convenience, I think this selection helped me evaluate important and often overlooked aspects of pedagogy of current events such as 9/11 and the War on Terror. For example, the small state-wide Muslim population (3,500–5,000 individuals) meant that many non-Muslims in New Mexico rarely interacted with this population, leading to fewer opportunities for teachers to interact with this population when teaching about the War on Terror. Furthermore, New Mexico is geographically far from the epicenter of 9/11, making it a good location to examine the dispersion of current event discussion on the War on Terror inside the classroom.

In order to investigate teacher pedagogy, I interviewed five social studies high school teachers. In selecting teachers, I used a purposive sampling method. For instance, I invited only those educators who had taught about 9/11 and the War on Terror to participate in the study. However, it was more challenging than I expected to find teachers willing to participate. I approached a social studies teacher colleague of mine and asked if he would be willing to participate. He refused without explaining why. I also hoped to interview social studies teachers who taught my Muslim American student participants during high school, which would have provided an interesting dual perspective on a shared lived experience; unfortunately these teachers also rejected my request without explanation. Frustrated, I used the snowball method "in which one participant leads to another" (Seidman, 2006, p. 55). My University of New Mexico professors offered to introduce me to social studies teachers who taught about these issues. I was finally connected with five teachers in the Albuquerque area who were willing to speak with me.

Linda, Patrick, Bill, Cain and George all selected their pseudonyms at the beginning of the study. All five teachers defined themselves as White Christians and were between the ages of 40 and 65 years old.

Their teaching experiences ranged between four to 35 years at various high schools throughout New Mexico. In terms of their teaching about the War on Terror and 9/11, they individually ranged from having four to 10 years of experience teaching these topics at the time of the study. All came from slightly different teaching disciplines and age groups, having taught a range of social studies courses such as U.S. history, world history, government, economics, and the Constitution, and a range of grades from 9th to 12th.

I based my question structure on Spradley's interview strategies. I developed what Spradley (1979) called "grand tour" questions (p. 86), "mini tour" questions (p. 88), and "open-ended experience" questions (p. 88). The goal of the grand tour question is to find out how people's personal experiences connect with broader themes, events, or history. Mini-tour questions are similar to grand tour questions but are more focused on obtaining detailed experiences related to a specific topic. Finally, open-ended experience questions are more focused on participants' unique experiences (Spradley, 1979). Each interview was audiotaped.

The participants selected the meeting locations, dates, and times. Several of them met with me at the university whereas many others preferred to meet in a nearby coffee shop. The interviews were semi-structured but conversational. I only interrupted when I felt that the conversations were deviating from the topic or when the interview time was running out. During the interviews, I frequently rephrased my participants' ideas to ensure that I understood their experiences accurately (Seidman, 2006). This helped in the data interpretation process.

The goal of conducting these interviews was to understand what some teachers currently do in order to teach effectively and in a non-biased way about current events such as 9/11 and the War on Terror. Transcripts of the interviews will be presented in this chapter for the readers to be able to judge for themselves where and how the teachers might improve their efforts.

Grading Rubric

In order to assess whether or not a teacher engages students in a critical pedagogy in regards to these current events, the following "grading rubric" may be useful. The grading rubric is based on the following categories (many of them originally described by Freire). These categories include the ability to (a) unveil reality, (b) engage in dialogue, (c) dismantle hierarchy, (d) regard students as agents of change, (e) evaluate praxis of others and oneself, and (f) work towards a more socially just world. It is important to remember that more than likely any given teacher may display elements of both banking education models and problem-posing education models. Reflecting on the stories and experiences of other teachers is an important tool in developing critical pedagogy for readers of this book.

Unveiling Reality

One of the main factors in determining whether or not pedagogy is banking or problem posing is how the teacher encourages students to understand reality. Some teachers lean more toward a banking model of education by prioritizing formal instruction geared towards success on standardized exams, while other teachers demonstrate a more of a problem-posing model of education that encourages deeper inquiry into reality, such as analysis of current events like 9/11 and the War on Terror. For example, banking education attempts to mythologize reality and "conceal certain facts which explain the way human beings exist in the world" (Freire, 1970, p. 83). Problem-posing education, on the other hand, "sets itself the task of demythologizing" (p. 83). Through demythologizing, teachers engage their students in an aspect of problem-posing pedagogy, whereas when teachers avoid questioning assumptions, or myths, this demonstrates a propensity towards banking education.

Engage in Dialogue

Problem-posing education insists on dialogue as an important process through which students and teachers reflect on the subject matter in relation to their experiences and become more cognitively aware of their position in society. Even when 9/11 or the War on Terror do come up, dialogue, a core element of problem-posing pedagogy, can be lacking in the instruction about 9/11 and the War on Terror. Indeed, Freire (1970) explained that dialogue is the process through which thinking, understanding, and learning happen. Freire (1970) made clear that dialogue could only be considered as such if it causes transformation, such as achieving a new realization. If a dialogue does not result in any type of transformation, then it is limited to *verbalism*. Freire defined *verbalism* as "unauthentic words" that are "alienated and alienating 'blah'" (p. 157). These words are empty because they "cannot denounce the world, for denunciation is impossible without a commitment to transform, and there is no transformation without action" (p. 157). Thus, a determining factor in evaluating whether or not the teacher truly engages the students in dialogue is its potential to transform into action. Whereas problem-posing educational models keep dialogue front and center, banking pedagogue avoid real and honest discussions which might lead their students to action.

Dismantle Hierarchy

In banking educational models, there is a strict and strong hierarchical relationship between teacher and student, whereas in a problem-posing educational model there is a greater sense that teacher and student are playing for the same team, understanding and unraveling reality together. Banking education figuratively turns students into receptors of information whereby a bank-teller teacher makes deposits of information in students' minds. Freire (1970) argued that this is a skewed system that dehumanizes students by perceiving them as lacking creativity, knowledge, and incapable of transformative action. In problem-posing education, the teacher is no longer an authoritative figure who controls knowledge. Instead, students are "co-cognitive investigators in dialogue with the teacher" (Freire, 1970, p. 80). In fact, teachers and students "are both subjects" bound by "the task of unveiling that reality" and "in the task of co-creating that knowledge" (p. 69). Thus, one of the key characteristics of problem-posing education is the opportunity for individuals to move beyond the traditional teacher-student relationship to become subjects working together.

Regard Students as Agents of Change

Teachers who use a banking model of education reinforce an alienation of students from an ability to change or make history, whereas teachers who work to use a problem-posing model of education empower students to become civically engaged. Students are not mere observers of history in a problem-posing classroom; they are agents of it. Whereas banking education "domesticates" consciousness by "isolating [it] from the world," the problem-posing education concept encourages "inquiry and creative transformation through which participants become fully actualized humans" (1970, pp. 83–84). In order to prepare students for the world, and the possibility that they might make it better, teachers must reinforce this notion.

Evaluate Praxis of Others and Oneself

Problem-posing teachers investigate the synthesis, or lack thereof, between the words and deeds of public figures, institutions, and even themselves, whereas banking educators neglect to draw attention to the difference between what is said, and what is done. The connection, or lack thereof, between reflection (often conducted through dialogue) and action is what Freire called *praxis*. It is an iterative process through which students and teachers reflect upon a topic and act based on this reflection, in a constant and consistent feedback loop. It is also a criterion upon which to evaluate the veracity, or potential for oppression, of public policies, public figures, and institutions. According to Freire (1970), the path to liberation "cannot be purely intellectual but must involve action; nor can it be limited to mere activism, but must include serious reflection: only then will it be a praxis" (p. 65). If the educational process involves strictly words, or empty dialogue, the teacher runs the risk of alienating the students through intellectualism. However, if the educational process involves only action without deep thought, the teacher will alienate the students through lack of reflection. Thus, students and teachers must continually reflect on the alignment between word and deed of those who either work to uphold or reveal oppressive systems at work around them, including themselves. Through questioning the underlying intent, the names of things (for example, is passing the Patriot Act truly an act of patriotism?) and how much individuals or institutions just talk the talk instead of walking the walk, helps students to unveil the world around them and serves as an important element of critical pedagogy. Critical teachers also constantly evaluate their own praxis, for example, taking time to reflect on how their words or hopes or ideals align with their pedagogical actions.

Work Towards a More Socially Just World

Both banking and problem-posing education shape liberation and the world of oppression, however, they do so in opposite ways. For instance, a banking model of education sees students' consciousness as empty vessels to be filled with a top-down knowledge from the teacher. Thus, the role of a teacher in a banking model is to instill in students particular information and ideology that silences their curiosity and adapts them to the world of oppression. On the other hand, problem-posing education rejects "the educational goal of deposit-making and replace it with the posing of problems of human beings in their relation with the world" (Freire, 1970, p. 79). A problem-posing education's primary goal is to help individuals becomes conscious of consciousness. In a problem-posing education, liberation is possible since "liberation education consists in acts of cognition, not transferals of information" (Freire, 1970, p. 79). Banking educational model maintains oppression and normalizes acceptance of it, while problem-posing education helps individuals to become conscious of their world and to imagine ways for liberation.

These elements of Freire's assessment of problem-posing versus banking educational models guide the analysis of each teacher. To make these ideas more concrete and easy to follow, I have also developed a self-reflection guide for the reader. In doing so, I have taken the core concepts of each of the main elements of critical pedagogy, and transformed them into questions that the reader may ask themselves as they read the transcripts. Again, these questions and transcripts are applicable for any teacher who wishes to evaluate themselves against Freire's golden standard. This is a useful jumping-off point for readers of this book to recognize where they stand in this process towards better professional development.

Self-Reflection Guide for Reader

Banking Educational Models

Failure to Unveil Reality. Do teachers fail to create sufficient time and space to discuss the present reality of current events with students? Do teachers fail to prioritize conversations about current events such as the War on Terror?

Non-Dialogue. Is the educational model an act of depositing, in which students primarily collect, catalogue, and memorize information issued from the teacher? Does the teacher fail to integrate dialogue as one of the main methods of learning?

Reinforcing Hierarchy. Is the teacher-student hierarchy reinforced, with the teacher believing he or she has all or most of the answers? Can the teacher recognize that they, too, learn from their students?

Alienation from History. Do teachers, knowingly or unknowingly, reinforce a false belief in a fatalistic history? In other words, do they neglect to spur a sense of civic engagement, a sense that students can and will shape history, or the future? Do teachers bolster the opinion that students are spectators, not creators?

Lack of Evaluation of Praxis. Do teachers fail to bring to the attention of students the separation between word and deed when it comes to how current events such as 9/11 and the War on Terror are discussed and politically addressed? Are teachers able to reflect concretely on the distance between their words and deeds? Does there seem to be a large separation between the two when it comes to their description of their pedagogy and what we know of the reality of their classroom?

Fostering Increasing Oppression. Do the teachers' methods, in any way, serve what Freire would call "the Oppressor?" In other words, do the teachers methods in any way lead to greater oppression of marginalized groups? In the case of critical education of current events such as 9/11 and the War on Terror, who is "the Oppressor"?

Problem-Posing Models

Success in Unveiling Reality. Do teachers build sufficient time and space to discuss the present reality of students? Do teachers prioritize conversations about current events, such as the War on Terror?

Dialogic Process. Is the educational model rooted in dialogic relations, in which students and teachers work together to develop their own opinions about reality? To what extent do teachers encourage discussions, debates, and human-to-human interactions?

Egalitarianism in the Classroom. Is the classroom more egalitarian, meaning do teachers recognize that they learn from students? To what extent does it appear that teachers and students are working together toward a common cause or goal? Do teachers and students appear to be on the same level? Do students take an active role in educating themselves, their peers, and their teachers?

Agents of Change. Do teachers encourage students to see themselves as a part of history? How do teachers model this? How do teachers encourage action on behalf of this knowledge?

Evaluation of Praxis. Do teachers succeed in bringing to the attention of students the separation between word and deed when it comes to how current events such as 9/11 and the War on Terror are discussed and politically addressed? Are teachers able to demonstrate a firm understanding of their own praxis? How accurately do they assess the difference between their words and deeds? Are their words and deeds mostly in alignment?

Liberation from Oppression. Do the teachers' methods help to liberate students from forms of oppression, whether it be intellectual, psychological, emotional, physical, or otherwise? To what extent do students and teachers appear empowered by the act of education?

Meet the Teachers

To understand the role of high-school teachers in shaping students' (and, therefore, society's) understanding of 9/11 and the War on Terror, please meet Linda, Patrick, George, Bill, and Cain. The following section will include excerpts of the teachers' interviews and provide an assessment of teachers' described pedagogies of 9/11 and the War on Terror through Freire's critical pedagogy framework.

Teacher #1: Linda

Educational Experience. Taught U.S. history Advanced Placement classes for 35 years

School Demographics. 75% of students are Hispanic and 15% are White

Teaching Philosophy. "You have to look at all the things that we did wrong so that you can grow from those and learn."

Linda was the first teacher I met with for an interview. Around 60 years old, Linda had many years of experience. At the time she was teaching Advanced Placement Social Studies classes, which she had taught in various New Mexico high schools for the past thirty years, and happily told me that 98% of her students graduate from her class. She stated that among her assets were her passion for teaching and her love for her students. With the 2011–2012 economic deficits and educational reforms that reduced funding for school systems, some teachers were laid off and others retired, but Linda was asked to teach part-time.

Linda: What I tell my kids at the beginning of the year is that, you know, when you teach AP you want them to be successful on this test at the end of the year, so you can't spend too much time on the details sometimes.

Me: The Terrorism in America chapter. I am just wondering how you teach this chapter?

Linda: I don't teach that chapter.

Me: You don't get to it?

Linda: No.

Me: But you said you discussed this issue.

Linda: We do talk all the time about things that are in the news, and unfortunately, all the things that are in the news about Muslims tend to be negative. I tell students at the beginning of the year that there are things that are not going to be on the AP tests, but I want them to learn them anyway because they are so important. I speak about these informally, as current events. I don't have things that I have my kids do. I don't have readings for them, but they sometimes bring in readings. Right now we are doing a lot of current events because it's the end of the year. They have taken the [AP] test on May the 6th and school does not end until May 21st. So the War on Terrorism, how we talk about that is of the Iraq War and how the misperceptions that our government tried to put on us, and how the war started and the Weapons of Mass Destruction and all that, and it is a war that if we have been given the truth, no one would have supported and didn't support anyway. And a lot of people did not support it and what my students feel is that Bush completely scammed us and completely lied to us about the reasons for the war. When we talk about things happening in the Middle East or Arab nations or whatever, and if we talk about terrorism—since this tends to be all the news that we get in the United States about the Arab nations and Arab people is about terrorism—it is wrong but that is the truth. So I try to maybe dispel that a little bit. If a fundamentalist Christian kills an abortion doctor, does this mean that all Christians are murderers? And unfortunately that is the kind of picture that is painted for us in America, for people that are from the Middle East. And so I try to dispel that myth, that terrorism is not a religious belief except for maybe fundamentalists that are on the edge. But the kids would go and research on their own. They would go, "Ms. Linda, I was looking at what you said about Arafat," and so they are interested in it. So that is the only thing that we can do, to educate the kids, and their parents. To educate Americans in general more about the War on Terror. In fact, one of the things that my kids come out of thinking, we discuss all this, that 9/11 was our opportunity to become world leaders in a peaceful way, and it was our opportunity to actually say to the world "this is wrong" and "this is not how we do things" and "we should be more civilized than kill-ing innocent people," and so, instead of going over there and killing innocent people like we are doing right now in the Middle East, that we could have provided such leadership by using diplomacy for all sort of things, and that is basically what my students continue to verbalize is that it was a missed opportunity that we had. Instead we took the John Wayne perspective and killed guys who were wrong and that is the kind of mentality when we lead the War on Iraq. (personal com-munication, May 29, 2010)

To offer another resource as a counterpoint to the textbook that Linda described as having "a slant on history" because the authors were "very highly historians from Standford," Linda told me she used Howard Zinn's, A *People's History of the United States*:

Linda: It is the most popular and famous revisionist history from the 1970s. Revisionist history is when everybody in this country was crazy in the 1960s, and we were questioning everything, and Nixon had trouble keeping everyone under control, and the Vietnam War had upset so many people, and it was chaos. And what happened is that out of questioning, people questioning things, came out a whole new genre of history. For example, there is a really famous and sad book writ-ten by a man named Dee Brown, who is not Native American, but the book is called, Bury My Heart at Wounded Knee [full name: Bury My Heart at Wounded Knee: An Indian History of the American West]. Which … do you know what Wounded Knee is? It is a terrible massa-cre by the United States army in 1890 of some Native Americans who are freezing and starving on their way to another reservation, just to get help. And the government literally first gives them shelter, and the next day they harass them and try to take their guns to make sure they are not going to cause any trouble, and then open fire on them and all these women and children and old people are killed because the younger men are mostly dead. And so the reference in the title, Bury My Heart At Wounded Knee, is it tells all the history of the American government contracts with Native Americans throughout our history and how the United States government broke all the treaties and mis-treated these people so badly and etc. … And so he [Dee Brown] is a revisionist and so is Howard Zinn. And so he [Zinn] tells the story of the American history from the people's point of view. So instead of talking about how there was a coal strike during Theodore Roosevelt's presidency and telling all the complaints of the companies, he would take it from the point of view of the strikers. So you get a completely different story here than what you get in this textbook. (personal com-munication, May 29, 2010)

Linda: Banking versus Problem-Posing Educational Analysis

Unveiling Reality, When Time Permits. Linda was an open-minded, kind person who genuinely hoped to impact her students' lives and help them to view the world with a critical eye. Certainly Linda expressed an understanding of hegemony in her description of the classroom textbook, media, and politics and a desire to catalyze positive change through her teaching. However, Linda's expressed priority was student achievement on standardized tests. She hoped to make a difference, but only within the cultural and political constraints provided. It could be argued that her pedagogical methodology is subversive, since she was encouraging critical thinking among AP students. However, inherent in Linda's teaching was a lack of unveiling reality through failure to prioritize current events. For example, by relegating controversial discussions, such as on the War on Terror, to the end of the school year and only if time permitted, and prioritizing standardized testing, Linda reinforced the adaption of critical thought around the prioritized state standards and exams.

Expressed Interest in Dialogue, Perhaps Needs More Follow-Through. Through her efforts, Linda noticed that some students begin to pursue learning more of their own volition. She told me that through the conversations she facilitated in the classroom, "the kids would go and research on their own. They would go, 'Ms. Linda, I was looking at what you said about Arafat,' and so they are interested in it." Nonetheless, doing so only when time allows defies the idea of dialogue as a process of thinking, learning, and understanding. Linda taught the students to engage in methods such as research, but there was no evidence of deep engagement in dialogue.

Authority of the State Standards. Although Linda spoke at length about her students and their insights, she made it clear that "what I tell my kids at the beginning of the year is that, you know, when you teach AP, you want them to be successful on this test at the end of the year, so you can't spend too much time on the detail sometimes." Therefore, Linda achieves her goal by maintaining her authority as a teacher, keeping students on task, and teaching them about historical issues that are part of the AP exam. This task is achieved through a clearly maintained teacher/student hierarchy in which the ultimate authority is the AP exam. Nevertheless, she demonstrated a clear love for her students, and pride in their successes on the AP exam.

Alienated from History. While Linda encouraged students to look back on the past with a critical eye, such as when she discussed the reasons behind the War in Iraq as well as the massacre at Wounded Knee, she did not describe ways that she encourages students to apply their knowledge and critical think-ing skills in the present, or the future. In this regard, Linda's students are alien-ated from their own agency in shaping the reality that they have inherited.

Evaluating the Praxis of Others, But Not the Praxis of the Self. Linda encour-aged students to evaluate the praxis of former President George Bush's invasion of Iraq—specifically how his spoken reasons for invading aligned, or did not align, with hidden motives. For example, she and her students discussed how President Bush used the media to deceive the American people into going to war against Iraq for a false claim of possession of Weapons of Mass Destruction (WMDs). Linda proudly stated that her students were "savvy that we did not go into this war willingly because we knew all of the facts and we had to punish the people for 9/11" and her students came to some different understandings of why the United States may have launched the War on Terror. According to Linda, the war in Iraq "is a war that, if we have been given the truth, no one would have supported and didn't support anyway. My students feel that [President] Bush completely scammed us and completely lied to us about the reasons for the war." It is evident that Linda encourages her students to evaluate the veracity and transparency of words and actions of political figures. However, through our interview Linda did not seem to demonstrate as much self-awareness in terms of her ability to measure the alignment of her educational methods and strategies, and her goal as a teacher. As she mentioned, the reason she teaches about the past is so that she and her students can "look at all the things that we did wrong" so that they "can grow from those and learn." However, in her teaching philos-ophy and her actions as a teacher she does not mention what steps she and her students can take to actually, physically, change the future based on the lessons learned in the past. Linda's goal as a teacher was to help students make bet-ter decisions based on understanding the mistakes of history. Yet, she relegated teaching about 9/11 and the War on Terror and other current events to the last few weeks of school, and instead prioritized teaching for the Advanced Place-ment Exam. This involved using a book that she deemed uncritical. In many ways, it seemed as though her ideals as a teacher and her actions did not align. However, much of this could be due to the pressure she felt as a part-time teacher with tenuous employment status. As she told me, she was worried that she would be fired just for speaking with me. Linda demonstrated an ability to evaluate the praxis of others, but did not demonstrate an ability to evaluate her own praxis, or encourage action among her students based on reflections on their learning.

Working Towards a More Socially Just World? Linda's teaching philosophy was for her students to learn and grow through studying the past. However, through prioritizing an arbitrary and industrial set of state standards and AP exams, rather than encouraging students to seriously consider how they might create positive change in the world, Linda can expect for most of her students to continue to participate in the strengthening of an oppressive status quo. Of course, there are other factors in these students' lives that may develop their sense of social justice and their abilities to foster it. However, Linda's classroom is likely not a source of that sense of the potential for true liberation.

Teacher #2: Patrick

Educational Experience. Four years teaching 10th grade world history, 11th grade
    U.S. history, 12th grade government and economics, and special education.
School Demographics. 94% of students are Hispanic and 4% are White.
Teaching Philosophy. "Helping adolescents develop the desire and skills to
    make the world a better place."

Patrick had a B.A. in International Relations and an M.A. in Special Education. Teaching was a second career for Patrick after almost 14 years of carpentry and home building. He changed his career out of a passion for education and his interest in helping adolescents develop the desire and skills to make the world a better place. Patrick was a White man of about 40 years old. Patrick had just finished his 4th year of team-teaching world history, government, and economics in classrooms which blend general and special education.

   Patrick, like Linda, brought 9/11 and the War on Terror into discussion "as current events and what not" predominantly because of issues with time:

> It is really difficult to get through with the content, so we try to make connections, instead of trying to force ourselves through the whole book. We try to make connections to the current world as well. ... Never did I have a lesson plan about it. So it may have come in a "Bell Ringer," which is our opening activity, or in a connection to a students' presentation, or as a question in class that we spent some time on. So it needs to move from a non-scheduled to a scheduled. ... We have not gotten to formally study about 9/11 and the War on Terror—mostly it's time. Getting to the present in world history is very difficult, given the standards and wanting to address topics in a way that is not flippant. So, wanting to spend some time on deeper issues, needing to spend some time developing skills, as well, so you can't just do worksheets all the time and get through world history and have students that can't write it again. So having to work on research skills, writing skills, and all that means that you have to dedicate time to units that will allow students to do that, which means that by the end of the year you get this kind of trickle out effect and you are always pushing to the end. Which, though, also speaks to prioritizing and planning. So if I put that

in the schedule at the beginning [of the year], then it gets done. And this is lacking in my teaching, like I said, that is one of the reasons I wanted to come and do this interview with you. Is to reflect on it a little bit. I would like to do a full-blown unit on it. That is something that is lacking in my teaching. I need to focus on it more particularly. That it's [the War on Terror] given so much resources, to some extent it's replaced the fear of a Cold War, have been replaced with fears of terrorism and now the justification for large military expenditures or abuses of citizens or abuses of people from other countries or loss of rights. Now instead of the fears of communism, it is the fear of terrorism. So, one of the things we have discussed is who is Osama Bin Laden? Who is he connected to? Why would we be after him? What's Al Qaeda and the difference between Al Qaeda and the Taliban? Why are we in Afghanistan? And that was more informal discussion versus formal teaching … Generally I try to keep discussions open as long as they are respectful and then try and point out what the consensus is in the education world and the news media and, like, try to get to a known fact as opposed to prejudices or misunderstandings. And I think one thing that is important for me is to discuss things in a respectful way, but deal with terrorism as not just a Muslim thing or Islamic thing, but an act that people have done through especially recent history that has a goal in mind and is trying to create some change. But we don't necessarily have to agree with the methods. But it is not a new thing, and it is not a thing that only one group has used—bring the IRA, for example, when we had the group present on the Irish Revolution we made connections between the IRA and current terrorists. And, so, like I am saying it [conversations about War on Terror related issues] has been more ad-hoc, but keeping it in mind as a connection that we can make to whatever topic we are dealing with today.

Me: So what are some challenges you find teaching this topic about the War on Terrorism?

Patrick: Challenges are when you're obviously working against what students have heard at home and or in media that may not be as reputable, let's say unbiased, so we are trying to dispel myths or misunderstandings. So trying to disassociate Al Qaeda, say, from Saddam Hussein. There is always this misunderstanding that we are in Iraq because of the attacks of September 11 … and then having it discussed in a respectful way that you don't end up with any kind of slurs or disrespectful speech, recognizing that it's probably going to happen and then responding to it appropriately so that it doesn't necessarily kind of squash everybody but that you at least stand up for respectful discussion and tolerance and understanding of people. So dispelling myths, dealing with how do you have a discussion with people on a topic that brings up a lot of passion and has, I think, a root of discrimination and what I think and racism involved.

Me: So how do you then help students to get past that kind of influence that they have from society? How do you do it?

Patrick: I don't know that we are that successful. (personal communication, May 30, 2010)

He closed our interview by saying, very kindly:

I am interested in seeing this research, for sure, and I guess I want to say thanks for the opportunity to reflect a little bit and I will make changes in my teachings based on that. It is a great topic. I want my students to walk away with a better understanding of the current world and the tensions involved and the tolerance we need to show one another, so that means I need to focus on doing it.

Patrick: Banking versus Problem-Posing Educational Analysis

Unveiling Reality, When Time Permits. Patrick, like Linda, brought 9/11 and the War on Terror into discussion "as current events and what not" predominantly because of issues with time. Large classrooms, heavy workloads, and the pressure of meeting state standards weigh especially heavily on newer teachers. Patrick wanted to support his students in developing characteristics such as a sense of right and wrong, and compassion for others. In fact, this is what motivated him to switch careers and become a teacher. And Patrick did try very hard. He gave an example on how he linked current events of the War on Terror to other units in the curriculum, discussing, for instance, the United States involvement in the Cold War and Afghanistan and the roots of U.S. support for Al-Mujahedeen and the Taliban. However, did his discussion of topics such as human rights issues due to 9/11 as informal "Bell Ringers" demonstrate to his students that they were less important than getting through state standards? Likely so. According to Freire, unveiling reality must be the priority and the focus if a teacher is to be considered problem-posing. Unfortunately, Patrick was unable to do so.

Disrespectful Dialogue: A Common Problem for New Teachers. Patrick struggled to maintain respectful dialogue in his classroom. He tried to prevent the use of "slurs or disrespectful speech," while "recognizing that it's probably going to happen." Clearly classroom discussions were not pleasant experiences for Patrick, and likely not for his students. While Patrick did encourage students to journal about their thoughts and opinions, which certainly helps develop an internal dialogue, Freire (1970) argued that "authentic thinking … does not take place in ivory tower isolation, but only in communication" (p. 77). The question remains, however, what kind of support Patrick needs to help him to develop the classroom management skills he needs in order to have the kinds of healthy, energized, and respectful discussions he would like to see.

Maintaining Hierarchy as a Method for Keeping the Peace. Patrick's lack of confidence and experience in classroom management and how to lead class discussions led him to rely upon an authoritative teacher/student hierarchy, potentially as a protective strategy to keep the order. Perhaps because of inexperience, he relied on activities such as worksheets and other activities for skill development, which may sound less like unveiling reality or co-creating knowledge and more like depositing knowledge in the students. Although his method might work in maintaining peace in the classroom, he missed out on the benefits of unveiling reality with students and accessing new levels of cognition.

Students Seen as Change-Makers, But Not Encouraged. Patrick's philosophy was to help adolescents be the change they want to see in the world, yet in describing his approach to teaching it did not seem like he met this goal. He did not mention any activities or lesson plans in which he encouraged students to be agents of change in regards to 9/11 or the War on Terror or in any other topic. This lack of encouragement in civic engagement is an element of the banking model of education.

Little Focus on the Praxis of Others, Deep Sense of Self-Awareness. Patrick did not explicitly mention how he called his students' attention to the separation of word and deed, or praxis, during our interview. Nor did he mention how he encourages students to act based on their reflections. He did, however, mention his efforts to clear up misconceptions, such as the connection between Al Qaeda and Saddam Hussein, which he said are purported in the media, but did not evaluate the praxis of political leaders. Still, despite these short-comings, Patrick's sense of self awareness, or his ability to evaluate his own praxis, is off the charts. An important element of problem-posing education is the ability to measure one's own praxis as an educator, or, in other words, to be able to reflect on how words or hopes or ideals align with pedagogical actions. Though he may have struggled to develop lesson plans and dialogue about the War on Terror, Patrick was very reflective and self-aware on the separation between what he hoped to accomplish in the classroom and what he was able to accomplish. He remarked several times about how 9/11 and the War on Terror was "lacking in my teaching, like I said, and that is one of the reasons I wanted to come and do this interview with you, is to reflect on it a little bit." Patrick told me that the interview had "given [him] more food for thought" in regards to the resources he was using in the classroom. He closed our interview by saying "thanks for the opportunity to reflect a little bit and I will make changes in my teachings based on that." Patrick demonstrated deep self-awareness in his desire to reflect on his ability to measure his own praxis, in other words, to reflect on how well his goals aligned with his curriculum.

Are Patrick's Students Being the Change They Wish to See in the World? The easy and short answer is likely not. Though Patrick has lofty goals and ideals, it is unlikely that he is fostering the skills, abilities, and beliefs necessary in his students so that he and they might go out and actually work towards ending oppression.

Teacher #3: George

Educational Experience. 9–11th grade U.S. History, 32 years of teaching experience.

School Demographics. 82% of students are Hispanic and 9% are White.

Teaching Philosophy. "*Perspectivism*: Recognizing, understanding, and respecting different points of view."

George is a White Catholic male who was 60 years old at the time of our interview. A social studies teacher, George explained that the theme of his school centered on the diverse cultural history of New Mexico, including the following: (a) the Spanish Iberian diaspora, (b) Spanish colonial presence, and (c) local Native cultures, as well as the arrival of people of European and African ancestry. The school intended to have students study all of those components and how they impacted the development of the state and, in turn, how the state had influenced cultures beyond its borders. He taught New Mexico history to 9th graders and world history to 10th graders. In his words:

> A key component in the curriculum that I deliver is trying to develop what I term as "perspectivism:" recognizing, understanding and respecting different points of view. Together with values, verification and skills, and deconstructing propaganda and appreciation for multiple causation and historical significance are critical thinking areas that are a part of every unit that I develop and share with my students. I think if you were to ask any of my students, "What did you get from textbooks in George's classes?" I think probably most of them would say, "Nothing," but those who would say something and would have thought about this would be able to tell you, "Well, I have learned how to be a critical reader or come closer to it." I think one of the best compliments I ever received was from a student at an assembly at Hills High School: "He taught us how to teach ourselves, how to become active lifelong learners."

> Me: Has the issue of the War on Terrorism or 9/11 come up in any of your teachings?

George: Of course, especially when it happened. I mean, I was in a U.S. history class at Hills High School at the time and we pretty much aborted our unit of study and immediately began to look at the events surrounding 9/11 and with a critical eye to deconstruct some of the propaganda that were dominating from a variety of sources. And it started with the announcement from our principal who paraded President Bush's statement to the nation, that they did this because they hate our freedom. And that was her only explanation for why students were witnessing what they were witnessing, dealing with the horrors of that awful time. But we used that as a springboard into looking for other explanations, other than the simplistic explanation of the President. So I focused the classroom on trying to accept this notion and drive home this notion that any time something big happens in personal life or in public life, if we want to learn from it, we should always look for more than one cause. Trying to explain a phenomenon such as a revolution, such as a war, such as migration of people, culture clashes, to always look for more than one explanation. And, of course, that involves the notion of *perspectivism* I was talking about where to fully understand the dynamics of a particular phenomenon you look at things from different points of view.

Me: So do you teach it [the War on Terror] as a unit by itself or do you— how did you teach it?

George: I have done it different ways. In that case of a unit, but we kept coming back to it when we went to study World War I and World War II. Some of the struggles for creation of true nationhood and sovereignty in Middle Eastern countries in the wake of World War II. So it does fit neatly into studies of other units because they are connected and at that particular time we focus on that as a unit, but then we kept trying to draw these links, those cords to the past as we studied that issue, but also later issues that succeed that, such as the United States leading the charge into Iraq to overthrow Saddam Hussein. And attacking Afghanistan and overthrowing the Taliban. Always looks to cords to the past and links between different regional developments. (personal communication, June 5, 2010)

George used a book called *Inside Politics* to help students recognize textbook propaganda and persuasion. In this book, George points his students to a specific passage:

The passage about the Palestine/Israel question is a great example of what I call "card castle" or "card stacking" wherein they offer, theoretically, two different points of view and yet the selection that they choose … The students have to look in the small print at the bottom of the page that people published in Tel Aviv and that the Palestinian spokesperson, their presentation is so laden with hatred and resentment and negativity; whereas the Israeli perspective seems to be magnanimous and peace-loving and you go "Wow, here, we presented both sides here." I want students to learn to recognize it—"No! This isn't fair, even though you did present both sides that are opposing. You stacked the deck, OK!" So, even when you get a text that pretends to be fair and balanced, there are underlying agendas, I think. What we want to do is to empower students to recognize this. I want them to be able to think for themselves, to be able to recognize propaganda, to be able to deconstruct it, to be able to sift through their own value structure to decide if they think it is good propaganda or bad propaganda. I think they should allow themselves to be called to action, or if they find this counter to their innate values and reject that call to action. Once they have a body of knowledge and have been exposed to the writing perspectives, I would like to have them then critique the textbooks treatment of the same subject matter and encourage them to write assignments where I asked them to write to the publisher of the book and tell him what they like about the coverage and what they think, and make suggestions for improvement. (personal communication, June 5, 2010)

George: Banking versus Problem-Posing Educational Analysis

"Perspectivism" as a Method for Unveiling Reality. George taught about 9/11 and the War on Terror by showing his students that the past is connected to the present, asking his students to see the complexity in every current event, and tying many of the units of the curriculum to the War on Terror. For example, he discussed the historical cords that connected World War I and II with the Middle East to issues of nation formation and the United States' interest in the region. Indeed, Kincheloe and Steinberg (2004) argued that the official knowledge in the United States approaches history as isolated events, unconnected to one another. In that case, every event seems new and it becomes hard to trace the cause and effect and to learn from the past. Understanding how official knowledge works, George often described time as a "continuum," and tried his best to demonstrate how past events impacted current ones. He also told me that when things happen, "we should always look for more than one cause" and "never be satisfied with simple answers to complex issues to problems." It could be argued that George relies too heavily on textbooks, which could be biased toward the dominant groups who wrote the history in the first place, so in an attempt to look for a historical continuum, George might be inadvertently looking at a historical continuum of a one-sided story. However, George seems to do a good job of teaching his students to look for bias within textbooks, which he calls "card-stacking," or "stacking the deck." All in all, George demonstrates a commitment to unveiling reality in his classroom, one of the key ingredients for problem-posing educators.

Good Development of Dialogue. Working at a diverse and bilingual high school made George encourage students to recognize, understand, and respect each other's perspectives. According to George, this approach helped students achieve critical thinking skills particularly as they discussed controversial topics such as 9/11 and the War on Terror. Although George allowed students to discuss the topics, it seemed he also relied heavily on lecturing students on how past historical events such as World War I and II are linked to 9/11 attacks, the War on Terror, and contemporary incidents that connect all the above to the United States invading of Iraq, toppling of Saddam Hussein, attacking Afghanistan, and overthrowing the Taliban. Also, George's focus on identifying the connection between historical events and 9/11 and the War on Terror does not engage students in a dialogue about their personal experiences and their own position in the world. While George demonstrates a commitment to encouraging dialogue in his classroom, he could employ it more often, and also encourage students to dialogue in greater depth about their personal experiences. Still, George does utilize dialogue in a way that galvanizes action—an important element of problem-posing pedagogy.

Unclear Teacher/Student Hierarchy. Generally, teaching for standards makes teachers focus more on the material rather than the students, but George's dedication to "empower[ing] students" to "be able to think for themselves" made him develop activities in which students and teachers co-create knowledge. However, it was unclear through our interview the extent to which he saw himself and his students at the same level, unveiling reality together.

Encourages Students to Act. George told me that once students understand a variety of perspectives, he engages them in activities in which they take an active role in critiquing certain resources. For example, George taught his students about card-stacking in textbooks. After learning about card-stacking, he encouraged them to write to the publisher about their opinions of the biases they discovered. During our interview, George at one point remarked that "if, as we are told, we are members of a democratic society, then we actually do have some kind of power and some role in decision making in public life as well as private life." He clearly saw his ability, and his students' ability, to write history. His belief in his students' agency is an example of problem-posing pedagogy.

A Deep Understanding of the Praxis of Others, Not of the Self. George demonstrated an ability to reflect upon, and encourage his students to reflect upon, the separation between words and actions of others. For example, George experienced an uncritical mindset from administrators, such as the principal, at his school, which merely reflected the uncritical statements issued by the

Bush administration during that time. George, in his own words, describes the school principal's response to the 9/11 attacks, and how George modified his teaching in response:

> I was in a U.S. history class at the time and we pretty much aborted our unit of study and immediately began to look at the events surrounding 9/11 and with a critical eye to deconstruct some of the propaganda that were dominating from a variety of sources. And it started with the announcement from our principal who paraded President Bush's statement to the nation, that they did this because they hate our freedom. And that was her only explanation for why students were witnessing what they were witnessing, dealing with the horrors of that awful time. But we used that as a springboard into looking for other explanations, other than the simplistic explanation of the President. (personal communication, June 5, 2010)

In this instance, George helped students to critique the praxis of both the principal and the president. Surprisingly, George also remarked that most students of his students would say they had learned nothing from the resources he shared and only a few would say they had become more critical readers. This seemed strange, especially since, per his descriptions, he is doing many of the right things in order to encourage liberation and action among his students. Based on this incongruency, one might expect George to be more reflective about what he might do to improve his pedagogy, so that he might truly develop critical thinking and reading skills among his students. However, he did not make any mention of how he could improve his teaching to align his pedagogical goals with his curricular activities.

Oppression or Liberation? It was unclear whether or not George's pedagogical efforts spurred positive change, or maintained the status quo. While he involved students in small assignments of speaking back to textbook authors, he did not mention how these may have translated into broader socio-political efforts for change.

Teachers #4 and #5: Cain and Bill

Cain and Bill were the only teachers interviewed together, since together they co-taught a class connected to a national competition called *We the People Constitution Law Program*.

Educational Experience. At the time of the interview, Cain had taught for 11 years and Bill had taught for 16 years.

School Demographics. 69% of students are Hispanic, 12% are White, and 7% Native Americans.

Teaching Philosophy. "We want students to be reading and finding things out about the world, then coming in and talking to [the things they learn], and then coming in with their own conclusions."

Cain and Bill are co-teachers. Bill was 58 years old with a B.A. in government and an M.A. in political philosophy. Cain was 55 years old at the time of our interview. He worked previously for the United States Postal Service (USPS) and was involved in the Union before becoming a teacher.

Bill: So our class, we participate in the national *We the People Constitution Law Program.* It is a competition which just got cancelled by Congress in the big budget cuts. It was a 24-year-old program, which started with the anniversary of our Constitutional Convention in 1987. And there were about 1200 schools around the country that participated in the competitive aspect. So there is a format, textbook. The students are grouped in different units associated with specializing in the textbook. There is a state competition. We won for nine out of 11 years. And the state winners go to Washington, D.C. to participate in nationals. And we have made the top 10 one time … So anyway, we have a particularly directed focus on constitutional issues … the students get questions sent out for state competitions and we focused intensely on those questions. There are 18 questions that are sent down. And that thing gives us the opportunity to bring in, for example, all that literature that we just gave you. Making the students aware of the violations of individual rights or violations of executive power and Congress not being able to check or a variety of things. It just all depends on the topic … This year the historical question was about Lincoln's use of executive power in the Civil War, but then President Bush used Lincoln as a precedent for things that he did and other presidents as well. So it begins with the historical analysis and then they start to understand that and its context.

Cain: So our pedagogy is based upon thinking about it in terms of Constitutionality and then the teaching of it comes in to discussion of what to read, how to read it, maybe the film clips, radio broadcast—things like that in terms of the actual dissemination of the information. And then for us there is a lot of writing involved for the students, but most importantly lots of talking. Our class is almost all the time small groups talking intensely and very focused about specific topics.

Me: Do you, for example, let the students take different sides and argue?

Cain: Surprisingly, we don't really foster too many debates. Debate—that happens, like, you were supporting the use of torture and we were all reading the same literature and we all go like, "No, that is not acceptable and here is why." That kind of debate happens all the time in our class, but do we have an organized activity enveloping that type of issue? Generally not. Every now and then we do, but it is very rare. In general, it is very historically based having to do with whether or not the Constitution should be ratified or not. That is a debate we routinely do every year, but we really don't do open debate in that format.

Me: What got you to think about developing the class that way?

Bill: Some of it is the legacy of the competition—which is why students are motivated to take this class, is that they want to be New Mexico State Champions and then they want to go to Washington, D.C. and have that whole experience. So there is an extra motivational factor that makes it easier for us to take that energy and channel it and some of our approach, too, is related to if we were in a big debate competition, then we would have regular debates but the model for this competition is based on Congressional Hearing where the committee and the Congress is sitting there and they call people to come testify and give information and they ask them questions. So that is the model for our kids. They begin with these research questions. They do a lot of reading. They prepare their testimony. Our class is different in that we are not necessarily teaching to the state's standards. Like if the state standards said you had to teach about the War on Terror, which they don't at this point, we would of course do that. (personal communication, May 29, 2010)

When I asked if they taught about the War on Terror and 9/11, Bill explained the different units in which they tie in conversations about the War on Terror:

In the curriculum there are 6 different units and 3 that are relevant to those issues. We have been doing it, 9/11 and the issues that arose in accordance with the War on Terror have been a strong part of our study. Even if we weren't interested in it, we know, given the questions the national organization has us work on for the competition, that the judges wanted that. So the kids become as expert as they can on the positive and negatives of different decisions—and they have perfect freedom to adopt their own individual perspectives on things—and when they compete in different units we encourage them on disagreements. The judges like to hear that, they give value to answers of a group that show understanding of both sides.

Me: What were student's reactions when you start talking about that [the War on Terror]?

Cain: Like their reaction to almost anything. When they see divergent voices and they get different information, they start making up their own minds. Often times, they are in conflict with what they hear at home or on TV, versus the research that is being done that shows them another reality. Over the years I have seen students that get angry, but they are very hungry to find out what the truth is. It seems once a student starts developing a taste for what is really happening, then it is kind of like the doors of perception start opening. It is very powerful. They get hungry for more information. They want to know what is going on. They don't care for Fox News or CBS. They want to know really what the facts are and what it means to them based on Constitutional study. One of our students that was on the team last year was writing a very provocative essay for her college application and scholarships and I think it is directly pertinent to your subject matter. She thought that she was ill-prepared in discussion and background regarding 9/11. So her concern was that all schools in the country should have some sort of standardized approach to the teaching of 9/11, because she was fearful that people don't know about it and would become intolerant to Muslim Americans. So very similar to like teaching the Holocaust, it took 40 years before it became an item that has to be taught to World History courses. Took a long time for schools and states to adopt those standards. She thought, "Well, 9/11 was one of those big issues that affect Americans that should be a concern for states to address." We try to give the kids an experience of not being in that passive mindset and in terms of their opinion formation, because of the competition, it's not like the kids would say if we were ordinary teachers doing ordinary things. Being a competition class they know that the judges will ask them and they want to win the competition, and this means understanding both sides and being able to articulate your position and that is an incentive for them to get more deeply into it than they would in an ordinary class. (personal communication, May 29, 2010)

Cain and Bill told me that they had their first Muslim student this year. They explained her experience of their classroom environment:

Cain: She just left for Michigan today and she competed for us at state but she didn't compete for us at national competition. We were highly disappointed because of personal issues that she was unable to compete. She is wanting to go to college and she is capable but there are cultural and, to put it in a nut shell—she wants to be free and her family won't let her be free. So I would love her to meet you. You would be a great role model for her. One of the things I noticed she went through a lot—she lived in a refugee camp and experienced heavy duty things. She came into class with preconceived notions on a lot of things, learning about the political science on the issue of the War on Terror, 9/11. Being a Muslim American young woman there were really new things to her and challenged her in a lot of ways. So I think she would be an incredible student. Not having grown up in the United States, we had a lot of information that she didn't have, and had learned. It is fascinating for us, I think, because we see our students, other Latin American countries often, to see if there are inner cultural biases often or to see the shape of how they view authority relations in the core. Because if you grew up here, you will have a very different mindset, no matter where you are at the political spectrum. And so we challenge for conventional thinking normally, and what she experienced as normal growing up in Iraq isn't like that here, and plus she experienced college-level expectations. Now it is very difficult. There is the reading and the writing that we were expecting from her to succeed. (personal communication, May 29, 2010)

They described how students often arrive in the classroom believing that torture is OK, based on the storyline of popular media:

Bill: A lot of students come in thinking torture is okay. So they start reading and understanding that torture is not okay. At least, that's, I think, kids come up to the decision that this is unacceptable in achieving the common good. But a lot of it comes from stupid media, popular shows. And they haven't thought what that means and my understanding is that every country has their nationalistic sort of TV—action shows especially. For boys it is to take it out of that realm of fantasy and confront what the reality of this is and also what's the Constitutional background on that and what the appropriate role of the courts is in terms of defending rights. And we have had some wonderful magnificent court decisions saying, "You can't do that, and you can't do that on the basis of the international law and you can't do that based on the highest traditions of America as a country." For example, in relation to torture, we would, if we got a specific unusual punishment question we would go back to some of the history of the landmark cases and see where was the court coming down on this. How did American judicial policy toward rights protecting one against cruel and unusual punishment develop? Were there different cases developed on torture and how did they happen? And what did the court say? So how did the judicial legal consensus against this develop? And then swimming in that for quite a while and seeing where the arguments are. The students just respond to the complexity, I think, and if they started out, "I think, oh yes, this is right," faced with those judicial and practical social realities that brought the case in the first place, sometimes their sympathy is opened up as well on an issue like that for the War on Terror related things and torture in Guantanamo, which has been a very contentious issue within the United States. It was made more difficult, harder for the kids initially, I think, to identify with because they are people outside the United States, so that raises the question of their citizen rights and what are human rights then—how seriously we take human rights. And then not only from outside the United States but in some cases Muslim or another religion, which is defining the other in a certain way, so what does our Constitution say about this and more importantly what are the ideas behind that, as well. Why do we have these rules to protect diverse religions? And minorities, as well. So the questions would get into Civil Rights law, would get into Constitutional Law on religious diversity and protection of religious freedom and issues of due process. … [The students] do quite a lot of reading, and they have got huge binders that are filled with stuff they have been assigned to research in their groups … there are articles from The Washington Post, The New York Times, but also on specific issues, articles trying to reflect the arguments of both sides. Often times we would begin the classes each day—and our class is about an hour and a half—with reading this. This is a particular summary that I put together based on a big file of Internet articles I have been collecting over the years, just to give them the sense of what the base line was on all of these issues and in fact War on Terror issues was complex and that there are 12 or so different topics.

Me: So what are your sources? So do you go online, do you have particular sources?

Bill: I would say everything. Past and current Supreme Court cases, congressional legislations, executive actions, everything that you see here is sourced. So it is not opinion or blog, it's as close to political science as—it is political science in the sense that it has some degree of validity and reliability. (personal communication, May 29, 2010)

In particular, the textbook allowed for many opportunities to tie in issues relating to the War on Terror in the classroom. Cain explained:

Well, it can reach all the different units. And all of our units are—if you look to the index [of the textbook], they start with basically political philosophy, and then how that shaped the early colonies and the structure of government on through. But the War on Terror would be one that everyone would know for contemporary issues. In particular it would be addressed with excessive executive actions, which would be Article Two in the Constitution. It would be in particular addressed in the Bill of Rights, having to do with violations of the Bill of Rights, getting into everything from search and seizure to cruel and unusual punishment. It gets into political parties and how political parties would differ in their approaches. It gets into the idea of classical republicanism—safety of the country verses individual rights and that is really big and then the effect of that. If you are protecting your right to go to the mosque and not be attacked to worship religion in your way versus a group of people saying that is dangerous and scary, you know, what is this about, what does the Constitution and Supreme Court say about those? (personal communication, May 29, 2010)

When Bill mentioned that the program had been de-funded by Congress, he surmised that the reason was as follows:

Maybe because there are political science students that are questioning the role that our government has had, sometimes in excessive force, in dealing with these issues ... The program is very resilient, so we are anticipating it will be back next year or the year after that. Because it is a 24-year-old program that is around the country, so there is a great deal of support for it. And when kids take classes like this they have a reaction, "Oh, political science is interesting. I wish I could have a career like that," so many of our national judges are ... would introduce themselves as, "I did this program in 1993," and now they are a local official or state somewhere or a congressional staffer so age-wise people who began in the early years are now working their way up the government ladders everywhere in their careers. So there is political support for this. They know how helpful the program is and it's bipartisan, which is unusual for the United States to have people from both sides agreeing on the value and things like this. (personal communication, May 29, 2010)

Cain and Bill: Banking versus Problem-Posing Educational Analysis

Unveiling Reality Through Constitutional Analysis of Real-World Events. Cain and Bill were unique among my interview sample in that they "were not necessarily teaching to the state's standards." Instead, they co-taught a class that focused on preparing students to compete in a national competition called *We the People Constitution Law Program.* Cain and Bill's teaching therefore focused on discussion of real-world events as refracted through the lens of the Constitution, in order to develop critical skills and generate individual opinion in preparation for the regional, state, and national competitions. The War on Terror and 9/11 are a major part of Bill and Cain's class. For example, one of the competition's questions in 2004 was, "How would you explain to one of the 9/11 victims' family members the importance of supporting due process rights for accused terrorists?" Bill told me that of the six units the class covers in the span of the school year, three of those units can be related to the War on Terror. Although Bill and Cain taught formally about 9/11 and the War on Terror, their analysis of the event and the aftermath was only through the lens of the Constitution, and while the Constitution is certainly representative of the United States' democracy, it is important to question a document that was written hundreds of years ago solely by White men, without the input of any women or people of color. All in all, it is clear that the main focus of the *We the People* program is a critical awareness of reality, and an ability to see this reality from a variety of viewpoints. Bill and Cain demonstrated that they successfully help their students unveil reality, an example of problem-posing education.

Rigorous "Testimony:" An Example of Dialogue. In Bill and Cain's class, students expressed strong opinions, based on evidence and a deep understanding of the counterargument. Bill mentioned that basing units in foundational elements of U.S. national identity and values, such as the Constitution, allowed the students to discuss various separate cases presented to the Supreme Court relating to torture, search and seizure, and war. Students analyzed courts decisions on these issues in various instances, gaining a greater understanding of history, culture, and discrimination. Bill and Cain told me that students were especially motivated by the competition aspect of the class and that the class demonstrated a high level of engagement predicated on this desire to win. Students were also responsible for representing themselves and their opinions during the testimony with evidence to support their claims. Students also had "perfect freedom to adopt their own individual perspectives on things," and spent "almost all the time in small groups talking." However, the potential problem in Bill and Cain's case is not whether or not they engage their students in dialogue, but rather what the dialogue is about. It could be argued that Bill and Cain's total focus on the discussions revolving around the Constitution to win a competition could limit the students' opportunities to share their personal experiences in relation to 9/11 and the War on Terror, potentially diminishing the possibility for personal transformation. Still, it was clear that dialogue, or, rather, testimony, was a keystone of their pedagogy, demonstrating again their knack for developing problem-posing methods.

Team Spirit, Most of the Time. With Bill and Cain, students were encouraged to make up their own minds about issues and defend their opinions with historical precedent. Though Cain and Bill certainly held authority as the teachers, the structure of the class somewhat subverted normal teacher-student hierarchies in that the grade or standardized exam was not the most important evidence of merit. Success was determined at the regional, state, or national championships by a panel of judges. In this way, Cain and Bill served more as facilitators and coaches, on the same side as the students and embarking on a joint goal as a team. However, when it came to students' lived experiences, especially the lived experience of the one Muslim American in the classroom, Cain and Bill may need to reflect more on their positions of power. Bill and Cain told me that since the Iraqi girl hadn't grown up in the United States, "[they] had a lot of information that she didn't have, and then learned." However, as a young woman who grew up inside a refugee camp, who must have seen and lived through things that none of her peers, nor her teachers, truly understood, I would have liked to see Cain and Bill describe all the knowledge to be gained from this truly remarkable story of survival and first-hand experience. Yet, the language used to describe the learning is very top-down, from teacher to student, echoing some of the typical rhetoric used in other banking educational settings. Cain and Bill mostly subvert the teacher-student hierarchy, yet they must learn more about cultural sensitivity and appreciation for the learning to be gained, particularly from marginalized Muslim voices.

Students Who Change the World. I couldn't help but think as we discussed the truly marvelous skill and knowledge that students clearly gained from Cain and Bill, why in the world would this program lose its funding? Bill said "maybe because there are political science students that are questioning the role that our government has had, sometimes in excessive force, in dealing with these issues." Clearly this means that Bill and Cain saw students graduate from the program who took an active role in civic engagement. This program set the foundation for changing society through providing students with a deep understanding of the Constitution, yet there is an opportunity for more of an understanding of activism's role in transforming society, rather that solely constitutional and legal precedent. Overall, Bill and Cain clearly sparked an interest in civic engagement among their students, and the evidence is there that these students do go out into the world and change it.

Great Evaluation of the Praxis Others. Bill and Cain successfully evaluated the praxis of political leaders who support certain policies, such as the Patriot Act, based on Constitutional study. Bill and Cain mentioned that basing units in foundational elements of U.S. national identity and values, such as the Constitution and international law, allowed the students to discuss various separate cases presented to the Supreme Court relating to torture, search and seizure, and war. Students analyzed courts decisions on these issues in various instances, gaining a greater understanding of history, culture, and discrimination. In the tradition of critical pedagogues, students were able to come up with their own opinion about the praxis of policymakers, based on co-interrogation with teachers and classmates and a close reading of the constitution and historical precedent. However, because of this, students were able to argue in favor of potentially oppressive laws and policies, as long as they knew how to defend their opinions. This is a challenge and delicate balance for critical pedagogues in general—how to encourage the development of opinions about praxis and how to encourage social transformation to end oppression. When it came to evaluating the relationship between their own words and deeds as educators, Bill and Cain were fairly successful in their self-awareness of the extent to which their pedagogical goals aligned with their actions. They both seemed passionate about teaching students and helping them unveil reality, and in many instances they were successful in this pursuit. However, they lacked a sense of reflection on their hierarchical stance towards the female Iraqi student. It may be useful for them to reflect on how they can build greater knowledge and understanding through the shared lived experience of individuals, especially those who come from the margins.

Working Towards Liberation. Cain and Bill's students often left high school for careers in public service, where, according to Cain and Bill, these very same students vocally challenged injustice where they saw it. These efforts towards liberation, in fact, was the main reason both suggested had led to the termination of funding for the We the People program. Fortunately, the program was quickly reinstated and remains to this day. It is an excellent example of a program that teachers may use in order to teach true democratic ideals.

Conclusion

The teachers interviewed ran the spectrum between problem posing and banking, and everything in between. It was clear through analysis of their interview transcripts that each had their own strengths and weaknesses. Most of the teachers could stand to improve (a) their ability to unveil reality through a greater and more formalized approach to teaching controversial current events, (b) build more dialogue into their classroom activities and perhaps learn some strategies to maintain respect, (c) check their assumptions about who is capable of passing along knowledge, (d) incorporate more experiential opportunities for students to recognize their own capacity to create change, (e) encourage greater reflection among the class, including themselves, on the separation between word and deed, and (f) remember that as teachers they either contribute to the continuation of oppression, or help to end oppression. Specific methods for improving teacher pedagogy in each of these areas will be addressed in Chapters 8 and 9.

However, the important element to remember through these analyses is that it is possible—and urgent—for teachers to improve. Without formal discussion of current events, consistent dialogue, egalitarian classroom environment, a sense that students can change the world around them, or a deep understanding of praxis, teachers can reinforce among their students an unbalanced dialectic about current events such as 9/11 and the War on Terror. This unbalanced dialectic can lead to further oppression of marginalized people. On the other hand, teachers who are able to develop a deep discussion of current events to unveil reality, sustain dialogue, use egalitarian learning styles, foster a sense of empowerment in students, and encourage praxis, can help students to make up their own minds about the world around them, thus leading to students' liberation. Based on this understanding of critical pedagogy, to what extent did each teacher utilize a problem-posing or banking education model? Do you believe that it is possible for teachers to still help their students attain intellectual freedom and personal liberation if they mostly use a problem-posing educational model, or must the teacher attain "perfect scores" in all of the categories?

Freire's philosophy, like any philosophy of education, has limitations. For example, Freire's method of discussion pins people in two opposing camps: oppressor versus oppressed or banking versus problem posing. Thus, educators who adopt critical pedagogy could be seen to be fighting traditional educators. This approach runs the risk of dehumanizing and dichotomizing, therefore creating an "us versus them" binary. Of course, there is a power dynamic at play here. Those who have more power, i.e. the oppressors, have more ability to maintain their dominance. However, what may happen when the tables turn? With binary-style thinking, when liberation for the oppressed comes, will we fall into a new social order of the haves and have-nots, of the powerful and the powerless? The either-or ideas presented by Freire are important in establishing poles, or extremes within a spectrum, but we must not forget that most people and ideas fall somewhere within the grey area.

Freire's conception of critical pedagogy is the touchstone that philosophers of education constantly return to, yet it is important that we recognize advances since his work in terms of critiques of binary thinking and ensuring that reformers who hope to liberate are not, in fact, oppressive. Therefore, I suggest an approach to education that breaks down these binaries. I call this a Critical Dialectical Pedagogy (CDP).

In regards to critical pedagogy of the War on Terror and 9/11, other scholars have called for presenting students with multiple perspectives, rather than two opposing ones. For example, Kincheloe and Steinberg (2004) argued for a broad understanding of 9/11 which included, but was not limited to, multiple and often contradictory strands of information from various sources that would therefore present the student with a plethora of competing view points on a single moment in time. In other words, indoctrination of any single perspective, or two opposing ones, is at odds with democratic ideals. Deploying a Critical Dialectical Pedagogy in this instance may help teachers usher students away from the intellectual and social limitations of binary thinking and introduce them to true the complexities of real life. Critical Dialectical Pedagogy (CDP) will be discussed in greater detail in Chapter 8.

As for teachers, not all are either critical or uncritical, problem posing or banking, but often demonstrate elements of both as they are still in the process of development. The element of dialectics reflects the diversity of ability and emphasizes that development of certain skills is a process, and that it is this path that should be emphasized, rather than the final outcome. For, has any teacher really and truly ever "arrived" as a problem-posing educator? One could argue that no one is perfect, and that there is always room for improvement. It is important for teachers to understand that it is acceptable to be in the grey area between problem posing and banking as long as they make effort towards improvement.

Dialectics is different than neutrality. It is the process of arriving at the truth through multiple perspectives. Through my approach, I do not mean to question or minimize the goals of critical pedagogy to achieve humanization or erase oppression, or criticize the great effort of critical pedagogues and theorists who saw education as political and demanded the interrogation of systems of inequality. What I attempt to do here is to mimic a democratic method and question binary thinking so that we might strip away cognitive limitations and be more compassionate towards educators and the processes necessary for developing critical pedagogy that truly liberates its participants.

Critical pedagogues have raised warning signs about the dangers of uncritical education and its role in the loss of democracy in the United States, calling teachers to action. I join their struggle by writing this book to demonstrate the urgency for changing the way teachers perceive and educate about current events such as 9/11 and the War on Terror into a critical dialectical approach that values multiplicity of perspectives. This method results in intellectual freedom for students, humanization of Muslims, and a reinstatement of democracy within society. One way for teachers to mend the lopsided dialectic is by including some of the missing pieces of this puzzle; Muslim voices and experiences. Muslim voices and experiences have been shut down for so long and adding them to the discussion about 9/11 and the War on Terror rectifies part of the lopsided dialectic. In the following chapter, Muslim American students will discuss their experiences in a post-9/11 world.

References

Freire, P. (1970). *Pedagogy of the oppressed*. New York, NY: Herder & Herder.

Kincheloe, J. L., & Steinberg, S. R. (2004). *The miseducation of the west: How schools and the media distort our understanding of the Islamic world*. Westport, CT: Praeger Publishers.

Seidman, I. (2006). *Interviewing as qualitative research: A guide for researchers in education and the social sciences*. New York, NY: Teachers College Press.

Spradley, J. P. (1979). *The ethnographic interview*. Belmont, CA: Harcourt, Brace, Jovanovich.

· 4 ·

LISTENING TO THE MISSING VOICES

So, I woke up and got ready to go to school and expected it to be like any other day to go to school, and then I went to my first class and everybody is talking like they are in a frenzy, and I don't know what's going on, and they turned on the TV in the classroom, and they turned on the news, and we saw what was going on. Apparently the US was under attack; there was a terrorist attack, the Twin Towers went down. And the whole time we were watching, I was in shock because I didn't know what was going on and why it was happening. And they were saying, like, some terrorist extremist groups is doing all this work and they are Muslims and it's their fault. … and the whole time I was scared because I knew that something bad is going to happen to all the Muslims here. And when they were saying that, everyone in the classroom, like all the kids in the classroom turned around and started staring at me.

—Heidi [student], personal communication (March 17, 2010)

Heidi is a young woman who I interviewed for my research. This was her experience of 9/11 feeling as though her classmates blamed her for events totally out of her control. She felt scared, alone, and very vulnerable. She "knew" that something bad would happen to "all the Muslims here." All of them. It wasn't just a sense that she was in trouble; it was a deep intuition that an entire people would be blamed for the actions of a few.

Heidi's story is not unique. As a high school educator and Muslim woman myself, I have seen and heard so many stories just like Heidi's. But these stories have not ended. They continue every single day within the school environment. The imbalanced dialectic of current events such as 9/11 and the War on Terror, which convinces peers, teachers, and regular citizens of the culpability of all Muslims, contributes to some Muslim American youth questioning their religious and cultural identities and the potential for the school environment on the whole becoming intolerant. Educators must understand the damaging impact certain narratives can have on innocent youth. These youth are rejected by the society to which they legally belong as American citizens. As a growing population of America's future, teachers must understand what has been done to them in order to prevent this unfair treatment from continuing in perpetuity.

When the media strung the words "attack," "terrorist," and "Muslim," together over and over in their description of the atrocities, the impact reverberated far beyond identifying and describing a singular moment in space and time. According to political philosophy and feminist scholar Judith Butler (1993), when images and words circulate and repeat, they eventually grow into an established norm. In this particular instance, the story that "Muslim Terrorists attacked the United States" echoed beyond New York City to pervert the perception of innocent Muslim American people just as stunned and shocked by the days' events in places far, far away. British-Australian postcolonial feminist and queer theorist Sara Ahmed (2004) argued that the emotions created through cultural discourse, like fear, are contagious. After the "other" is isolated, they are perceived and treated as threatening. The post-9/11 shock-waves carried with them some heavy assumptions about who is a "real" American, made unfair accusations about who can and should be considered a threat to society, and instigated fear. This moment redefined the lives of millions of innocent Muslim Americans across the country. This new treatment affects each particular individual's self-recognition, according Charles Taylor (1994), a political philosophy scholar influenced by the work of Hegel and Aristotle. The "othered" person may adopt the perceptions or resist them, or some amalgamation of the two. For example, Heidi, as a Muslim, felt shocked to learn that the terrorists were Muslims, just like her. This recognition elicited fear—fear of her peers' stares, fear of her teachers' potential response, and fear of the school environment. Clearly she was not responsible for the attacks, but she felt a sense of blame because of her identity. She was so afraid in that particular moment that, according to what she told me during our interview, she can't remember anything else from that day.

Meet the Muslim American Students

Through this chapter, it becomes clear that one of the elements missing in this lopsided dialectic is, of course, the voices of Muslims, particularly Muslim American youth. When teachers silence, denigrate, or ignore these voices in the classroom, it contributes to the wonky dialectic, as well as very serious repercussions for Muslim American youth and their identity formation. In order to reinstate this dialectic, teachers and researchers in the field of critical pedagogy must saturate themselves in the voices of the unheard and the marginalized. This chapter will breathe life into the silenced, and focus in on the marginalized through analyzing interview transcripts of nine Muslim American youth recounting the very real impacts of this unequal debate on their emotional, social, and psychological well-being. Through their eyes, the reader will recognize how the school environment on the whole runs the risk of becoming intolerant of critical thought, and the everlasting impact on their individual sense of identity.

To investigate the impact of the imbalanced conversation of 9/11 and the War on Terror on Muslim American students' identities and belonging, and the potential for the school environment on the whole becoming intolerant and oppressive towards Muslims, I conducted interviews with nine Muslim American students. I used purposive sampling and selected Muslim Americans who are second-generation or beyond between the ages of 18–26. All had been in attendance at a public school in New Mexico, United States, during the 9/11 attacks. The decision to select second-generation students ensured participants were born and raised United States citizens, who also had cultural, religious, and familial ties to Islam and/or the Arab world.

This study was conducted in New Mexico, a state located in the Southwest of United States. According to the Islamic Center of New Mexico, the Muslim population of New Mexico is small, with only seven mosques in the entire state and 3,500–5,000 Muslim inhabitants. New Mexico's dominant Muslim populations include South Asian and Palestinian Arabs. Other ethnicities exist in very small numbers and include Algerians, Afghans, African Americans, Caucasians, Egyptians, Iraqis, Latinos, Moroccans, Native Americans, Sudanese, Syrians, Yemenis, and mixed ethnicities. New Mexico's Muslim population is not representative of the larger Muslim population of the United States because of the limited number of individuals of each ethnicity.

I was an active member of the Muslim Student Association at the University and an active member of the Muslim community of New Mexico. Being involved in projects such as *Project Share* to help feed the homeless and *Prison Dawa*, which offers visits to Muslims in prison to lift their spirits, helped me build a positive rapport with many Muslims and facilitated the selection Muslim student interviewees. I generated a list of 22 potential participants to represent the diverse ethnic pool of the New Mexico Muslim community and approached them either in person or through email. I interviewed the nine participants who agreed to the study. I recorded participants' demographics via a pre-interview survey. The nine participants selected were given the following pseudonyms: Henry, Wayne, Young, Bridget, Mary, Francis, Mark, Heidi, and Darla. Eight of them are second generation, and only one, Young, is a third generation Muslim American. Participants included eight Sunni Muslims and only one Shiite Muslim (Mary). Even though not all participants were practicing Muslims, they considered themselves Muslims because of their affiliation with the Islamic religion. Participants came from diverse ethnic origins: two mixed race participants (Heidi is the daughter of a Lebanese mother and Turkish father, and Darla has a Palestinian father and Anglo-American mother), two Palestinians (Young and Francis), two Hispanic (Bridget and Mark), one Iranian (Mary), one Pakistani (Henry), and one Afghani (Wayne).

All participants are from middle class families. Their parents have all received college degrees; three of them have fathers who own businesses or are self-employed, and five of them have mothers who are housewives. Three of them have at least one Christian parent. All of them know how to speak their parents' ethnic languages as a second language after English. Even though some participants are not proficient in their second language, they use it in communication mainly at home or with people from similar ethnic backgrounds. For example, Young, Heidi, Darla, and Francis speak Arabic because they have at least one parent who speaks the language at home. They all joined Arabic classes at the University. Mary's parents are both Iranian so she knows how to speak Persian. Wayne's parents are both Afghans and both speak Persian and Pashto. Bridget and Mark have Spanish-speaking parents so they are both proficient in Spanish.

Muslims: A New Enemy

When people say "terrorists," people automatically think "Arabs" and "Muslims." It is just one of those things they are pretty much brainwashed Americans' minds, incorporating those two words together. "Terrorist" and "Muslim." So by incorporating these two words together it's like when you say "park" people think "grass," you know, so a lot of image and connection between these two and this is why we Muslims are up against this ideology that everybody is thinking Muslims are horrible. (Darla, personal communication, April 3, 2010)

The uneven debate surrounding 9/11 and the War on Terror presents Muslims, including Muslim Americans such as Darla, as a dangerous enemy of American and Western culture. According to Michael Lipka, Senior Editor of Pew Research Center, almost half of Americans believe that some Muslim Americans are anti-American (Lipka, 2016). Even political figures vocalize negative opinions of Muslims, such as Presidential candidate Donald Trump, who called for a "total and complete shutdown of Muslims entering the United States." According to representatives integral to his campaign, this would mean tourists and even American citizens living abroad (Casselman & Enten, 2015, para. 1). Christian religious leaders in the United States often deeply oppose Islamic belief and draw connections between Muslims and terrorism. For example, Jerry Farwell, an influential Baptist, said on 60 Minutes, "I think Mohammad was a terrorist … Jesus set the example for love, as did Moses, and I think Muhammad set an opposite example" (Nimer, 2007, p. 85). These hostile statements of Islam slander all Muslims and are used to distinguish the flawless America from the evil Muslim world. It is interesting to note here what Freire (1970) would call the relationship between oppressed and oppressor—the two serving as each other's antithesis. In Freire's opinion, "without [the oppressed] the oppressor could not exist" (1970, p. 49). After 9/11, Muslims have been seen as oppressors, inflicting great violence towards Western nations, however, this binary thinking makes it easy to convince a populace of an over-simplified view of the world where one side is good and the other is bad. Without this "other," who is deemed bad, the dominant culture would not seem good, or as good. Thus, portraying Muslims as an enemy makes America seem like a victim and in turn Western nations seem like heroes in the fight against global terrorism. As a result of the one-dimensional debate, it has become normative to see Muslims as individuals capable of inflicting great violence towards Western nations.

The problem with the way America views terrorists is that this view is mapped onto how society views and interacts with Muslims. According to Freire (1970), oppression is "any situation in which 'A' objectively exploits 'B' or hinders his and her pursuit of self-affirmation" (p. 55). This situation "constitutes violence … because it interferes with the individual's ontological and historical vocation to be more fully human" (Freire, 1970, p. 55). Applying Freire's quote shows that presenting a false perception of Muslims as oppressors facilitates discrimination against Muslim Americans in daily life. After 9/11,

Muslim Americans, particularly those who fit a certain physical profile, were labeled as terrorists and were often treated as a threat to American national security by authorities (Van Driel, 2004). Among other policies, the Patriot Act paved the way for numerous acts of discrimination and marginalization for Muslims. Because of the Patriot Act, tens of thousands of Muslim and Arab immigrants must submit to a call-in interview which is not required for other immigrants (Ahmed, 2004) and the FBI collect data and conduct surveillance predominantly on Islamic centers and mosques across the country (Ahmed, 2004). Besides a discriminatory political framework, direct acts of discrimination and violence against Muslims and their businesses have become more frequent nationwide (Haque, 2004). Inflamed by Islamophobic rhetoric in the media and in political discourse, many Muslims living in the United States have experienced verbal and physical abuse. Mostafa Abu Sway, Associate Professor of Philosophy and Islamic Studies at Al-Quds University in Jerusalem, added that there is much "discrimination in employment" and "in the provision of health services, exclusion from managerial positions and jobs of high responsibility and exclusion from political and government posts" (2005, p. 15). Further, emergency medicine physician, Dr. Aasim Padela, and Dr. Michele Heisler, University of Michigan Professor in the Department of Internal Medicine, conducted a study that gathered face-to-face data from Arab American adults in the greater Detroit Area to assess the relationship between abuse and discrimination with stress levels in a post-/911 world. They found that post-9/11 discrimination directly impacted the rise of psychological disorders among Arabs (Padela & Heisler, 2010). Further, psychology professors Selcuk R. Sirin of New York University and Michelle Fine at The City University of New York confirmed that discriminatory acts challenge Muslim Americans' ability to attain an education, improve socio-economic status, and their development of a sense of identity and belonging (Sirin & Fine, 2008). Because of the crooked perspective that generalizes Muslims as oppressors, many face persecution or experience systematic discrimination that hinders their self-affirmation. This systematic discrimination is also prevalent within public schools.

The Results of Banking Education: Dehumanization of Muslims

Banking education, which perpetuates this uneven conversation, contributes to a cycle of intolerance and fear of Muslim Americans in the classroom, which can lead to their dehumanization.

They would be behind our back, so they are like, "Look at them, they are Muslims, blah blah, they are sand diggers. ..." they have a few words with sand. (personal communication, April 1, 2010)

Just like Francis, other interviewees experienced discrimination and intolerance by their peers after 9/11. Heidi's peers "would still consider us outsiders or foreigners. We [Muslims] had a hand in this [9/11], it was our entire fault. A lot of people would start picking on me about it." She even threw punches over disputes with her peers who verbally harassed her. Darla's peers called her a "sand digger" and said that, "if you are a Muslim and you speak Arabic, you are a terrorist." She was so miserable at high school that she rearranged her schedule to be able to spend the least amount of time possible there. Mark noticed his peers developing an anti-Muslim attitude in his private Christian High School. He said the following:

Because this was a Christian school, but it became even more like, you know, "We are on the side of God and these people [the Muslims] they worship the devil," you know, or something like this. We had a weekly chapel service and at the end of the service, one of the students he went up there and he said, "I want to make an announcement." So he was such a good Christian and all these things. So, he said, "I want everybody who is on the side of God who is a Christian, so if you are not a Christian, you are obviously not on the side of God." He said, "I want everyone who is on the side of God who is a good Christian to come up here and show that you are a good Christian." People started going up one by one, you know. Some people didn't want to go, but then I could tell they saw other people going and so they are like, "Oh, wow, I'd better go or else I will be like some kind of outcast or something." Almost everybody went up except maybe me and four other people that I knew. And they were all like staring at us like, "What is wrong with you guys? How dare you not be on the side of God?" (personal communication, March 19, 2010)

Mark clarified that after 9/11, even though he did not notice any Muslim students at the school, his peers at the school started adopting an "us" versus "them" mentality. He added:

There was a strong anti-Muslim sentiment and that it was kind of like people were adopting this, "We have to go fight against these people who are Muslims," and, you know, "They don't believe in God or anything," like this. (personal communication, March 19, 2010)

Mark's observations indicate the conflation between a religious and a national identity that defines an Americans as being a Christian. This form of nationalism is exclusive of others who do not fit this category. Also, Wayne explained that:

Most people knew I was from Afghanistan, and so one kid was giving me a hard time, but the kid was smaller than me, so I didn't let it affect me too much. He would call me kind of like "terrorist" and stuff like that. (personal communication, April 11, 2010)

In college, Francis described a situation in which a University professor was trying to explain that Islam is a peaceful religion. She was upset when students refused to listen and three left the class in protest. Francis stated the following:

Some of the students were arguing with him [the professor] like, "How could you say that [Islam is a peaceful religion]?" Because 9/11 and what had happened and he was trying to explain and saying—of course it was just him and I against the whole class. And we were just trying to explain, "Why would you pin this on a whole religion and a whole people, like 1.3 billion people?" (personal communication, April 1, 2010)

A banking educational model allows for the perpetuation of an uneven dialectic about 9/11 and the War on Terror which unfairly associates Muslim American youth with acts of terror. Through this association, they are dehumanized—called horrible names, beaten, hated. Dehumanization is "the result of unjust order that engenders violence in the oppressors, which in turn dehumanizes the oppressed" (Freire, 1970, p. 44). The treatment of Muslims as sub-human is exacerbated in particular when the individual in question is more obviously Muslim-looking.

Symbols of Islam Heighten Discrimination. Dehumanization of Muslim American students heightens in the classroom when they display visible symbols of their Muslim identity. Muslim Americans who wear typical "Islamic clothing" at school or who are from transnational communities that have a contentious relationship with the United States typically experience additional racism within the school system. In the aftermath of 9/11, Naber (2008) described the rise of two new types of racism: nation-based and culture-based racism. In nation-based racism, immigrants or children of immigrants are perceived as potentially criminal and immoral, and therefore must be removed or controlled. Cultural racism is an "othering" process that creates a perception that certain cultural (i.e., Arab), religious (i.e., Muslim), or civilizational (i.e., the Middle East) differences are natural and insurmountable. Naber (2008) argued that when these two forms of racism dovetail together, they serve as the backbone for the argument to go to war "over there" and support racist and exclusionist policies "over here" under the guise of national security. It is clear the interviewees felt the weight of nation-based racism mapped onto the cultural racism they already experienced as Muslim Americans. It was also clear that cultural symbols, such as the *hijab*, exposed Muslim Americans as easy targets for the "othering" process that Naber described. For example, Francis described being Muslim and Palestinian as a "double violence" against her "because of the Qu'ran," or her religion, and "because of being Palestinian, being people that they [the media and U.S. government] portray as terrorists." She dealt with peers who refused to acknowledge the existence of a Palestinian state, attempting to deny Francis of her own sense of identity. One student responded "You are Arab," every time Francis described herself as Palestinian, and said such things as "There is no such thing as Palestine." When I asked Francis how being Palestinian American was a different kind of experience than other Muslim Americans, she referred to how the United States financially and politically supports Israel and presents the conflict as "a one-sided issue. Like, you will never open the TV and find Fox News talking from a Palestinian side" (personal communication, April 1, 2010). This is an example of how Muslim stories, experiences and voices are silenced in the media and politics, thus enforcing a disproportionate dialectic. In other words, her experience as a Palestinian American student is refracted through the lens of American media's portrayal of a land conflict in which the United States has a clear vested interest.

When Wayne's family discovered that a Muslim extremist group based in Afghanistan was responsible for the 9/11 attacks, they rushed to pick him up at elementary school. His family felt the need to tell this young child, "If anybody asks you, we are not Muslims and not from Afghanistan. Say you are Mexican or Italian or something like that" (personal communication, April 11, 2010). His family was concerned about the repercussions of both their religious and national identities.

The Muslim American students who wore Islamic clothing also faced additional discrimination. For example, Mark said that sometimes he wears a *thobe* (an ankle-length garment with long arms, similar to a robe that Muslim men typically wear to the mosque) or a *kufi* (a hat most commonly worn in parts of Africa and Asia) to university. He had an uncomfortable experience due to his Islamic dress, which he describes as follows:

> There was one lady, she came up to me one time and she said, "You need to take off that kind of clothing. We don't want people dressing like this around here," something like that. ... (Mark, personal communication, March 19, 2010)

Muslim women who wear *hijab* are portrayed in the media as oppressed, backwards, and uninterested in education (Zine, 2007). This portrayal, according to ethnic studies and sociology scholar, Jasmin Zine (2007) of

Wilfrid Laurier University, can lead their teachers and school administrations to discriminate against them and, occasionally, even place them in lower academic tracks. Darla, Francis, Heidi, and Bridget also noticed that women who wear the *hijab* experience heightened discrimination.

Heidi explained that her experiences of discrimination were nothing compared to those of her Muslim friend who wore the *hijab*. This friend "felt discriminated because of the students and some of the teachers." When this friend came to her crying "about something that was happening to her ... I would nearly get into a fist fight over it for her." Heidi confided that during the situation "we [were] not sure what to do to help alleviate that tension" which "[kept] us in fear" (personal communication, March 17, 2010).

Bridget, who converted to Islam after 9/11, reported feeling like "the little ugly duckling that no one wants to talk to" when she wore her *hijab* at university (personal communication, March 24, 2010). As a new Muslim, wearing the *hijab* was not easy for her. Bridget noticed how much the *hijab* isolated her from others, and described this experience as follows:

> Wearing the *hijab* already singles you out. It makes you a symbol, and it is very different between men and women, you know, between men, you can't really tell unless they tell you that they are Muslims. Or if they have a long beard, but with women, the way you dress and just wearing the *hijab* or the veil already singles you out because you are a walking symbol of a new religion, something that sometimes people fear. (personal communication, March 24, 2010)

Francis also noticed that her school peers treated Muslim girls wearing the *hijab* differently than they treated her. She said, "I knew this one girl that was in high school who used to wear the *hijab*." Apparently, the young girl "took it off after 9/11" because "she felt like she was more bullied, more looked down upon. ..." Francis' cousin, who wore the *hijab*, experienced more harassment than other Muslim girls not wearing it. Francis said the following:

> I think it is different for someone wearing the *hijab*, like our cousin who wore it. She got a lot more assaults for wearing it. They [students] were like, "Terrorist." They didn't respect her as much as they respected me because of the fact that she was wearing that. They thought she was an outcast, "She is not like us, she is weird," you know? Even though she is our cousin and we are the same religion, you know. I think they accepted me more because of the fact that I don't wear it. And they were just like, "We can kind of connect to you more than we could connect with her." (personal communication, April 1, 2010)

Francis tried to stick by her cousin's side. She stayed with her during lunch and they would usually partner for classroom activities. Francis noticed a change in their classmates' behavior as the year progressed and "you could tell [the students] were more open to her, like, compared to the beginning of the year." Their peers "started talking to [Francis' cousin] and she started having more friends and she didn't have as much problems" (Francis, personal communication, April 1, 2010). As the high school students got to know Francis' cousin, they realized she was a young girl similar to them, and stopped treating her with the disrespect and "othering" they had somehow and somewhere previously learned she deserved.

Wearing the *hijab* can be very eye-opening, especially for non-Muslims. Heidi's "typical American white girl friend ... wanted to experience what it's like to be a Muslim." So Heidi gave her some clothes to wear, including a *hijab*. When the young woman put the clothes on, "she saw a different reaction towards her" than normal, as "people were staring at her" and trying "to walk the other way." Heidi's friend was surprised, "because she thought that people would be a little more open minded and liberal ... She never expected people to be like that" (Heidi, personal communication, March 17, 2010).

As Francis and I discussed the *hijab*, she brought up a very relevant point about why the *hijab* elicits such strong responses from non-Muslim people. Since Francis does not wear the *hijab*, she said people would be more open-minded about her religion since they will see her as "a normal looking girl." She contrasted this with me, as I sat in front of her in *hijab*, by saying, "They will probably look at you and that's it. They have this image, opinion about you already without speaking to you" (personal communication, April 1, 2010). As a Muslim woman who wears hijab in a post-9/11 United States, I can personally attest to a sense of heightened discrimination due to wearing this particular article of clothing.

For many Muslims—men and women alike—physical symbols of their religion preclude them to greater mistreatment than their peers who are able to blend in more. While this is a frustration experienced by men and women alike, there tend to be more overt symbols of religion worn by women, and therefore the burden of heightened discrimination and isolation often falls on their shoulders.

The Results of Banking Education: Intolerance and Ignorance

Intolerance of certain populations, such as Muslims, is on the rise, and it is in part due to the educational system. Intolerance results from the notion that many Americans believe that their culture is superior to other cultures in all aspects of life, including their perspective and ways of living. Francis was seen as a "normal looking girl," whereas others who dress in a non-normative way are discriminated against. Where does this intolerance come from? American anthropologist and professor at the State University of New York, Mark Nathan Cohen (1999) argued that the American educational system fosters it through "a lack of positive exposure to, or education about, other people and their cultures" (p. 298). For example, when students threw punches or insults, Heidi knew that her teachers would do all that they could to defend her personally. However, the initial effort teachers made post-9/11 to correct misinformation about Islam was not carried over into the classroom curriculum. When I asked her if there "were any teachers who tried to teach them [the students] something about Islam. ..." Heidi responded in the following way:

> No, none of them did, so everything the students heard or read, it was from home. Outside the school. The teachers had nothing to do with it. If they tried to teach them anything it was very vague. Like they only taught whatever was on the curriculum. (personal communication, March 17, 2010)

Heidi correlated curricular lessons on Islam with vagueness. According to her, these lessons were insufficient to truly abate misconceptions about Islam and Muslims among her classmates.

Henry described similar experiences. In his religious studies class in which the teacher talked about all sorts of religions, Henry said, "the teacher, she introduced Islam ... she didn't go into too much details about it." Fortunately she didn't have to, since, according to him, the following occurred:

> There was a huge talk about it from the MSA [Muslim Student Association] from the University of New Mexico. They came out there and answered a lot of questions for students. So our class from that period went to MSA. (personal communication, April 6, 2010)

Though Henry believed the teacher presented the information on Islam "in a fine way," the information would have been cursory and incomplete if not for a timely visit from the MSA to Henry's school. Still, the fact that the MSA was invited in the first place is certainly commendable. Henry believed that lack of education about Islam in the United States fosters extremism among Americans. Henry perceived the American definition of extremism to be "anything that is against America ... anyone against America's government or policy is an extremist."

In high school, Francis felt that Islam was a taboo subject. She described the situation as follows:

The teachers wouldn't talk about it. The topic you can't talk about, which made it worse because the kids were so ignorant during that time. I think it would have been better if somebody actually sat them down and had a discussion with them and, you know, just had some dialogue to understand what is going on. (personal communication, April 1, 2010)

Francis also believed that more time was allocated for learning about Christianity and Judaism, whereas "[the teacher] only gave us like three days to learn about Islam."

Francis initially told me she had no problems with educators. However, as our interview continued she remembered more and more incidents. For example, she recalled a memory of when her sixth grade social studies teacher introduced the topic of Islam to the class, Francis described the interaction as follows:

She was like, "Let's talk to Muslims about it," but she said it sarcastically, and we were trying to say the five pillars and how we go by, basically a discussion on how is Islam and what is it perceived by us compared to them. And she just basically blocked us out. She kept asking the most basic questions, like, she kept being like, "Are you forced to wear this? Are you forced to pray? Are you forced to say this by your parents? Are you forced to lie?" And the whole time, we were like, "No, we are not." She was an old Social Studies teacher and it shows, like she was ignorant. And the class was like, "Dang, you need to back off these kids," because she was bashing us. She is not listening to us when she was asking us. The whole topic wasn't about what we think, she just turned it around, like, her own words. It was more of a fight instead of a discussion. (personal communication, April 1, 2010)

The askew dialectic perseveres even in the classroom, as Muslim voices are shut down by some teachers. For instance, the teacher's interaction with Francis and her Muslim peers demonstrates cruelty and domination and "dialogue cannot exist … in the absence of profound love for the world and for men" (Freire, 1970, p. 158). Freire insisted time and time again that without dialogue, without care and commitment to other human beings, liberation cannot be achieved. In subsequent years, when Francis and her Muslim American peers attempted to provide their perspective on Islam in her high school social studies class, she described how the teacher "blocked" them in the following way:

We tried to say that the Qu'ran is one of the most poetic books in the world, and she would just block me off and block my cousin off. It was something positive and something interesting, people actually want to hear it. She twists it around and turns it negative. (Francis, personal communication, April 1, 2010)

When I asked Francis if this particular teacher discussed 9/11, her response was the following:

> When she brought up violence, she did. When she said that in our book it teaches us to be, she said that people say, or she has heard, that people say that in our book, it teaches us to be violent since we were born. She would just say basically Muslims are violent and stuff. The only thing she had to back this claim with was 9/11. (personal communication, April 1, 2010)

Dialogue requires humility. And humility cannot exist where there is hierarchy, where people and cultures are not seen as equals. At the heart of educational systems are two questions: "How do we know what we know? And by what warrant can we call our knowledge true?," according to educator and activist Parker Palmer, who has written several books focusing on teaching and social change (2007, p. 51). Dominant cultures ultimately decide what knowledge is important and how we measure what is true. However, the dominant ways of knowing are often rooted in arrogance and fear. The superiority of the dominant knowledge disguises a fear of other ways of thinking, being, and living. This fear of diversity is based on the rejection that anyone else's view of the world is as equally valid as the dominant one. This view fosters intolerance, as it overlooks the existence of other views, and often other peoples. As a result, for example, contributions of other societies and minorities are not taught in World and American History, and there is an overlooking of mistakes Americans and/ or the dominant culture made in history. There is a general fear of encountering cultures that are different because they threaten a hegemonic American view of life and therefore the white, heterosexual, male, capitalistic America's hegemonic national identity. When teachers invalidate Muslim students' experiences and epistemologies, it enforces an "us versus them" mentality, leading to an intolerant classroom and furthering a shallow narrative. This narrow viewpoint eliminates broader perspectives, thereby preventing a balanced dialectic. In this case, an imbalanced dialectic of current events such as 9/11 and the War on Terror funneled through teachers and school systems often contributes to the potential for a hostile educational environment towards Muslim students and intolerance of discussions that embrace alternative opinions or thoughts.

What is important to note is that teachers have a choice as to whether they perpetuate this warped discussion. This decision will have very real consequences not only for general intolerance, but also for the identities of specific Muslim American students. Broad, negative stereotypes of an entire religious group indelibly lead to significant psycho-social challenges. In my research, I found that the uncritical dialectic contributes to Muslim American youth questioning their sense of belonging in the United States, thereby complicating their connection with their American nationality, religion, and transnational communities.

Muslim American Identity: How Isolation and Discrimination Impact the Self

Identity is a complex and ethereal concept, and it is created and impacted by a variety of factors. According to Özlem Sensoy (2010), professor of education at Simon Fraser University, identity can be defined as "characteristics, beliefs, behaviors, ways of being, and ways of making meaning" that represent an individual and can be shared within a community (p. 123). As such, identity is a mix of influences between self and society, according to Maja Miskovic (2007), Associate Professor of research at Concordia University in Chicago. Due to identity's nature, its development is a process (Miskovic, 2007). But who or what determines the processes by which this identity is shaped? Literacy and discourse analysis professor of Arizona State University, James Paul Gee (2001) insisted that identities could either become assigned or acquired and both have consequences. For instance, among ascribed identities are those seen through social lenses such as *essentialism*. In social science, essentialism is defined as seeing all members of a racial or gendered or other group as having specific permanent biological, genetic, or mental traits and abilities that do not vary among individuals or over time (Aulette & Wittner, 2015). For instance, it could be argued that the fixed perception of blacks as dangerous led to the killing of an innocent boy, Trayvon Martin.

Therefore, it comes as no surprise that minority identity formation is a different process than dominant group identity formation, and this difference is especially apparent among Muslims. For example, Muslims are portrayed as a homogenous group, with no individual, cultural, or religious diversity, with fixed qualities such as violence and ignorance (Zine, 2007). Despite many spheres of influence, such as the religious, national, and transnational identity, identity is often projected onto Muslims through a lens of Orientalism or Islamophobia (Zine, 2007). Muslim American identity formation is vastly different than that of their white peers, or even that of other minorities.

Can Muslim Americans Claim American-ness?

In a post-9/11 world, the essentialist lens through which Muslims are viewed leads them to often feel a sense of disconnection to their American identities.

For example, Mary, who holds an American and Iranian passport and was born in the United States, responded, "I was born at the States but I am originally from Iran." She told me she felt "more Iranian than American." As she described heightened security checks post-9/11, Mary wondered why she was often selected for random screening, surmising that maybe it was "because they know I am not a one-hundred-percent American ..." Though she said, "when I am around American people I kind of feel like one of them" she also told me that "I don't think I have too much of an American culture in me" (personal communication, April 2, 2010).

Despite being born in the United States and holding an American passport, she still does not see herself as one-hundred percent American.

When I asked Francis if she had dual citizenship for the United States and Palestine, she responded, "No, I don't. I can get an ID, but it is just a long process." Part of the challenge was getting it through the Israeli government. She lived in Jerusalem for 5 years in order to take care of her sick grandparents and "learn about our culture, learn Arabic." In this instance she clearly identified her culture as Palestinian culture. When describing the 9/11 attacks, she seemed confused about whether to consider Arabs or Muslims fully American:

> We are not all terrorists and we come from different countries and have different backgrounds. But we are all Americans. We didn't want this to happen especially ... it wasn't only Americans who died, too, there were also Arabs and Muslims who died too in 9/11. (personal communication, April 1, 2010)

At first Francis located herself among other Muslim Americans, when she said, "We are all Americans." In the following sentence, she separated Americans from Muslims and Arabs, as if belonging to either the religion (Islam) or culture (Arab) negates American citizenship. This is also an example of identity confusion (Zine, 2004), as well as religion and culture confusion. Perhaps a lot of this confusion stems from the fact that she felt "left out, in American terms, like an outcast, basically, because of how they thought of us." Once when she was out driving with her mother, who always wore *hijab*, people in a passing car rolled down their windows and yelled, "Go back home, terrorists." Though only having American citizenship, Francis described herself exclusively as Palestinian, or a Palestinian Muslim. When Heidi told me she considered herself a Muslim American, I asked her to identify why and how she felt connected to her American-ness. She replied that having "lived here a long time" she had absorbed "bits and pieces of the American culture" yet also "completely rejected" others. Still, she ultimately "considers [herself]

American" because she "grew up here, this is [her] country, [she] is a citizen of this country." Unlike her peers, Heidi still defined herself as an American because of her citizenship, despite the discrimination she faced. When I asked Mark how he identified himself, he responded, "As a Muslim … I would identify myself as a Muslim who happens to be an American." Mark clearly identified first and foremost with his religion, but still saw himself as a citizen of the United States. When I asked if he thought other Muslim Americans felt that their citizenship was denied or questioned by others, he said:

> When they [Muslim Americans] see over and over again that they are being misrepresented and portrayed in this way it makes alot of people say, "Well, you know, I guess I am not even like an American basically," because you don't feel like it actually because of these images and the messages being broadcast. (personal communication, March 19, 2010)

In his opinion, the stereotypical representations of Muslim Americans makes all American citizens (Muslims and non-Muslims) question if Muslims are true Americans.

Darla, whose mother is a Christian from Texas and father a Palestinian Muslim, said "I am an American Muslim … but I am Palestinian American, who is Muslim, that is what I say." Darla struggled with her identity, unable to fully express her connection to Islam at home due to her mothers' disapproval, and her sense of both connection and dissimilarity to her father's Palestinian culture. This struggle was evident in the way she described herself. Still, she demonstrated a clear and unwavering connection to her American identity, likely due to the fact that her mother is from Texas.

Wayne's stories about how his family tried to blend in demonstrate the extent to which many Muslim Americans feel fear in their communities because of the identities ascribed to them. He said:

> On the anniversary of 9/11, my mom went to Target and bought all these American T-shirts, and she brought them to us, and we wore them that day. My parents were really trying to blend in and making all of us blend in. (personal communication, April 11, 2010)

When I asked Wayne to talk more about his own sense of identity as a dual citizen of Afghanistan and the United States, he said if someone were to ask him where he is from, he would respond, "San Diego." Only if someone asked where his parents were from would he say, "Afghanistan." When I asked Young to identify himself, he said "I am proud of my Arabic name. I am a Muslim."

He did not mention his American citizenship at first. When I asked him "How does your American identity fit with all that? Do you consider yourself American?" He responded, "I consider myself Muslim American." The American part, for him, was the fact that he has "video games … can socialize with other people around the world," and "we have American friends come over sometimes and we hang out at my place." Only after he mentioned these other things did he finally say "I do, I think of myself as American, you know, being born in America I consider myself American" (personal communication, March 14, 2010). It is almost as if the location of his birth were an afterthought in determining his American-ness. Still, Young seemed to feel secure in his Muslim American identity. When I asked him to "tell me a story in which you were proud to be a Muslim American," he paused for a second and then said, "I guess I don't have a story about that. I am always proud to be one." Bridget seemed to separate her identities, describing herself "as a Muslim and an American Hispanic individual." She closed by saying "I definitely have a lot of self-identification" (personal communication, March 24, 2010), which could mean that she has thought deeply about who she is, perhaps through her conversion experience, or it could mean that her identity is multi-faceted, or both.

Can I Belong Here?: Discrimination and the Right to Citizenship

Navigating questions of personal identity are especially difficult for individuals who experience racial profiling, harassment, and hate crimes (Haque, 2004). Students who belong to groups alienated in society experience an unhealthy amount of stress due to discrimination, their minority status, and the process of negotiating their identities within multiple, competing cultures, according to Associate Professor of Women and Gender studies Thea Renda Abu El-Haj of Rutgers, School of Arts and Science and Sally Wesley Bonet, Visiting Professor of transnational citizenship and migrations at Colgate University (2011). When it comes to a connection to American citizenship and sense of belonging, Muslim American students question their ability and desire to lay claim to it. For some, the idea of citizenship "confers membership, identity, values, and rights of participation and assumes a body of common political knowledge" (Abowitz & Harnish, 2006, p. 653) and that "a citizen derives his/her rights and obligations through a social contract of the nation-state" (p. 680). However, there are emotional layers to this social contract "because democratic participation is related to the emotional experiences of inclusion and exclusion" (Abu El-Haj & Bonet, 2011, p. 32). It is clear through my students' interviews that many of them defined citizenship in ways that went beyond merely holding an American passport. These other ways of defining or determining their sense of belonging center around a sense of acceptance that was so often denied them on behalf of peers, teachers, airport security personnel, and many others. As a result, the students covered up aspects of their religion, dialed up their American-ness, or isolated and removed themselves from American culture and citizenship, leaving many confused as to who they really were.

The Important Role of Teachers in Helping Muslim Students

Despite the many cultural forces at play that lead to these identity challenges among Muslim Americans, teachers do have power that influences marginalized students' identities and sense of belonging. According to Erikson (1968), when people see you differently than how you see yourself, it often leads to identity consciousness, or awareness about a certain aspect of one's identity (Erikson, 1968). For example, Muslim American youth did not equate their religion with terrorism, as did the world around them. This dissonance between external perception of identity and internal understanding of identity can lead to a temporary identity crisis, or war within oneself (Erikson, 1968). When the person or system that produces and maintains the external perception of identity is in a position of power—such as a parent, teacher, or the dominant culture—the dissonance between a positive internal identity and a negative external one can be especially great, and lead to more personal challenges for the individual (Erikson, 1968). However, there is also an opportunity for liberation from the alienating negative external identity through greater awareness of the self (Erikson, 1968) as well as affirmations from adults or authorities, such as teachers.

Examples of Problem-Posing Teachers

There were many examples given by the Muslim American students of how their teachers demonstrated a problem-posing model of teaching in which ignorance and intolerance were not accepted. Remember Heidi, who felt the intensity of all her peers staring her down in her classroom? Thankfully her teacher, in her words, did not allow the students to blame her for 9/11. Heidi described the situation as follows:

> My teacher was telling them [her peers] this is not my fault or anybody else's fault. This is some other group that took things in their own hands and they were being vigilantes. (personal communication, March 17, 2010)

Immediately following 9/11, Heidi's teachers tried to help teach the students about Islam by doing the following:

> ... tried to get them to be more open about their feelings and opinions about Islam and talking to them about it and try to show them the better way of seeing things. For example, if someone says, "Yeah, I think all Muslims worship the wrong God," and the teacher corrects them and translates that the word "God" is "Allah" in Islam, so they [Muslims] worship one God. (Heidi, personal communication, March 17, 2010)

When Wayne became more religious and started praying 5 times a day during his senior year of high school, he described how his teacher supported his religious decision as follows:

> I prayed during class and my teacher was like, "Yeah, you could go ahead and pray in his office," it had an extension and a backroom. He was like, "Go ahead and pray whenever you want." He was nice. (Wayne, personal communication, April 11, 2010)

These demonstrations of tolerance, understanding, and acceptance are examples of problem-posing educational methods. These demonstrations are extremely important for affirming positive associations with religious identity, and helping Muslim American youth to feel less alienated by the dominant culture in which they live.

Why Teachers Struggle to Help Muslim Students, and Why They Must

Seeing Muslims as a problem prevents teachers from sympathizing with Muslim American students. The Swiss Professor of English of Brooklyn College, Moustafa Bayoumi (2008) argued that Islam and Muslims are perceived to be a problem for the West, and therefore it is hard to see them as victims of oppression. Christopher Stonebanks, professor of Education at Bishop's University (2010) insisted that "to teach against" a prejudice requires that the person engaged in teaching that "acknowledges that the discriminatory practice in question actually exists and, if so, is worth teaching against" (p. 35). Since discriminating against Muslims is not seen as a problem in society, it gets similar attention in the classroom (Stonebanks, 2010). Just like the rest of humanity, teachers harbor personal ideologies, biases, and intolerances (Apple, 2004; Sleeter, 2005). Unsurprisingly, Islamophobia could potentially be reproduced through teachers (Stonebanks, 2010). Distorted representations of Islam and Muslims in a post-9/11 world influence teachers' material choices and pedagogies. For instance, negative per-ceptions of Muslims are supported by several myths, including the following: (a) Muslims are a monolithic and homogenous group (Zine, 2007), (b) Arabs and Muslims are the same people (Elbih, 2015), (c) Islam teaches terrorism and all Muslims are terrorists (Elbih, 2015), (d) Muslims hate the West and democracy (Nasr, 2004), and (e) Muslims want to rule the Western world (Nasr, 2004). Teachers need to look beyond what is presented to them, reflect on their posi-tion, and understand that true social justice education may mean some personal risk (Stonebanks, 2010). Just as Linda, one of the teachers I interviewed, was afraid to get fired just for speaking with me about 9/11 and the War on Terror, other teachers must understand that when they teach against injustice they are taking a risk of challenging the status quo. Freire (1970) argued that the solution is not to integrate the oppressed in the oppressive system, but to transform that system itself to become socially just. However, since the banking model of edu-cation serves the oppressive system, such transformation will not be in the inter-est of the oppressor. Nevertheless, the goal of problem-posing education is not to oppress the oppressor and free the oppressed, instead the goal is to restore "the humanity of both" (p. 44). If educators do not recognize and teach against the unidimensional rhetoric, they will likely foster an intolerant classroom environ-ment that dehumanizes Muslims and impedes healthy identity formation among Muslim American youth. Becoming educated and recognizing unfair stereotypes directed at Muslim youth will assist critical teachers and educators to fight in solidarity with Muslims to restore their humanity.

When encountering another who is different, teachers might fear con-flict of divergent truths, or losing one's ideas, or sense of self. Sometimes teachers fear encountering difference that would compel them to reassess and even change their lives. However, according to Palmer (2007) teachers must understand that diversity "always invites transformation, calling us not only to new facts and theories and values but also to new ways of living our lives" (p. 39). Many teachers try to control encounters with diversity to minimize this transformation. However, these changes and transformations can be posi-tive, ones that lead to personal and professional growth. Channeling this fear of diversity in their classroom towards greater inquiry and learning is what critical educators do. Educators who listen to the discrimination experiences of marginalized groups can see things in different ways, often developing "a cognition of empathy" (Kincheloe & Steinberg, 2004, p. 3). Palmer supported the idea that "fear can play a positive role in students' lives … the fear we feel when we encounter something foreign and are challenged to enlarge our thinking, our identity, our lives—the fear that lets us know we are on the brink of real learning" (2007, p. 40). In fact, embracing difference is the bedrock of democracy (McLaren, Kincheloe, & Steinberg, 2005). Embracing diversity, just like embracing dialectical perspectives, expands thinking and assists teachers and students in exploring issues from divergent viewpoints. The goal is to understand people who are Muslims and break the cycle of intolerance.

Conclusion

In the wake of the 9/11 attacks, the media repeated the terms "Muslim" and "terrorist" together so many times that both terms now go together as an ingrained norm. Generalizing Muslims as terrorists impacts the way society perceives and interacts with Muslims. This phony analysis of 9/11 characterizes millions of Muslim Americans as violent, causing others, including teachers and peers, to fear them and classify them as a threat to national security. Ultimately, this leads to disrespect and discrimination against Muslims, and leads Muslim youth to develop self-doubt and question their identities, citizenship and sense of belonging. Whether they have Muslim students in their classroom or not, teachers need to become aware of Muslim youth experiences in order to stop the pervasive discrimination against them.

Identity is a challenging concept to pin down and is shaped by many competing factors. As a minority group, Muslim identity formation is different from dominant group identity formation in many ways. For one, the taunting, bullying, and physical abuse of peers, colleagues, and even authority figures add a layer of complexity to a Muslim person's understanding of self. Specifically, disapproval by authority figures often leads to identity crises among youth. Teachers are authority figures, and they have the power to mold students' identities either by affirming or disapproving of them through their interactions and teaching methods.

Many Muslim students at some point in their school careers encounter teachers who utilize a banking model of education that upholds a crooked conversation of 9/11, the War on Terror, and of Muslims themselves. These teachers silence Muslim voices or insult them. Seeing Muslims as the problem prevents the teachers from recognizing that their Muslim students might be on the receiving end. Some teachers recognize injustices against Muslims and support them during challenging times, but many failed to realize or teach against the existence of Islamophobia in society. Sometimes fear not of Muslims, but of change, causes teachers to ignore other perspectives so as not to lose their own ideas and sense of self. Nevertheless, if teachers embrace this fear as a positive opportunity to assess and challenge their preconceived notions, they can contribute to true democracy that celebrates plurality and diversity.

When a teacher uses a problem-posing model of education, it enhances dialogue and contributes to tolerance in the classroom, thus affirming Muslim students as equal human beings. This contributes to their positive self-identification and wellbeing in the classroom. On the other hand, a teacher who utilizes a banking model of education restricts dialogue, shuts out the voices of Muslim American youth, fosters intolerance in the classroom, and therefore can contribute to an identity crisis or confusion among Muslim American youth. It is up to teachers to decide whether to reinforce a disproportionate conversation or to encourage tolerance and critical thinking among their students.

But what can teachers do if they are surrounded from all directions by a lopsided dialectic? How can they teach critically about 9/11 and challenge misperceptions of Muslims if the curriculum itself includes misinformation and biases? The next chapter analyzes how the curriculum can contribute to the skewed discourse, particularly textbooks. Once teachers learn to recognize this bias in their teaching materials, it will be easier to support Muslim-American students as they struggle to have their voices heard.

References

Abowitz, K. K., & Harnish, J. (2006). Contemporary discourses of citizenship. *Review of Educational Research, 76*, 653–690.

Abu El-Haj, T. R., & Bonet, S. W. (2011, March). Education, citizenship, and the politics of belonging: Youth from Muslim transnational communities and the "war on terror." *Review of Research in Education, 35*, 29–59.

Ahmed, S. (2004). *The cultural politics of emotion.* New York, NY: Routledge.

Apple, M. (2004). *Ideology and curriculum.* New York, NY: Routledge Falmer.

Aulette, J., & Wittner, J. (2015). *Gendered worlds.* New York, NY: Oxford.

Bayoumi, M. (2008). *How does it feel to be a problem? Being young and Arab in America.* Toronto: Penguin Press.

Butler, J. (1993). *Bodies that matter: On the discursive limits of "sex."* New York, NY: Routledge.

Casselman, B., & Enten, H. (2015, December 7). Most Republicans have negative views of Muslims—And toward a religious test. *Five Thirty Eight: 2016 Elections.* Retrieved October 6, 2016 from http://fivethirtyeight.com/features/donald-trump-muslim-religion/

Cohen, M. N. (1999). *Culture of intolerance: Chauvinism, class, and racism in the United States.* New Haven, CT: Yale University Press.

Elbih, R. (2015). Teaching about Islam and Muslims while countering cultural misrepresentations. *The Social Studies, 106*(3), 112–116. Retrieved from http://www.tandfonline.com/doi/pdf/10.1080/00377996.2015.1015712

Erikson, E. H. (1968). *Identity: Youth and crisis.* New York, NY: W. W. Norton.

Freire, P. (1970). *Pedagogy of the oppressed.* New York, NY: Herder & Herder.

Gee, J. (2001). Identity as an analytic lens for research in education. *Review of Research in Education, 25*, 99–125.

Haque, A. (2004). Islamophobia in North America: Confronting the menace. In B. Van Driel (Ed.), *Islamophobia in educational settings* (pp. 1–19). London: Trentham House.

Kincheloe, J. L., & Steinberg, S. R. (2004). *The miseducation of the west: How schools and the media distort our understanding of the Islamic world.* Westport, CT: Praeger Publishers.

Lipka, M. (2016, July 22). Muslims and Islam: Key findings in the U.S. and around the world. *Pew Research Center.* Retrieved September 15, 2016 from http://www.pewresearch.org/fact-tank/2016/07/22/muslims-and-islam-key-findings-in-the-u-s-and-around-the-world/

McLaren, P., Kincheloe, J. L., & Steinberg, S. (2005). *Teachers as cultural workers: Letters to those who dare teach* (expanded ed.). Boulder, CO: Westview Press.

Miskovic, M. (2007). The construction of ethnic identity of Balkan Muslim immigrants: A narrativization of personal experiences. *The Qualitative Report, 12*(2), 514–546. Retrieved from http://nsuworks.nova.edu/tqr/vol12/iss2/1

Naber, N. (2008). "Look, Mohamed the terrorist is coming!" Cultural racism, nation-based racism and the intersectionality of oppression after 9/11. In N. Naber & A. Jamal (Eds.), *Race and Arab Americans before and after 9/11: From invisible citizens to visible subjects* (pp. 276–305). Syracuse, NY: Syracuse University Press.

Nasr, S. H. (2004). *The heart of Islam: Enduring values for humanity.* New York, NY: HarperCollins.

Nimer, M. (2007). *Islamophobia and anti-Americanism: Causes and remedies.* Beltsville, MD: Amana Publications.

Padela, A., & Heisler, M. (2010, February). The association of perceived abuse and discrimination after September 11, 2001, with psychological distress, level of happiness, and health status among Arab Americans. *PMC US National Library of Medicine National Institutes of Health.* Retrieved September 15, 2016 from http://www.ncbi.nlm.nih.gov/pmc/articles/PMC2804633/

Palmer, P. J. (2007). *The courage to teach: Exploring the inner landscape of a teacher's life.* San Francisco, CA: Jossey-Bass.

Sensoy, O. (2010). "Mad Man Hassan will buy your carpets!" The bearded curricula of evil Muslims. In J. L. Kincheloe, S. R. Steinberg, & C. D. Stonebanks (Eds.), *Teaching against Islamophobia* (pp. 111–133). New York, NY: Peter Lang Publishing.

Sirin, S., & Fine, M. (2008). *Muslim American youth: Understanding hyphenated identities through multiple methods.* New York, NY: New York University Press.

Sleeter, C. E. (2005). *Un-standardizing curriculum: Multicultural teaching in the standards-based classroom.* New York, NY: Teachers College Press.

Stonebanks, C. D. (2010). The inescapable presence of "non-existent" Islamophobia. In J. L. Kincheloe, S. R. Steinberg, & C. D. Stonebanks (Eds.), *Teaching against Islamophobia* (pp. 29–48). New York, NY: Peter Lang Publishing.

Sway, A. M. (2005). Islamophobia: Meaning, manifestations, causes. *Palestine-Israel Journal of Politics, Economics & Culture, 12*(2/3), 15–23.

Taylor, C. (1994). *Multiculturalism: Examining the politics of recognition* (pp. 25–75). Princeton, NJ: Princeton University Press.

Van Driel, B. (Ed.). (2004). *Confronting Islamophobia in educational practice.* London: Trentham Books.

Zine, J. (2004). Anti-Islamophobia education as transformative pedagogy: Reflections from the education frontlines. *The American Journal of Islamic Social Sciences, 21*(3), 110–118.

Zine, J. (2007). Deconstructing Islamic identity: Engaging multiple discourses. In A. Asgharzadeh, E. Lawson, & K. U. Oka (Eds.), *Diasporic ruptures: Globality, migrancy, and expressions of identity.* New York, NY: Sense Publishers.

· 5 ·

YOU ARE WHAT YOU READ

Textbooks and the Lopsided Dialectic

The textbook writers are very highly historians from Stanford, as we say, are dead white men. So they have a slant on history that is very traditional. It plays down, for example, the genocide of the people who came here from Europe towards the Indigenous people in America. "That is progress," you know. "You can push those people to the side so you can build your farms, and we can become a great and successful country." It sort of does that in this book. … And so in terms of this textbook, it has a history, because it is a common textbook for AP courses. And this textbook, when it talks about OPEC, the founding of OPEC, it almost makes it sound like it is so unfortunate for the United States. Whenever there is a story of a leader in the Middle East or India, it always makes it sound like it is unfortunate that they have these nationalistic aspirations for themselves, you know? Like, that is what people should have! Everyone has love and dreams for their country and why shouldn't we encourage that? And so I talk about the CIA when we talk about Central and Southern American nations that the United States had influenced, like killing leaders in Chile and other places. So I try to show them the textbook isn't ideal on that because it makes it sound like everything should be for America.

—Linda [high school teacher in New Mexico],
personal communication (May 29, 2010)

Linda, one of the teachers I interviewed, recognized that the very same textbooks she used in her classroom played a significant role in normalizing and reproducing the unidimensional narrative about Muslims, the War on Terror, and many other historical or current events. Linda mainly used *The American*

Pageant: 13th Edition (2008) by Mifflin, Kennedy, Cohen, and Bailey. She observed that the textbook she used for the AP U.S. History class was written predominantly by those who tend to have a more conservative and nationalistic perspective on history that glosses over past wrongdoings to uphold the ideal of American *exceptionalism* which sees White America as a unique society that is sophisticated and developed above all other. Linda even hinted that the textbook authors represent people of color, including American Indians and African Americans, as lesser human beings whose lives have no value and whose physical presence is seen as an obstacle to progress. This imperialistic perspective is not unusual or unique. Imagine how many more teachers use this textbook in their classroom every day and what kind of impact such ideas might have on students and society?

The purpose of this chapter is to investigate a possible existence of an ideology in representations of 9/11 and the War on Terror within the textbooks that might serve the interests of some groups in society at the expense of others. Through analyzing the selective tradition by which these textbooks represent 9/11 and the War on Terror we can answer questions such as the following: (a) Whose knowledge (ideology) is included in the curriculum?, (b) What other knowledge is blocked?, (c) Why is this particular knowledge seen as legitimate?, (d) What feelings does the content trigger?, (e) What actions do the textbooks authors want the readers to take? Whose interest does this benefit? This allows us to relate the knowledge in the curriculum (and the knowledge missing from the curriculum) to economic and political power. Textbook analysis will complement the interviews with teachers and students in this book to provide a full picture of how schools and teachers run the risk of proliferating harmful ideologies. The goal is to help educators and curriculum developers to reflect on the content that is presented and normalized by textbooks and society about certain targeted groups such as Muslims. My hope is that they consider using alternative material that would present holistic perspectives about 9/11 and the War on Terror to alleviate stereotypes about Muslims in textbooks and society. In the following chapter, I will analyze commonly used high school U.S. history textbooks to understand what kinds of belief systems they may be constructing within the hallowed walls of our public schools.

Textbooks and Curriculum Have Many Influences

Textbooks are heavily used in classrooms, and, in many ways, they represent the curriculum. If you are a teacher, especially a new one, then a textbook is most likely your first choice to locate subject-specific content knowledge related to state standards. Textbooks, in many ways, *are* the curriculum. In fact, Thomas W. Hewitt, former chair of the Department of Elementary and Early Childhood Education at the University of South Alabama, indicated that textbooks are sometimes referred to as the implicit or formal curriculum (Hewitt, 2006). Imagine that "a number of studies have found that students engage in textbook-related activities 70 to 95% of the time that they spend in classrooms" (Wade, 2012, p. 232). Thanks to the textbook publishing companies, textbooks represents an economically cost efficient curriculum needed for schools (Hewitt, 2006). Indeed, textbooks are important tools in the classroom—so important that, in many ways, textbooks are synonymous with schooling or schools.

However, this textbook curriculum is strongly influenced by conservative political and economic interests who often have ties to societal elites. Schools' dependence on textbooks creates a thriving market for the textbook production business. With up to $4 billion in annual sales of elementary and secondary education textbooks, it comes as no surprise that textbooks production is a profitable industry. *Publishers Weekly* named the world's 57 largest book publishers of 2015 and included Pearson, and McGraw-Hill Education among the biggest textbook-producing corporations in the United States and the world (*Publishers Weekly*, 2015). On the other hand, as a flourishing business, textbook production creates many job opportunities and connects people in different professions, including academics, teachers, students, parents, curriculum developers, and other practitioners. Textbook production is a profitable, complex industry that involves a network of professionals across different institutions.

Despite being informed by a broad-based network of professionals, the textbook industry is especially influenced by political conservatives. Private publishers handle textbook production in the United States under the direction of the government, which controls and regulates all stages of production, including textbook content knowledge and the provision process. In the past, California and Texas, with a large population of school-age children who needed to buy textbooks, vied for control of the nation's textbook production. However, American journalist and *The New York Times* columnist, Gail Collins wrote that in recent years it became evident that Texas has become more influential, with 4.8 million textbook-reading children as of 2011 (Collins, 2012). Now national publishers alter their books to align with Texas, meaning many children may have a reflective disdain for the separation of church and state, and a firmly held belief in the positive influence of the National Rifle Association (NRA) on American history (Collins, 2012).

Clearly, the national textbook production industry is influenced by the conservative state of Texas; nevertheless, the state is only one aspect of this market.

Remember that textbooks are written by and for people. They are written by historians and curriculum developers and go through layers of editing until the text reaches final production stage and is ready to be used by schools. Often textbooks represent the authors' perspective of curriculum. Textbook authors are expected to "articulate the knowledge that exists about curriculum," (Hewitt, 2006, p. 62) however knowledge is subjective, not objective. Thus, textbooks are written for particular readers and to create particular political subjects. In a report by the National Center for Educational Statistics (NCES) that provides Fast Facts regarding Back-to-School Statistics (n.d.), it was reported that in the fall of 2016 nearly 50 million students will attend U.S. public elementary and secondary schools. This complicates the textbook selection and adoption process per state and per district. Consequently, textbook sales are dependent upon consumers' expectations and satisfaction (Anyon, 1979). This makes the job of textbook authors even harder since they have to present the content knowledge in ways that reflect an understanding of the "curriculum-teacher relationship, with secondary attention to others, like the curriculum supervisor or specialist in the school district" (Hewitt, 2006, p. 62). This also means that textbook customers—such as school boards, committees, teachers, school administration, students, and their parents—all can indirectly impact textbook content since their satisfaction influences the selection and adoption of textbooks. Textbook content reflects a blending of state standards, the author's initial perspective on the curriculum, and customer expectations.

Textbooks: Political and Ideological Tools

Textbooks do not just provide knowledge and pedagogic strategies, they play other important roles. But what are these roles? Textbooks often reflect the basic ideals of the national culture, many of which are positive. However, the flipside of these ideals is that they may exclude many individuals or belief systems. Often the pages of textbooks are filled with controversy writhing just barely beneath the surface, in what deputy director of the Georg Eckert Institute for International Textbook Research, Falk Pingel, would call "a flashpoint of cultural struggle and controversy" (2010, p. 7). The importance of textbooks lies not only in conveying knowledge, but also in defining the sociopolitical norms of a society as well as positioning that society in a global historical context. In other words, much of what American citizens know about the United States has to do with the comparisons to other countries, and even comparisons between a modern and an historical United States. Textbooks construct such norms through presenting geography and history in a "mesh of reference points in time and space" (Pingel, 2010, p. 7). Geography textbooks help individuals learn about themselves, their roots, the reasons and methods of movements of their people to a particular geographical location, and the characteristics of that location. History textbooks create a sense of national unity and identity through a presentation of accomplishments and critical events and through comparisons with other countries. Textbooks help students learn the norms of society and to adapt to its culture.

Textbooks are also political documents and are even used as tools to serve political agendas. For example, Hewitt (2006) explained that any presidential candidate or political party "includes ideas about the purpose and use of education, and the schools are a conduit for implementing those ideas through policy making and curriculum development" (Hewitt, 2006, p. 14). Even historically, during colonization, the curriculum was modeled after colonizing nations. However, whenever a nation gained political and economic independence, such as the case of countries in Africa and Asia in the mid-1900s, these new nations developed new textbooks that reflected their independent status and their own national beliefs, accomplishments, and aspirations. Textbooks serve many political purposes, including being a "means to order society and build loyalty to it, a pillar of nation building capable of creating unity, conformity, and performance of civic duty" (Hewitt, 2006, p. 14). Notions of nationhood and nationalism are highly stressed in textbooks of American history, civics, and literature. Recognizing their political power has led to constant disputes over what content to include in the textbooks and what purpose they serve (Hess & Stoddard, 2007). For instance, there are disputes over presentations of women, racial minorities, and homosexuals in the United States curriculum. Historical events such as national independence and presidential campaigns assert the social and political importance of textbooks. However, disputes over what information to include in textbooks demonstrates the role of ideology in deciding what is kept in and what is left out.

Textbooks contents reflect ideologies that can serve the interests of the elites. Many educators have argued that textbooks reflect the ideology of the dominant groups in society. Ideology is defined here as a lens that helps interpret reality or "what a group holds as truth" (Sleeter, 2005, p. 34). For instance, the French sociologist and philosopher, Emile Durkheim, claimed that between the seventeenth and twentieth century in France the secondary educational curriculum served the interest of the church (Durkheim, 1977). When describing the role of schools in the American capitalist society, Bowles and Gintis (1976) argued that schools prepare students to take their role in the division of labor in the economic system of society because this role helps the smooth reproduction of the hierarchy of labor and maintains the system of inequality that favors the elites. In both of these instances, the benefit of encouraging blind religiosity or unquestioning faith in a man-made economic system resulted in quantifiable benefits for a socio-political elite. Though there are now many wonderful public education systems across the globe nowadays, they are still rife with similar challenges.

Students are convinced of the acceptability of these world views through subtle messaging. Much like a child is convinced that sugary cereals are delicious and good for them through the usage of cartoon characters, so, too, are many youth convinced of the viability of a particular worldview through symbols. Bourdieu and Passerson (1977) contended that the dominant group's knowledge and culture are seen in society as *symbolic capital* whereas the cultures and knowledge of other non-dominant groups are not seen as equally valid. In the example of food advertising, children from immigrant families may reject their traditional breakfast foods in favor of foods, like sugary cereals, that represent what children should want to eat within that particular culture. Symbolic capital then translates to economic capital, only increasing the power of dominant groups. Since the elite's culture and knowledge represents capital, it makes sense to only include their ideology in the curriculum in order to raise the intellectual and cultural competency of others in society to match that of the elites. In other words, why even advertise for foods like chapatti or rice and beans in the United States, when this is not what the dominant group eats for breakfast? The delivery of the elite's knowledge and culture is distributed at schools by a gatekeeper, such as teacher, through a hidden curriculum which is described by Hewitt (2006) as a covert and informal curriculum exemplified through classroom rules and a teacher's interactions. Including the elite's knowledge and culture in textbooks while making their capital hard to achieve for those students who do not belong to the elite conceals an uneven relationship of social and cultural power and maintains the dominance of the elites. In that sense, the ideology within textbooks distorts and hides an uneven social and cultural power relationship of dominance and subordination. In a worst-case scenario, the role of schools becomes to reproduce such relationships and serve the power of dominant groups.

Over time, the repetition of social norms through the lens of dominant society constructs a collective memory that may not portray the true or full story. Though many unwittingly participate, some dominant individuals and institutions do actively create social and culture recollections that tell history in a way that favors groups in which they are a part. This is evident within the school curriculum. Williams (1962) suggested that to legitimize the elite's knowledge and culture, the curriculum is involved in a process called the "selective tradition." Selective tradition operates by selecting and presenting particular aspects of history while eliminating others. Specifically, textbooks include a collection of "certain meanings and aspects" that "are chosen for emphasis, and certain other meanings and practices" that "are neglected and excluded" (Apple, 2004, p. 5). The selective tradition manipulates information to serve a particular purpose—to either "support" or "not contradict other elements within the effective dominant culture" (Apple, 2004, p. 5). An example of the selective tradition in textbooks is demonstrated through an article published by *The Washington Post* in 2014 regarding the controversial revision of Texan U.S. History textbooks in 2010, which is an issue still being discussed among scholars and academics in the fields of education and curriculum development. The revised textbooks removed aspects of religious tolerance and replaced founding fathers such as Thomas Jefferson with John Calvin, while tracing democracy to the Hebrew Bible. The textbooks clearly exaggerated a Judeo-Christian ideology and eliminated the separation of church and state while also concealing aspects of history such as how Christianity was spread through violence and conquest and the United States government's role in uplifting the capitalist economic system Finally, the textbooks demonstrated high levels of essentialism in the way they downplayed slavery and through the negative portrayal of Native Americans, African Americans and even more aggressively demonstrating the violence, terrorism, and incivility of Muslims. What is even more problematic is that the board members assigned to revise the curriculum were non-experts (Strauss, 2014). Textbooks are subjective, ideologically charged documents that become common knowledge through the selective tradition (Apple, 2004). In this regard, the role of the selective tradition is to train students to absorb and adapt to the dominant culture's beliefs and see them as the only valid worldview. This helps to continue the dominance of one culture over another, and thereby maintains inequality. The contents of textbooks are not neutral; instead they reflect the interests of the dominant group in society.

The Problem with Textbooks: They Are Seen as Unbiased and Truthful

Despite the slanted viewpoint textbooks have demonstrated in historical and modern times, many individuals consider textbooks to contain indisputable truth. If you are a teacher that uses textbooks often in the classroom, you may look to the textbook to define a particular word, or to give a summary about a particular historical event. You and your colleagues may see the textbook as the number one source of information, and you likely pass that message along to your students. This is a powerful belief. A belief through which ideologies and universalized and masses of people homogenized, in many cases ultimately achieving the interests of the dominant group. To understand what kind of ideologies, and whose interests they may serve, it is important for teachers and critical pedagogues to conduct close readings of the messages sent to impressionable youth through these revered educational documents.

It is also important for teachers and critical pedagogues to dispel the myth—first and foremost—that textbooks are objective and completely honest. For example, the authors of *America's History* by Bedford-St. Martin (2004), one of the textbooks I analyzed for bias, compare the writing of history to the creation of a movie.

> When you go to see a movie and the film ends, the credits roll, the lights come on, and you go home. The movie is over. But for the writers of a history textbook, there is no "end" because history does not stop. (pp. 939–940)

A movie, like a history textbook, is told by a narrator who has a particular perspective or ideology. The narrator paints a picture for the reader of the context in which the story takes place that includes a description of the place, the people, and the culture. The narrator constructs characters and their relationships by giving lead roles to some and bit parts to others. Just as in every movie, there is a moral of the story; so, too, there is one in every textbook. Most of the time, this message has an emotional and psychological impact on the viewers/readers that calls them to take action. The more gripping the story or the underlying moral, the more it sticks in people's minds. Both textbooks and movies rely on the narrator's ability to use words and images that stimulate the viewers' or readers' senses. These stories are powerful because they are passed down from one generation to the next. They become part of a collective national history and transform from words on a page or actors on a screen to an integral part of culture. This culture then influences identity and dictates perceptions of

and relationships with people different from us. The late professor of literature at Columbia University, Edward Said (2003), shared similar thoughts in
his argument about the role of literature in imperialism. In his words, "Little
attention has been given to narrative fiction, as stories are at the heart of what
explorers and novelists say about strange regions of the world; they also become
the method colonized people use to assert their own identity and existence of
their own history" (p. xiii). Said argued that "nations themselves are narrations" (p. xiii) and that to become a narrator of the story of a nation is a privi-
lege given to some at the expense of others whose narratives are blocked from
developing and evolving. Said (2003) contended that the stories that are being
blocked from history are those stories of people rising up against colonialism or
who have been emancipated from colonial rules. It could be argued that textbooks construct similar views of certain nations outside of the United States
borders, or of certain individuals still considered not quite American. Unfortunately, these subjective elements are not made explicit in textbooks, which
many teachers and youth read as the objective truth. Consequently, the ideologies textbooks engrain among readers become hard to change once normalized.

So, what truth do textbooks currently in use by New Mexico's Bureau of
Education convey about 9/11 and the War on Terror? Who do these textbooks
consider to be an American and who do they see as an outsider? What views
do these textbooks construct about Muslim people and nations? To find out,
we now turn to the textbooks themselves.

To examine how textbooks address the above questions, I analyzed seven
textbooks, all of which include older and newer versions except for one. These
consist of recent editions of three widely used U.S. History 11th-grade textbooks, adopted in contract with the New Mexico department of education
from 2011–2017:

- *The American Vision* (2005) by Glencoe McGraw-Hill
- *The American Vision Modern Times* (2010) by Glencoe McGraw-Hill
- *A History of the American People: Revised third Edition* (2002) by Pearson–
  Prentice Hall
- *United States History: Reconstruction to the Present* (2010) by Pearson–
  Prentice Hall
- *The Americans: Reconstruction to the 21st Century* (2005) by Holt
  McDougal
- *The Americans: Reconstruction to the 21st Century* (2012) by Holt
  McDougal
- *America's History* (2004) by Bedford-St. Martin

I selected these textbooks based on teacher recommendations of text-books that have been adopted by their schools. The questions to guide the analysis were inspired by models developed by educational specialists such as Hess and Stoddard (2007), Hess, Stoddard, and Murto (2008), Hess (2009), Pingel (2000), and Sleeter (2005). What I found is that American high school textbooks cover current events such as 9/11 and the War on Terror in a way that reinforces bias, ignorance, and the banking model of education, thereby contributing to an uneven discussion of current events related to 9/11 and the War on Terror so often funneled through teachers.

Findings: Textbooks Prop Up an Unbalanced Dialectic through Bias

Textbooks prop up a one-sided conversation in regards to current events such as 9/11 and the War on Terror. This is exemplified through examples of bias such as nationalism, American exceptionalism, and language that foments the ideas of a culture clash between the East and the West.

Examples of Bias: Nationalism

Similar to Linda's observation of the AP textbook she used, the U.S. history textbooks I analyzed showed extreme levels of nationalistic influence, espe-cially in the discussion of 9/11 and the War on Terror. For example, many textbooks dedicated a significant amount of space and words—pages and pages—to long and dynamic descriptions of the actual attacks. Textbook rhet-oric itself demonstrated an infusion of American patriotism. A strong empha-sis was placed on the number of Americans who died and comparisons to Pearl Harbor attacks abound. For example, the Pearson-Prentice Hall book *A History of the American People* from 2002 describes the 9/11 attacks as "a huge explosion followed by fierce fires" where "the death toll soon reached 189, including 64 people who had been on board the hijacked airliner" (p. 986). Former Mayor Rudolph W. Giuliani was quoted in the textbook, calling the attack "horrendous" (p. 986). The authors of the Bedford-St. Martin (2004) textbook described how "almost three thousand men and women from over eight countries perished" (p. 941) While mentioning the number of the dead is certainly relevant, and important, none of the textbooks mentioned the total number of Afghani and Iraqi deaths as a result of the War on Terror, which are above and beyond 130,000. While the textbooks were used to teach U.S. history, and therefore may have focused more so on the attacks on American soil, it seems appropriate to at least make some mention of the atrocities on both sides in order to present a balanced picture. According to Alfie Kohn (2001), including these numbers would serve as a much needed sign of respect, thereby demonstrating that their lives are just as valuable as those Americans who died in the 9/11 attacks and the War on Terror. Their omission demonstrates bias in the form of nationalism.

However, the U.S. history textbooks seem to connect feelings of nationalism with Christianity by infusing the sense of unity and connectedness that Americans felt immediately after the attacks with a quote by Billy Graham. In doing so, the textbook certainly overlooks the fact that the United States is a diverse society, not just Christian. For example, Glencoe McGraw-Hill *The American Vision* (2005) stated:

> *America Unites.* ... Then, on September 11, 2001, terrorists struck again, hijacking four American passenger planes and executing the most devastating terrorist attack in history. ... If the terrorists had hoped to divide Americans, they failed. As the Reverend Billy Graham noted at a memorial service: "A tragedy like this could have torn our country apart. But instead it has united us and we have become a family." (p. 1033)

The question that should be asked here is: who has the event united and who has the event divided? The discussion in the textbook and in Billy Graham's quote seem to do just the opposite. The 9/11 attacks divided the American society into Muslims versus Christians, and "Who is with us?" versus "Who is against us?" The events of 9/11 redefined who or what an American is, and therefore united those who became redefined as Americans. Including Reverend Billy Graham's quote affirms the role Christianity plays in the cultural identity of the United States, and also disregards the citizenship held by many Muslim Americans and their allies. Instead, this quote asserts that Muslims are the enemy of America, and that the war is a religious and political one. Pushing such religious intolerance violates the First Amendment of the United States Constitution, and including these loaded words sends a strong message to readers about what religions deserve protection and respect and which ones do not.

The family that Billy Graham described in the quote above seemed to be led by the father figure of President Bush, who was quoted at length in many of the books.

> The president then issued an ultimatum to the Taliban regime in Afghanistan, demanding they turn over bin Laden and his supporters and close all terrorist camps.

He also declared that although the war on terrorism would start by targeting al-Qaeda, it would not stop there. "It will not end," he announced, "until every terrorist group of global reach has been found, stopped, and defeated." The president also announced that the United States would no longer tolerate states that aided terrorists. "From this day forward," the president proclaimed, "any nation that continues to harbor or support terrorism will be regarded by the United States as a hostile regime." The war, President Bush warned, would not end quickly, but it was a war the nation had to fight: "Great harm has been done to us. We have suffered great loss. And in our grief and anger we have found our mission and our moment. ... Our Nation—this generation—will lift a dark threat of violence from our people and our future. ..." (President George W. Bush, Address to Joint Session of Congress, September 20, 2001 as cited in *The American Vision* Glencoe McGraw-Hill, 2005, p. 1034)

President Bush's quote indicates that it is the role of every individual in the United States as a nation to launch this war against terrorism. It is unclear from this quote, however, what terrorism means and who terrorists are. As Hess (2009) wrote, "An old saying goes, 'One person's terrorist is another person's freedom fighter.' Countries define the term according to their own beliefs and to support their own national interests" (p. 151). Bush announced that the War on Terrorism was not punishment for those terrorists who committed the attacks of September 11, but instead it would become an ongoing war against any individual, any group, or any nation that specifically dislikes the United States or in other words stands against the United States interests. This sends a message that acts of terror from one group are reason enough to preemptively strike and kill members of another.

Textbooks encouraged symbolic acts of nationalism through textbook assignments. For example, the Glencoe McGraw-Hill (2005) *The American Vision* textbook asked students to "work in pairs to design a memorial to the victims and heroes of the September 11, 2001, terrorist attacks" (p. 1033). Recognizing and memorializing innocent people who died is an honorable thing to do. However, there are no lesson plans that ask students to make memorials for the hundreds of thousands of innocent Iraqis or Afghanis that died as "collateral damage" in the many U.S.-led airstrikes. It is likely that there would not be any such exercise for any of the wars in which the U.S. has fought.

Examples of Bias: American Exceptionalism

Disregarding innocent people who perished in gruesome bombings and attacks perpetrated by Americans sets Americans, or a certain kind of American, apart as special, or somehow more important. American exceptionalism is another example of bias that props up a cockeyed perspective of 9/11 and the War on Terror. There were many examples of American exceptionalism which shows white Americans as an exceptional civilization, but these examples seemed especially pronounced in the discussion of why and how the United States decided to invade Iraq, despite the United Nation's admonishment that the U.S. not do so. The Bedford-St. Martin's *America's History* (2004) book described how "President Bush presented his case to the United Nations" in order "to garner international support for the war on Iraq" (p. 943). However, despite the importance of this international support of the United Nations, the United States "still reserved the right of unilateral action" and "when [the U.S.] failed to obtain international, U.N.-sanctioned support for a pre-emptive strike, the United States and Britain launched an armed attack against Iraq without it" (p. 943). The United Nations, of which the United States was a founding nation, is considered the forerunning international peace organization. How does the textbook treat the opinion of the U.N. in this paragraph? Initially, they mention how "important" it was for the United States to "garner international support for the war on Iraq." However, when only Great Britain was left standing by America's side, the United States went forward with its war plans since it had "reserved the right of unilateral action." The use of the term "right" here is a confusing one. Typically, rights refer to laws. However, there is no "right" granted to the United States or any other nation to act unilaterally, especially when it comes to the drastic and deadly measures of war.

But American exceptionalism in these high school textbooks was not limited to excluding humanizing information about Muslims over there, but it also applied to Muslims over here, many of whom were citizens of the United States. Discussions on the civil rights abuses of Muslim and Arab people as a result of the Patriot Act were cursory at best. Glencoe McGraw-Hill *The American Vision* (2005) described the Patriot Act as a piece of "legislation to help law enforcement agencies track down terrorist suspects" (p. 1035). The textbook said that "drafting the legislation took time. Congress had to balance Americans' Fourth Amendment protections against unreasonable search and seizure with the need to increase security" (p. 1035). Telling readers that "drafting the legislation took time" since "Congress had to balance American's Fourth Amendment protections against unreasonable search and seizure with the need to increase security" signifies that Congress and the President were successful in this process. There is no indication in this textbook that the Patriot Act was and remains highly controversial. Perhaps it may not seem controversial to the authors, who in many of the textbooks demonstrate extreme fear of home-grown terrorism. For example, Holt McDougal's *The Americans: Reconstruction to the 21st Century* authors (2005, 2012) described how "Al-Qaeda network has used 'sleepers' to carry out its terrorist attacks" (p. 897). The textbooks described sleepers as "agents who enter a country, blend into a community, and when called upon, secretly prepare for and commit terrorist attacks" (p. 897). It seems only reasonable that "U.S. officials detained and questioned Arabs and other Muslims who behaved suspiciously or who violated immigration regulations" (p. 897). The paragraph begins with how al-Qaeda definitely used sleeper cells in the United States to carry out their attacks, thereby providing a real and terrifying need for the Patriot Act. However, the potential for civil rights implications remains cast in doubt. Glencoe McGraw-Hill *The American Vision* (2005) textbook authors write, "Critics claimed that detaining these people violated their civil rights," but provide no concrete examples of any such civil rights abuses, the way the authors provided concrete examples of the need for this kind of legislation. Pointing out "that limiting civil liberties during wartime to protect national security was not unusual" (p. 1035) rather than recalling how detrimental racist treatment was to entire populations, demonstrates a sense of infallibility. What about the detainment of the Japanese during World War II—could the textbook instead engage the reader in an honest discussion of these "not unusual" but also hugely cruel methods? The textbook also discusses how "suspicious foreigners" were detained and spied upon, but does not mention how American citizens, who were also Muslim, were targeted. Neglecting to mention this fact feeds into the idea of a culture clash, whereby an individual of a particular religion couldn't possibly also be considered American.

Examples of Bias: The Language of Culture Clash

The language of a culture clash between the West and Islam also contributed to bias within many of the textbooks, and skewed the rhetoric about 9/11 and the War on Terror. Textual analysis revealed that most of the focus on the history of 9/11 or the rise of terrorism rested on Osama bin Laden's hatred of the United States, the spread of Western ideals, and a rise of Islamic fundamentalism—in other words, a clash of cultures. Only in a minimal way do the authors of the various textbooks mention the role the United States played in arming Osama bin Laden, or the long-term oil-based relationship the Bush family had with the bin Laden family, and the economic frustrations of people coping with U.S.-backed free trade agreements that supported the growth of a small but elite ruling classes worldwide. As Hess et al. (2008)

wrote, "deliberating contemporary issues stemming from 9/11 requires at least some modicum of historical understanding" (p. 3). Unfortunately, rather than actually describing the historical events which led to the hatred and desperation that fueled terroristic acts, the textbooks by and large glossed over these historical facts. For example, Glencoe McGraw-Hill *The American Vision* (2005) on the first page of the War on Terrorism section (p. 1031) provides a small infographic called Preview of Events. The timeline spans from 1980–2000, and highlights four events in this timeline. They are as follows:

1. "1979: Soviet Union invades Afghanistan
2. 1988: Al-Qaeda is organized
3. 1998: Bombs explode at U.S. embassies in Kenya and Tanzania
4. 2001: Attacks on the Pentagon at the World Trade Center"

Not mentioned is the United States' involvement in arming the precursor to al-Qaeda. The use of the passive voice here ("al-Qaeda *is* organized") removes the presence of any actor in its manifestation, as if it appeared out of thin air. Without the training, money, and weapons the fighters received via the United States, would al-Qaeda have formed, and would they have had the power and capacity to fly an airplane into the World Trade Center? Glencoe McGraw-Hill *The American Vision* (2005) continues to describe the rise of al-Qaeda and Osama bin Laden as follows:

> He used his wealth to support the Afghan resistance. In 1988 he founded an organization called al-Qaeda (al KY-duh), or "the Base." Al-Qaeda recruited Muslims and channeled money and arms to the Afghan resistance. (p. 1033)

Again, there is no admission that much of bin Laden's access to power came also from the United States' previous support. The textbook authors use the word "Muslims" to describe al-Qaeda members in Afghanistan, a country which is already nearly 99% Muslim. Why did the textbook authors not use another more specific term, such as fighters, terrorists, or soldiers, to clarify which Muslims in the almost entirely Muslim country to which they were referring?

Clash of culture rhetoric is also evident in the way 9/11 transforms from a war against al-Qaeda to a war on the Middle East. For example, when President Bush and the FBI "identified the attacks as the work of Osama bin Laden and the al-Qaeda network," instead of writing that these groups were attacked, the textbook authors chose to write "Secretary of Defense Donald Rumsfeld began deploying troops, aircraft and warships to the Middle East" (Glencoe McGraw-Hill, 2005, p. 1034). The term "Middle East" is a socially constructed political term used to group together countries that are in conflict with the United States. This is evident in the way that countries that have constituted the Middle East have changed over time. For example, Koppes (1976) pointed out that before World War I, the Middle East included non-Arabic speaking countries such as Iran, Afghanistan, and Central and South Asia. However, after 1958, the term Middle East became reserved only for Arab countries located in Asia including: Egypt, Syria, Palestine, Lebanon, Jordan, Iraq, Saudi Arabia, Kuwait, Bahrain, and Qatar and not those located in North Africa such as Libya, Algeria and Morocco. Professor of Asian American Studies at University of California Davis, Sunaina Maira (2009) noticed that before 9/11, the United States used the category of "Middle Eastern" to indicate Arab and Muslim, but after 9/11, South Asians were added to this category of "Middle Eastern" to represent the terrorist Muslim enemy of the United States even though South Asians do not speak Arabic. In that sense, the category "Middle Eastern/Arab/Muslim" chunks together a mixture of people such as "Arabs and Iranians, including Christians, Jews, and Muslims, and all Muslims from Muslim majority countries, as well as persons who are perceived to be Arab, Middle Eastern, or Muslim, such as South Asians, including Sikhs or Hindus" (Naber, 2008, p. 279). So, using the term "Middle East" in the textbook without the historical explanation of how the term developed and evolved is misleading and confusing for students because it is left to them to figure out which countries constitute the Middle East. Consequently, what do you think of the use of the term "Middle East" instead of "Afghanistan" in the previous paragraph? The Bedford-St. Martin's *America's History* textbook (2004) describes the rise of terrorism as follows:

> How can the growth of such religious extremism be understood? As historians grapple with this question, they will need to take into consideration U.S. foreign policy, including its efforts to secure and protect American access to Middle Eastern oil, an objective made clear by its role in unseating Muhammad Mossadegh in Iran in 1954 as well as its support for Kuwait against Iraq in the Gulf War of 1991. And, despite U.S. efforts to broker peace between Israel and the Palestinians, long-standing American support of Israelis constitutes yet another major source of resentment throughout the Muslim world that historians will have to consider. So, too, they will have to assess the circumstances that led the United States during Jimmy Carter's and Ronald Reagan's presidential administrations to support radical Islamic fundamentalists, including Osama bin Laden, in their efforts to drive the Russians out of Afghanistan in the 1980s. As part of the long-standing cold war tactic of resisting Communist encroachment in developing countries, the CIA trained and partially funded many

leaders who eventually formed the Taliban. This is certainly one of the tragic ironies
of recent history. (p. 944)

While it is commendable that the authors of this textbook do actually mention these historical facts, look at how few lines of text are dedicated towards
the explanation of how the United States' CIA was involved in training and
arming Osama bin Laden. Though the authors in this particular textbook did
mention it, very little space and attention is provided to this important piece
of history. Imagine if this detail was given as much space and attention as the
events of 9/11, over and over again, in all of the texts.

Some textbook authors compared and contrasted religion and politics, as
if democratic states and Muslim societies existed at the opposite ends of a cultural spectrum. For example, in both Glencoe McGraw-Hill textbooks (2005,
2010), the authors stated:

> The reason Middle Eastern terrorists have targeted Americans can be traced back
> to events in the early twentieth century. As oil became important to the American
> economy in the 1920s, the United States invested heavily in the Middle East oil
> industry. This industry brought great wealth to the ruling families in some Middle
> Eastern kingdoms, but most people remained poor. Some became angry at the United
> States for supporting the wealthy kingdoms and families. (p. 810)

This is one of the few admissions that free trade policies pushed onto other
nations by the United States may have led to the same unequal distribution
of wealth we see worsening every day in America. However, this admission
of some accountability in the economic woes of a country is short and quick.
The quote continues:

> The rise of the oil industry also led to the spread of Western ideas in the region,
> and many Muslims feared that their traditional values were being weakened. New
> movements arose calling for a strict interpretation of the Qu'ran—the Muslim holy
> book—and a return to traditional Muslim religious laws. These Muslim movements
> wanted to overthrow pro-western governments in the Middle East and create a pure
> Islamic society. Muslims who support these movements are referred to as fundamen-
> talist militants. Some militants began using terrorism to achieve their goals. (p. 810)

Unlike the two sentences used to describe the poverty created partially through
U.S. economic policy, the clash of civilizations between Western ideas and
Islamic fundamentalism is given an entire paragraph. The above quote also
raises important issues that requires an explanation of what is meant by strict
adherence to Islam. Glencoe McGraw-Hill's (2005, 2010) authors implied

that the strict interpretation of the Qu'ran by either Muslims or non-Muslims brings ignorance, falsehood, and extremism (Zine, 2007). The word strict is misleading because it could imply either that the Qu'ran does call for a pure Islamic society and for fundamentalism and interpreting it in this way would lead to such understanding. If the authors meant so, they did not provide any evidence to back up such a claim. However, the other way the term strict could be understood is as a literal interpretation of the Qu'ran, which means that interpreting the Qu'ran out of context by either Muslims or non-Muslims brings ignorance, falsehood, and extremism (Zine, 2007). This is accurate since a literal interpretation of the Qu'ran is banned by the religion. To understand the Qu'ran requires rigorous education, and, to that end, Islamic universities and institutions graduate scholars of Islam on a daily basis. Interpretation of the Qu'ran requires comprehensive knowledge of the Qu'ran, its historical context, and the sayings and methods of the Prophet (pbuh), which only such scholars possess. In that sense, any groups or movements in Muslim societies calling for a literal interpretation of the Qu'ran are warned against and even fought in Muslim countries.

The second issue with Glencoe McGraw-Hill's *The American Vision* (2005) and *The American Vision Modern Times* (2010) quote is the presentation of Muslims as intolerant of Westerners and incapable of living side-by-side with people of other faiths and religions. If Glencoe McGraw-Hill's authors had researched the history of Muslims, they would have found that there were Christians, Jews, and people of other religions who existed and lived side-by-side in these countries for millennia. In fact, there are Christians and Jews who still live in Muslim societies today freely practicing their religions (Moore, 2006). Therefore, a purely Muslim society has never existed at any point in history, not even during the time of Prophet Mohamed nor his companions when Islam reached its peak (Moore, 2006). Therefore, Muslims are tolerant and coexist with people of other faiths.

The third problem with this quote is the indication that Muslim societies dislike pro-Western governments for religious reasons. Muslim societies have suffered from a long history of Western colonialism that divided its societies and exploited its resources at the hands of puppet leaders who were truly tyrants. Many people in Muslim societies perceive the American hegemony as an extension to Western imperialism, so it makes perfect sense for them to want to overthrow such governments and oppressive ideologies. However, many societies, including non-Arab/non-Muslim societies, worldwide have also suffered from Western interventions in their countries' affairs. For example, as a response to the Cuban government's nationalization of U.S. corporations during the Cuban revolution, the United States punished the Cuban government and people through an embargo that prevents U.S. corporations from conducting any business in Cuba (BBC News, 2009). Cuban society has suffered from this ban since 1959, particularly children who could not access vital medicine (BBC News, 2009). Indeed, many people around the world have suffered from the United States and Western countries' neoliberal ideology. According to Norman Fairclough (2003), emeritus Professor of Linguistics at Lancaster University, neoliberalism increased the gap between rich and poor, increased labor exploitation, and resulted in disastrous financial restructuring and sanctions against less fortunate countries by the United States and its rich allies. Even inside the United States, neoliberalism has contributed to weakening of public debates and democracy and widening the gap between the super-rich (1% of Wall Street and major corporations) and the middle and lower class (who represent the 99% of the American population). Therefore, by focusing on Muslims as the problem for being anti-modern religious fundamentalists instead of focusing on global ideologies that have oppressed Muslims and others around the world to achieve global imperialist agendas is misleading. The quote continues:

> American support of Israel also angered many in the Middle East. In 1947 the UN divided British-controlled Palestine into two territories to provide a home for the Jews. One part became Israel. The other part was to become a state for Palestinian Arabs, but fighting between Israel and the Arab states in 1948 left this territory under the control of Israel, Jordan and Egypt. In the 1950s, Palestinians began staging guerilla raids and terrorist attacks against Israel. Since the United States gave aid to Israel, it became the target of Muslim hostility. In the 1970s, several Middle East nations realized they could fight Israel and the United States by providing terrorists with money, weapons, and training. This is called state-sponsored terrorism. The governments of Libya, Syria, Iraq, and Iran have all sponsored terrorists. (p. 810)

In the above quote, the textbook mixed facts with assumptions to make a case for Muslim hostility towards the United States. For instance, Glencoe McGraw-Hill's *The American Vision* (2005) and *The American Vision Modern Times* (2010) claim that one of the reasons for the "Middle Eastern" terrorist movements and terrorist attacks on the United States is American support of Israel that angered many in the Middle East is true, however, Muslims are not the only ones disappointed about this support. According to Haddad (2004), many Christians also felt angry about Zionist aggression toward Palestinians in Palestine and against neighboring Arab countries during the Israeli strike against Egypt, Syria, and Jordon in 1967. In fact, many people around the world, regardless of their religious beliefs, were angered by the establishment of Israel and the American support for the country at the expense of the Palestinian people. Many pro-Palestinian organizations have been established worldwide to advocate for the rights of Palestinians who have been exiled by the global community. In fact, many individuals from across the world have decided to band together to breach Israel's naval blockade of the Gaza Strip, one example being The Freedom Flotilla Coalition. This international group made up of individuals from Canada, Greece, and South Africa, among others, sent several ships in 2014 that delivered food and aid to the Palestinian people, defying Israeli embargos (Jewish Virtual Library, 2016). However, by including the establishment of Israel as one of the reasons behind terrorism against the United States, this quote pits religion against politics. Thus, they also stereotyped all these nations as anti-modern and constructed them as enemies of the United States and Israel. It seems that the textbook was scrambling for reasons to justify the attacks and ultimately vilified all Arab/Muslim/Middle Eastern people.

Palestinians fighting to retain their homes may not consider their efforts as "terrorism." Who defines what is terrorism is? Why is the attack on the World Trade Center considered terrorism, but the death of over 100,000 civilian Iraqis as a result of the U.S. invasion not? Authors of both Glencoe McGraw-Hill textbooks have written that "although there have been many acts of terrorism in American history, most terrorist attacks on Americans since World War II have been carried about by Middle Eastern groups" (p. 810). These quotes by Glencoe McGraw-Hill (2005, 2010) could be interpreted through the Ugandan academic, author, and political commentator Mahmood Mamdani's (2004) discussion of what he calls "culture talk," which "qualified and explained the practice of 'terrorism' as 'Islamic'" (p. 17). In this way, Islamic terrorism becomes "both description and explanation" (p. 17) for 9/11, and it is "no longer the market (capitalism), nor the state (democracy), but culture (modernity) that is said to be the dividing line between those in favor of a peaceful, civic existence, and those inclined to terror" (p. 18). The Bedford-St. Martin's *America's History* (2004) concludes melodramatically that "so much international anxiety about the future tied to Muslim extremists also raises the alarming specter of a world divided in two, of the followers of Islam pitted against the rest of the world" (p. 944). But as the textbooks highlight the speeches of President Bush and Colin Powell and Mayor Rudy Giuliani, there are many voices absent from this written dialectic. Who has the right to speak on these pages? Whose voices represent the guiding light, the "truth"? And what parts of the story might be told if the silenced voices could speak?

Findings: Textbooks Prop Up an Unbalanced Dialectic through Ignorance

Linda, one of the teachers I interviewed, had some very insightful things to say about the role of ignorance in feeding the unbalanced perspective of 9/11 and the War on Terror. As an experienced educator who had spent the bulk of her adult life teaching, Linda's words really struck a chord with me. What truly resonated with me was her perspective, as a teacher, looking back on the kind of education she had received about Muslims, Islam, and the Middle East.

Me: Why do you believe there is this intolerance of Muslims?

Linda: Ignorance, I mean it is something that Americans aren't comfortable with in general, they are not familiar with it, and I think it may just be education. I never taught World History, but I know that, over the years, when you teach World History, you teach Western Civilization, you don't teach Eastern Civilization as much. It's gotten better, but the parents of my children had Western Civilization, and I think, until we understand as a nation, history of the world, we are so bigoted and biased I guess to look at something different. (personal communication, May 29, 2010)

Linda blamed intolerance of Muslims on ignorance and arrogance and explained that historical textbooks focus predominantly on Western civilization. She saw improvements in the way these topics are taught now, with how she learned them herself many years ago. However, there are still vast improvements to be made. One of the students I interviewed, Francis, noticed that "there isn't as much information in the textbook for Islam. There is not as much textbook wording about Islam as there is for Christianity, Judaism, and Buddhism" (personal communication, April 1, 2010). Francis observed that even today, ignorance about non-Western civilizations is found within the classroom. Little space—in terms of sheer wording—is given to Islam in comparison to other world religions such as Christianity, Judaism, and Buddhism. This lack of information leads to confusion about the relation between weapons of mass destruction and terrorism and also creates fertile soil for illogical claims about an existence of a cultural clash between Muslims and Western nations as reasons for the 9/11 attacks. Some American textbooks perpetuate a crooked dialectic by contributing to ignorance through the omission of other points of view about history, religion and the diverse cultures of Muslims.

Reinforcing Ignorance about History

In the textbook analysis, there was a clear confusion of historical facts such as whether or not Iraq held Weapons of Mass Destruction (WMDs), the reality of the "collateral damage" at the hands of U.S. troops, or what other motives may have spurred the War in Iraq, which all contributes to a disproportionate consideration of these current events. For example, in a timeline of the war on terror, Glencoe McGraw-Hill (2010) includes that by October 2005, "American deaths in the war in Iraq surpass 2,000" (p. 817). There is no mention here of Iraqi deaths. According to the Iraq Body Count (IBC), an independent research firm based in the United States and UK, by December 2005, around 39,646 Iraqi civilians had died as a direct and indirect result of the conflict, only two months after the textbook authors reported that American deaths surpassed 2,000. In the discussion of the launching of the war in Iraq, the Glencoe McGraw-Hill textbook describes how in the initial attack, "the coalition forces quickly seized control of the country, and on May 1, President Bush declared that the major combat was over" (p. 1037). Of the dead, the textbook authors write, "about 140 Americans, and several thousand Iraqis, had died … more Americans died after May 1 than had died in the six weeks of major combat. As American deaths and expenses mounted, President Bush began to seek support from the UN and other countries to help stabilize and rebuild Iraq" (Glencoe McGraw-Hill, 2005, p. 1037). Several thousand Iraqis died during this short time frame, around the same number of people who died during the 9/11 attacks. As of 2015, over 100,000 Iraqis have died due to direct and indirect violence from the war in their country. How would you compare the description of the deaths of these innocent people at the hands of U.S. forces to the description of the deaths of innocent people in the World Trade Center? Concern over mounting American deaths and expenses are mentioned, but nothing is said of the thousands of innocent Iraqis who died in the repeated bombings.

The personal hardships faced by individuals from these war-torn countries are also rarely mentioned, and, if they are, there tends to be an upbeat comment about the positive outcomes of the war on Afghani and Iraqi citizens. For example, the Bedford-St. Martin's *America's History* book "celebrated how Afghani women were freed from an exceptionally repressive way of life" (p. 942) due to the war. What message does it send to students when only positive outcomes of the U.S. invasion, such as women voting, are described in these textbooks? What remains missing from the dialectic? How might ignorance about these facts impact students? Focusing on positive outcomes of war leaves the absence of information in regards to the destructive impact of wars on Iraqi and Afghani civilians such as facing shortage of food, inability to access medicines, and their schools were destroyed.

Textbook analysis also revealed obfuscation of the truth and blatant misinformation, especially in regards to the conversation around Weapons of Mass Destruction (WMD), Iraq, and terrorism. Specifically, textbooks repeatedly connected the ideas of terrorism, 9/11, and WMDs, even though the three are not related. Weapons of Mass Destruction, according to the FBI, are any destructive devise intended to kill or seriously injure its target. This includes chemical, biological, radiological, nuclear, and explosive weaponry, the emphasis being the relatively large-scale destructive capacity. The countries that have access to this kind of advanced weaponry technology are as follows: (a) the United States, (b) China, (c) France, (d) India, (e) North Korea, (f) Pakistan, (g) Russia, and (h) the United Kingdom. The only country to ever use a WMD was the United States, dropping two atomic bombs on Hiroshima and Nagasaki during World War II. However, through the textbook authors' depictions of WMDs, cited below, terrorism and WMDs become inextricable. The textbook authors' rhetoric mirrors the media and politicians deflection of the American people's fear of terrorism onto another as of yet totally unrelated national security concern.

Textbooks conflated terrorism and WMDs even though there was no specific or actual evidence that terrorist groups had access to materials and technology at such a high level, encouraging ignorance among readers. For example, the Glencoe McGraw-Hill *The American Vision* (2005) textbook describes the "fear that groups such as al-Qaeda might acquire nuclear, chemical, or biological weapons" that "could kill tens of thousands of people all at once" (p. 1036). Because of this fear, "President Bush warned that an 'axis of evil,' made up of Iraq, Iran, and North Korea, posed a grave threat to the world" (p. 1036). No mention is made of Afghanistan, or Saudi Arabia, the two countries with citizens considered complicit in the September 11 attacks. Yet the textbook continues to conflate these acts of terror and these horrific weapons by saying "each of these countries had been known to sponsor terrorism and was suspected of trying to develop weapons of mass destruction" (p. 1036). Therefore, "The president promised to take strong action: The United States of American will not permit the world's most dangerous regimes to threaten us with the world's most destructive weapons" (p. 1036).

There is an uncertain and speculative thread connecting WMDs and 9/11 attacks; this was that the attacks "created fear that groups ... *might* [emphasis added] acquire nuclear, chemical, or biological weapons." Again, at this point in history, a rogue group of terrorists had not yet succeeded in procuring and deploying such advanced weaponry. Suggesting its possibility may lead readers to believe that that this false information is true. It seems that the textbook attempted to conflate the two, just as the Bush administration and the media did. Another textbook, the Bedford-St. Martin's *America's History* (2004) textbook conflated terrorism and weapons of mass destruction:

> President Bush stressed that the world still faced the threat of an international web of radical Muslim terrorists, ranging from Somalia to Bosnia to the Philippines and beyond. He signaled an intention to carry the fight to other nations that harbor terrorists or develop weapons of mass destruction—hence his characterization of Iran, Iraq, and North Korea as 'an axis of evil.' By the first anniversary of September 11, President Bush was threatening to attack Iraq, a controversial plan that divided his advisors and provoked heated public debate. (p. 942)

The proliferation of WMDs is alarming. However, conflating WMDs with terrorism is nonsensical. President Bush was often criticized for connecting the two. The textbook recreates and reinforces this connection, with no critical inquiry. Over and over textbooks drill this idea into students, even asking questions at the bottom of the page such as, "Why did the United States think stopping the spread of weapons of mass destruction was linked to the War on Terror?" (Glencoe McGraw-Hill, 2010, p. 817). The nonsensical connection between terrorism, September 11, and WMDs in the textbooks mirrors the hysterical and totally non-factual rhetoric of politicians and the media during this time period. The textbooks aligned with the majority of media sources and President Bush's insistence on the connection between 9/11, terrorism, and WMDs without providing any logical explanation justifying such a connection. These extrapolations run the risk of furthering ignorance among readers about these important issues.

Textbook analysis also revealed obfuscation or confusion of the truth surrounding whether or not Iraq had weapons of mass destruction. Textbooks also repeated possession of WMDs as the main reason for going to war with Iraq, rather than mentioning any historical conflicts or economic gains to be made by the United States. For example, some textbook headings read "Confront Iraq" and describe how "President Bush considered Iraq a more immediate threat than North Korea in developing and distributing weapons of mass destruction" (Glencoe McGraw-Hill, 2005, p. 1036). The textbook then describes how "U.N. inspectors found evidence that Iraq had developed biological weapons and was working on a nuclear bomb" (p. 1036). Unmentioned here is that post-Gulf War, Iraq was under strict economic sanctions and scrutiny. Their ability to create this kind of weaponry was seriously diminished. The Iraqi military was also crippled and forced to comply with frequent weapons investigations. There was little evidence to support the idea that this defeated military at the mercy of the U.N. would be capable of threatening a military powerhouse like the United States. However, despite these factors, the textbook described only how "in the summer of 2002, President Bush increased pressure on Iraq, calling for a regime change in the country" (p. 1036). Though the textbooks describe how he attempted to garner support from the U.N., Bush "made it clear, though, that the United States would act with or without U.N. support" (p. 1036). Again, echoes of American exceptionalism. Prior to launching the U.S. attack, the Glencoe McGraw Hill *The American Vision* textbook wrote as follows:

> Weapons inspectors returned to Iraq, but some Americans doubted their effectiveness. The Bush administration argued that the Iraqis were still hiding weapons of mass destruction that were ready or nearly ready to use. Others had more confidence in the inspection process and wanted to give the inspectors more time. (p. 1036)

President Bush and Colin Powell felt concerned about the potential of WMDs, but unnamed others were not so concerned. Why do you think these others were not mentioned by name? What is the effect of not naming and not quoting the critical opposition to the Bush administrations' belief that Iraq had WMDs? Of a total of 700 inspections after the end of the Gulf War, chief weapons inspector Hans Blix says that nothing indicative of a growing WMD program was ever found. Additionally, Blix has said repeatedly that Saddam Hussein complied with weapons inspectors (Powell, 2004). Yet, despite evidence to the contrary, "in 2002 President Bush decided the time had come to deal with Iraq" (Glencoe McGraw-Hill, 2010, p. 817), as if "dealing" with Iraq is considered a foregone conclusion by the textbook authors, as if the United States "dealing" with Iraq were reminiscent of an adult scolding a petulant and chronically misbehaving child. Of course, Saddam Hussein was a cruel dictator who severely mistreated his people, yet there were and are many other violent leaders across the world. Why focus on Hussein?

What is missing from most of the textbooks are ulterior motives, such as financial or personal ones, for justifying the attacks. Some textbooks mention how, President Bush wanted "to help stabilize and rebuild Iraq" (Glencoe

McGraw-Hill, 2005, p. 1037) after the invasion. What the authors neglect to mention is that "rebuilding Iraq" was a serious money-making venture for many American corporations, especially those with connections to the Bush administration. As former Senator (R.-AZ) John McCain said, "It's like a huge pot of honey that's attracting a lot of flies" (Edsall & Eilperin, 2003). One lobbyist who preferred to not be named said, "One well-stocked 7-Eleven could knock out 30 Iraqi stores; a Wal-Mart could take over the country" (Edsall & Eilperin, 2003). Why is nothing of this mentioned in the textbooks? It is almost as if the authors want to eliminate economic drivers for invading Iraq and to base the premise of the invasion fully on preventing terrorism. Why would they do this? Another un-named element in the rising fear over WMDs is the contentious relationship between Bush Sr. and Saddam Hussein—namely, the accusation made often by George Jr. that Saddam Hussein tried to kill his father. George Bush said in multiple occasions "After all, this is a guy that tried to kill my dad at one time" (King, 2002). This accusation, of course, was made after George Sr. waged war against Iraq in the Gulf War. How might this personal and political history also have impacted George Bush Jr.'s desire to go to war with Iraq? The Gulf War is also not mentioned in any detail—a war that occurred only ten years prior to September 11. Why is this not also mentioned in the history books? Although textbooks insisted that the reasons the United States attacked Iraq post-9/11 was due to its possession of WMDs, textbooks authors did not provide proper evidence to back up such claims. They also failed to mention other potential contributing factors, leading to more ignorance among readers and furthering an uneven conversation about these current events. Eliminating details about the conflict-ridden historical relationship between the United States and Iraq distorts the history and reasons for the 9/11 attacks.

The textbook summaries also made it confusing whether or not Iraq actually had WMDs. For example, a "Reading Check" asked "Why did President Bush decide to confront Iraq?" The answer provided in the book is "Answer: Iraq had developed and used weapons of mass destruction, supported terrorism, and refused to comply with U.N. resolutions" (Glencoe McGraw-Hill, 2005, p. 1037). This information is completely wrong. Iraq had not developed weapons of mass destruction at this time. Alarmingly, even the textbook authors themselves seemed confused on this point, since they had written on the same page that it was discovered that Iraq had no WMDs whatsoever. In their words: "By December 2003, Americans had found no evidence that Iraq possessed weapons of mass destruction" (McGraw-Hill, 2005, p. 1037).

At best, perhaps the textbook authors are referring to Iraq's use of biological weapons in the early 90s. However, the statement can easily be confused as referring to present-day concerns. Additionally, the United States also previously used WMDs, most notably in Japan during World War II. Citing previous WMD deployment as a precedent for disarmament would necessitate the United States' inclusion in this international scrutiny. The textbook summaries failed to paint the socio-economic and historical contexts that lead the Bush administration to accuse Iraq of having weapons of mass destruction. The books also failed to critique the United States' false claims and aggressive attitudes about sovereign nations.

In summary, the textbook authors often connected WMDs with terrorism, much like politicians and the main sources of media. Though the sense of inevitability for an attack on Iraq is loud and clear, there is a startling silence when it comes to recognizing the death and destruction experienced by Iraqi civilians. The effect of highlighting certain untrue assumptions, such as WMDs, while omitting other facts, such as the historical relationship between Iraq and the U.S. or the total number of Iraqi dead, gives credence to an unfair bias about current events such as 9/11 and the War on Terror.

Reinforcing Ignorance About Religion and Culture

The U.S. history textbooks I reviewed also contributed to ignorance through the lack of a clear explanation or understanding of who Muslims are, making it easy for students to jump to conclusions about Islam and its followers. For example, the perpetrators of the 9/11 attacks are described interchangeably as Muslims, Arabs, and Middle Easterners. Blame is attached to the Taliban, Afghanistan, Osama bin Laden, and "sleeper cells" in the United States. Textbook authors for Holt McDougal *The Americans: Reconstruction to the 21st Century* (2005, 2012) wrote that "Nineteen Arab terrorists had hijacked the four planes and used them as missiles in an attempt to destroy predetermined targets" (p. 894). Later on, the textbook authors wrote, "the Afghan government was harboring Osama Bin Laden and his al-Qaeda terrorist network believed responsible for the September 11 attacks" (p. 867). In subsequent chapters, the textbook authors wrote that "the government soon discovered that al-Qaeda network had used 'sleepers' to carry out its terrorist attacks" (p. 897). In other words, they blame al Qaeda, bin Laden, Afghanistan, and terrorists living within the United States. As a result, "U.S. officials detained and questioned Arabs and other Muslims who behaved suspiciously or violated immigration regulations" (p. 897). Arabs and Muslims are conflated in the above descriptions. Naber (2008) argued that after 9/11, the popular media associated the terms "Arab" and "Muslims" with a specific group (p. 5). However, since not all Arabs are Muslims and not all Muslims are Arabs, this association demonstrates a serious lack of knowledge. Indeed, the largest Muslim populations live in Indonesia, Pakistan, India, Turkey, and Iran, all of which are non-Arab countries. Also, many Arabs are not Muslim, but are, in fact, Christians. The mixing of the two in the textbook, without any distinction between them, further ingrains the belief that these identifiers are the same.

There is also clearly ignorance about who Osama bin Laden was and what he represented to other Muslims. For example, the older Pearson-Prentice Hall book A History of the American People (2002) wrote that "U.S. intelligence sources insisted that only bin Laden had the resources to carry out such a sophisticated operation and sufficient motivation" and that "Bin Laden had issued a decree that granted religious legitimacy to all efforts to expel the United States from the lands of Islam in the Middle East" (p. 988). These quotes make Osama bin Laden seem very powerful and influential and respected. However, Osama bin Laden did not hold any legitimate position of power within any political organization in Afghanistan, nor in his home country, Saudi Arabia. What kind of message does it send to students to use the phrase "issued a decree that granted" in connection with one of his statements? The textbook treated Osama Bin Laden as a leader, yet bin Laden was little known to the Muslim world before 9/11 happened since he was neither a recognized politician nor scholar. Even if he had issued such a decree as the textbook stated, many Muslims would not have known nor cared since he was considered an outlaw, dangerous and wanted by Muslim countries (Mamdani, 2004). This misinformation about who Osama bin Laden was—apparently, a powerful and respected political leader—masks the truth: Osama bin Laden was and is considered an outlaw by many Muslims. Lack of understanding of who Muslims are, especially key figures like Osama bin Laden, leads to ignorance about an entire religion and its people, thereby continuing to skew the dialectic.

In summary, these U.S. history textbooks lack clarity on who Muslims truly are, misrepresent religious fanatics as popular or well-loved within the international Muslim community, and avoid deep analysis of the political or financial gains to be made in the Middle East through these wars. The perpetrators were described using the seemingly interchangeable terms of Muslim, Arab, and Middle Easterner. Osama bin Laden is mischaracterized as a political and religious leader, rather than the ostracized outlaw that he represented and continues to represent for many Muslims. Little to no information about the political history and economic gains to be made through invading the Middle East are discussed. All of these elements contribute to an absence of information, which encourages ignorance, and makes it easy for students and teachers to pass judgment about all Muslims, and lack a critical awareness of the War on Terror that may never end. This ignorance, bias, and lack of encouragement of critical thinking among readers increases the veracity of the askew discourse and subsequently supports a banking model of education.

Findings: Textbooks Spur a Lopsided Dialectic through Banking Education

What message does it send students when they are compared to an audience at a movie theater? When I imagine someone in watching a movie, I imagine someone who is mentally checked out, someone who has paid their 10 dollars and passively waits for the action, suspense, and magic to wash over them.

> When you go to see a movie, the film ends, the credits roll, the lights come on and you go home. The movie is over. But for the writers of a history textbook, there is no "end" because history does not stop. (Bedford-St. Martin Epilogue, 2004, pp. 939–941)

According to the authors of this U.S. history textbook, it is not the students who create history, but, in fact, the writers of it. While this is insulting, in many ways, it is also true. We remember the stories that are told to us. There is a collective amnesia of the stories that are neglected, or the stories that are retold to favor a dominant ideology. This is why social activists exist, and this is also why many teachers teach. It is to make sure that the stories told to children reflect an honest accounting of what happened in their nation's past, so that they might learn from it and build a better future. However, the textbooks analyzed did not pass the baton to the students. The textbooks did not make it explicit that the students, and the students alone, would need to determine for themselves what was right and wrong about the past. Instead, the textbooks mostly reflected the sentiment of the Bedford-St. Martin's *America's History* (2004) text, and reinforced a banking model of education that supported existing systems of power on the one hand, and discouraged critical thinking among readers on the other hand.

Banking education models are ones that strip students of the ability to think for themselves; models which provide all the answers that students are meant to accept and absorb. Banking education not only dehumanizes those who we perceive as the enemy but also dehumanizes all students since according to Freire (1970), "apart from the inquiry, apart from the praxis, individuals cannot be truly human" (p. 72). Freire insisted that knowledge develops only through inquiry and investigation. The textbooks analyzed in this study provide students with the so-called "right" answers and therefore do not promote such investigations. Instead, the textbooks analyzed did not encourage students to think or develop critical consciousness. As a result, students might not think of transforming society but adapting to the inequality within it. As Freire said, "the more the oppressed can be led to adapt to that situation, the more easily they can be dominated" (Freire, 1970, p. 74). These textbooks indicated a strong effort toward adapting students to biased and ignorant forms of thinking through a banking system of education, which legitimizes other unjust elements of society. The oppressor establishes a system that resembles the good, organized, and just society, and individuals who adjust to the system are good individuals, while those who think otherwise are deviants at best and dangerous at worst.

Discouraging Critical Thinking and Supporting Existing Systems of Power

How did textbooks turn students into mere audience members rather than agents of history? First and foremost, through discouraging critical thinking skills. For example, students were asked in *The American Vision* to "write a descriptive essay explaining how they think the terrorist attacks united Americans and brought a great sense of patriotism to the country" and "have them consider the many acts of heroism and sacrifice that followed the attacks" (Glencoe McGraw-Hill, 2005, p. 1035). Teachers were then encouraged to "have volunteers read their essays to the class," (Glencoe McGraw-Hill, 2005, p. 1035) seemingly cementing these forced expressions of patriotism through groupthink.

In some of the textbooks, students were encouraged to learn how to find media sources, but never encouraged to think deeply about what might be influencing what these media sources report or how. For example, the Glencoe McGraw-Hill *The American Vision* textbook (2005) provided the following "Critical Thinking" Activity for students:

> *Analyzing.* Have students find and bring to class an example of an article that uses both primary and secondary sources to tell the story of the September 11, 2001, terrorist attacks or of the mass-relief effort that followed. Have students write a one-page

summary of their article identifying various points of view and explaining how the writer used a variety of source material to paint a picture of the events. As a class, discuss the importance of both types of sources in explaining historical events. (p. 1035)

Certainly it is important for students to understand the difference between primary and secondary sources, but shouldn't students also learn about where and how media sources develop opinions? This superficiality in regards to the media continues, as Glencoe McGraw-Hill (2005) encouraged teachers to request that students use "good sources" when conducting their research:

Creating a Fact Sheet. Have small groups of students create fact sheets about weapons of mass destruction, including information about the types of weapons that exist, the countries that have or are developing them, and the attempts at controlling their existence and proliferation. Remind the groups that they should use good sources for their information. Have students submit a separate bibliography citing sources used. (p. 1036)

The admonishment to have students use "good sources" is loose and undefined. What exactly is a "good source?" The New York Times, supposedly a "good source," faultily reported the presence of aluminum tubes in Iraq, said to be the building blocks of WMDs. Students categorize what WMDs are, but don't assess how the idea of them was used politically. The lesson plans continue with a "Critical Thinking" exercise on why the U.S. went to war with Iraq: "6. Organizing. Use a graphic organizer similar to the one below to list the reasons why President Bush declared war on Iraq." The answers provided were: "Iraq sponsored terrorism and had used chemical weapons; inspectors had found evidence of biological weapons and nuclear bomb making" (Glencoe McGraw-Hill, 2005, p. 1037). Is it critical thinking if the "correct" answers are already provided for students? How could this question be improved to truly engage more critical thinking skills? These questions fit Paulo Freire's description of "banking education" models in which "students patiently receive, memorize, and repeat" information provided to them, becoming "collectors or cataloguers of the things they store" (Freire, 1970, p. 72). The textbook continues with an assignment on the Patriot Act:

Writing About History. Persuasive Writing. The attacks on New York City and Washington, D.C. convinced many Americans that more security was needed, even if it meant giving up some freedoms. Write a letter to a newspaper explaining why you are for or against increased security. (Glencoe McGraw-Hill, 2005, p. 1037)

How was this question set up? What do you think the authors believe about the Patriot Act, based on how they introduced the question? Introducing the question with the fact that many Americans are convinced that security is more important than freedom could be considered a leading question.

In general, there are few, if any, opportunities for critical thinking in the textbooks. The assignments were modeled after what Freire would call a banking education model, in which students are discouraged from developing their own opinions and asked to repeat the answers provided to them by experts. Through discouraging critical thinking, the textbook authors inadvertently support existing systems of power and inequity, while also disempowering students to feel as though they may change these systems.

Conclusion

This study draws teachers' attention to the underlying ideologies and messages found in textbooks relating to 9/11 and the War on Terror, and to the role of selective tradition in educational textbooks. The textbook authors almost universally seemed to push an ideology that contrasts American identity with a stereotypical and conflated Arab/Muslim/Middle Eastern one. This identity is often characterized as uncivilized, undemocratic, terror-inducing, irrational, and oppressive to women. The presence of such an ideology is evident in (a) the illogical connections between 9/11, terrorism, and WMDs, (b) the grouping of Muslim/Arab/Middle Easterners into one category while overlooking the geographical, historical, political, religious, or linguistic differences among them, and (c) the exaggerated push for nationalism and exceptionalism for Americans while downplaying the destruction of Iraqi and Afghani people and society as the just deserts of those who are the enemies of modernity. These sweeping generalizations and glaring absences make it that much easier for students already saturated in the bombastic rhetoric of a conservative-leaning press to develop hate against all Muslims and their cultures. Consequently, the ideology embedded in the textbooks seeks to normalize and adapt students to accept and approve of the oppression against Muslims in the United States and to normalize and support the War against Muslim societies abroad. At the same time, the textbooks hide the fact that Muslims are human beings who suffer just as any American would when a family member is blown senselessly to bits, or when an errant bomb demolishes their most beloved museums and cultural centers, or when a family member is detained for weeks on end by the FBI despite the fact that this family member is a citizen of the United States of America. This information, missing, skewed, or glossed over in the textbooks, could help non-Muslim students to sympathize with their peers and with the victims of this never-ending war. Its absence strengthens an already strong and growing hatred against Muslims and a belief in their complicity in a political situation far beyond their control.

Teachers must challenge this selective tradition, and demonstrate to students how and where these beliefs are born. One place to look is the media. But, isn't the media supposed to be fair and just? Doesn't the media cover a current event from a balanced perspective? Unfortunately, there is a lot of evidence of media bias, especially in conservative media, when it comes to 9/11, the War on Terror, and Muslims. Chapter 6 will discuss media coverage of 9/11 and the War on Terror and its role in the creation of a public pedagogy that hides American imperialism through transforming Islamophobia into entertainment, rather than rectifying the skewed discourse.

References

Anyon, J. (1979, August). Ideology and United States history textbooks. *Harvard Educational Review, 49*(3), 286–361.

Apple, M. (2004). *Ideology and curriculum.* New York, NY: Routledge Flamer.

Armitage, S. H., Czitrom, D., Buhle, M. J., & Faragher, J. M. (2002). *Out of many: A history of the American people.* Upper Saddle River, NJ: Prentice Hall College Div.

Bourdieu, P., & Passerson, J. (1977). *Reproduction in education, society and culture.* Thousand Oaks, CA: Sage Publications.

Bowles, S., & Gintis, H. (1976). *Schooling in capitalist America: Educational reform and the contradictions of economic life.* New York, NY: Basic Books.

Collins, G. (2012, June 21). How Texas inflicts bad textbooks on us. *The New York Review of Books.* Retrieved September 16, 2016 from http://www.nybooks.com/articles/2012/06/21/how-texas-inflicts-bad-textbooks-on-us/

Durkheim, E. (1977). *Evolution of educational thought: Lectures on the formation and development of secondary education in France.* Boston, MA: Routledge & Kegan Paul.

Edsall, T. B., & Eilperin, J. (2003, October 3). Lobbyists set sights on money-making opportunities in Iraq. *The Washington Post.* Retrieved from https://www.washingtonpost.com/archive/politics/2003/10/02/lobbyists-set-sights-on-money-making-opportunities-in-iraq/88048fc3-3852-4ac5-90f7-edf34381823d/

End Embargo on Cuba, US is Urged. (2009, September 2). *BBC News.* Retrieved February 11, 2012 from http://news.bbc.co.uk/2/hi/8232907.stm

Fact Sheets: Israel's "Blockade" of Gaza. (2016, May). *Jewish Virtual Library.* Retrieved September 25, 2016 from http://www.jewishvirtuallibrary.org/jsource/talking/62_Blockade.html

Fairclough, N. (2003). *Analyzing discourse: Textual analysis for social research.* New York, NY: Routledge.

Fast Facts: Back-to-School Statistics. (n.d.). *National Center for Educational Statistics (NCES)*. Retrieved September 24, 2016 from http://nces.ed.gov/fastfacts/display.asp?id=372

Freire, P. (1970). *Pedagogy of the oppressed*. New York, NY: Herder & Herder.

Glencoe McGraw-Hill. (2005). *The American vision modern times, student edition*. Columbus, OH: Author.

Glencoe McGraw-Hill. (2010). *The American vision modern times, student edition*. Columbus, OH: Author.

Haddad, Y. Y. (2004). *Not quite American? The shaping of Arab and Muslim identity in the United States*. Waco, TX: Baylor University Press.

Hess, D. (2009). *Controversy in the classroom: The democratic power of discussion*. New York, NY: Routledge.

Hess, D., & Stoddard, J. (2007). 9/11 and terrorism: "The ultimate teachable moment" in textbooks and supplemental curricula. *Social Education, 71*(5), 231–236.

Hess, D., Stoddard, J., & Murto, S. (2008). Examining the Treatment of 9/11 and Terrorism in High School Textbooks. In J. S. Bixby & J. L. Pace (Eds.), *Educating Democratic Citizens in Troubled Times* (pp. 192–225). Albany, NY: State University of New York Press.

Hewitt, T. W. (2006). *Understanding and shaping curriculum: What we teach and why*. Thousand Oaks, CA: Sage Publications.

Holt McDougal. (2005). *The Americans: Reconstruction to the 21st century*. Boston, MA: Houghton Mifflin Harcourt.

Holt McDougal. (2012). *The Americans: Reconstruction to the 21st century*. Boston, MA: Houghton Mifflin Harcourt.

James, H. A. (2004). *America's history* (5th ed.). New York, NY: Bedford-St. Martin.

King, J. (2002, September 27). Bush calls Saddam "The guy who tried to kill my dad." *CNN*. Retrieved October 10, 2016 from http://edition.cnn.com/2002/ALLPOLITICS/09/27/bush.war.talk/

Kohn, A. (2001). Teaching about Sept. 11. In War, Terrorism, and our classrooms: *Teaching inthe aftermath of September 11 tragedy*. http://www.rethinkingschools.org/speial_reports/sept11/pdf/911insrt.pdf

Koppes, C. R. (1976). Captain Mahan, General Gordon, and the origins of the term 'Middle East'. *Taylor & Francis Online, 12*(1), 95–98.

Maira, S. (2009). *Missing: Youth, citizenship, and empire after 9/11*. Durham, NC: Duke University Press.

Mamdani, M. (2004). *Good Muslim, bad Muslim: America, the Cold War, and the roots of terror*. New York, NY: Random House.

Moore, J. (2006). Teaching about Islam in secondary schools: Curricular and pedagogical. *Equity and Excellence in Education, 39*, 279–286.

Naber, N. (2008). "Look, Mohamed the terrorist is coming!" Cultural racism, nation-based racism and the intersectionality of oppression after 9/11. In N. Naber & A. Jamal (Eds.), *Race and Arab Americans before and after 9/11: From invisible citizens to visible subjects* (pp. 276–305). Syracuse, NY: Syracuse University Press.

Pearson Education. (2010). *US history: Reconstruction to the present, student edition*. Upper Saddle River, NJ: Prentice Hall.

Pingel, F. (2000). *The European home: Representations of 20th century Europe in history textbooks*. Strasbourg: Council of Europe.

Pingel, F. (2010). *UNESCO guidebook on textbook research and textbook revision* (2nd ed.). *United Nations Educational, Scientific and Cultural Organization (UNESCO)*. Retrieved September 16 from http://unesdoc.unesco.org/ulis/cgi-bin/ulis.pl?catno=117188&set= 4BA09A1F_2_261&gp=1&mode=e&lin=1&ll=1

Powell, B. A. (2004, March 18). U.N. weapons inspector Hans Blix faults Bush administration for lack of "critical thinking" in Iraq. In *UC Berkeley News*. Retrieved September 3, 2017, from https://berkeley.edu/news/media/releases/2004/03/18_blix.shtml

Said, E. (2003). *Culture and imperialism*. New York, NY: Vintage Books.

Sleeter, C. E. (2005). *Un-standardizing curriculum: Multicultural teaching in the standards-based classroom*. New York, NY: Teachers College Press.

Strauss, V. (2014, September 12). Proposed Texas textbooks are inaccurate, biased and politicized, new report finds. *The Washington Post*. Retrieved September 16, 2016 from https://www.washingtonpost.com/news/answer-sheet/wp/2014/09/12/proposed-texas-textbooks-are-inaccurate-biased-and-politicized-new-report-finds/

Wade, R. C. (2012, July 11). Content analysis of U.S. history textbooks: A review of ten years of research. *Theory and Research in Social Education*, XXI(3), 232–256.

Williams, R. (1962). *The long revolution*. New York, NY: Columbia University Press.

The World's 57 Largest Book Publishers. (2015, June 26). *Publishers Weekly*. Retrieved September 16, 2016 from http://www.publishersweekly.com/pw/by-topic/international/international-book-news/article/67224-the-world-s-57-largest-book-publishers-2015.html

Zine, J. (2007). Deconstructing Islamic identity: Engaging multiple discourses. In A. Asgharzadeh, E. Lawson, & K. U. Oka (Eds.), *Diasporic ruptures: Globality, migrancy, and expressions of identity*. New York, NY: Sense Publishers.

· 6 ·

HOW ISLAMOPHOBIA BECAME
ENTERTAINMENT

Unfortunately, all the things that are in the news about Muslims tend to be negative. When we talk about things happening in the Middle East or Arab nations or
whatever, and if we talk about terrorism … this tends to be all the news that we
get in the United States about the Arab nations and Arab people is about terrorism. It is wrong, but that is the truth.
                    —Linda [teacher], personal communication (May 29, 2010)

The vast majority of images broadcast through the United States televisions
and other news media about an entire religion and region relate to terrorism.
The obviousness of this is not lost on the high school teachers I interviewed,
such as Linda, quoted here. And it is not just a few stories here and there.
In Linda's words, "all." All stories. This means that in a post-9/11 world, an
American will almost never be exposed to a positive story about a Muslim.
These images infiltrate homes, schools, and minds like noxious gases. Far from
subliminal messages, the explicit nature of the association between terrorism
and Islam means that many Muslims and Arab-looking people walk around
feeling as though they have a target pinned to their backs. For obvious reasons,
the images and associations perpetuated by the media and the culture at large
leave an impact on viewers who consume them without a second thought.
This is why education—and particularly critical dialectical pedagogy—is so

important. Educators can help themselves and those around them to read these messages and images with greater knowledge, understanding, and freedom of thought. But first, educators themselves must be able to see the role the media and culture plays in blaming an entire religion for the acts of a few. Only through this—a greater understanding of the role of the media and American culture in influencing the West's understanding of Islam post-9/11—can students begin to determine their own opinions about the War on Terror and how they choose to interact with their Muslim and Arab peers.

Through this chapter we will evaluate common misperceptions presented by the media and culture fueled by *Islamphobia*. The term Islamophobia generally means a dislike of or prejudice against Islam or Muslims, especially as a political force, and can lead to assumptions such as "Muslims are the enemies of the United States" or "9/11 is the fault of Islam."

It is important to take stock of this based on the obvious holes in the conversation, which will be discussed at greater length in the following chapter (Where are Muslim voices? Who are Muslims? What is the history of the Muslim-Western relationship? What is the role of imperialism in maintaining and encouraging Islamophobia?). Through a deep analysis of various sources—such as teachers, students, and the media and culture itself—it becomes clear that growing Islamophobia contributes to the lopsided dialectic about 9/11 and the War on Terror through bolstering stereotypes, ignorance, and fear.

What Is Islamophobia?

The correlation between Muslims, Arabs, and terrorism has left many Americans fearful. This fear has led to harsh commentary and strong political action. For example, many influential American thought leaders vocalize strong religious beliefs, predominantly Christian ones, which are often placed in moral opposition to Islam. These opinions indelibly impact public opinion and the shape of American democracy. In the wake of the Paris and Brussels terrorist attacks of 2016, Ted Cruz blurred the line between Muslims and Islamic terrorism by saying that the United States enemy was "radical Islamic terrorism" and calling on police to "patrol and secure Muslim neighborhoods" in search of "homegrown" terrorism in America (Saletan, 2015). In response to the same events, Donald Trump quoted The Pew Research and said that Muslims hate America, and agreed that "violence against America is justified as part of a global jihad." As a result, he called for "a total and complete shutdown of Muslims entering the United States until our country's representatives can figure out what the hell is going on" (BBC News, 2015). Right-leaning Christians often deeply oppose Islamic belief and draw connections between Muslims and terrorism. For example, William G. Boykin, United States Deputy Undersecretary of Defense for Intelligence under President George W. Bush from 2002 to 2007 said "Islam is evil … it calls for brutality that is alien to us as Christians" (SPLC, n.d., para. 6). These deeply problematic understandings of Islam vilify Muslims and are used to hold up an infallible "Christian" America against a fear-mongering Muslim world. Perhaps because of this fear, it has been relatively easy for many Americans to accept the ongoing wars abroad in predominantly Muslim countries, as well as the mistreatment of Muslim Americans in the United States. Fear of Islam, or *Islamophobia*, is evident in the media and American imperialist culture through representations of Muslims in the news, popular culture, and politics, as well as treatment of Muslims in everyday life.

The current fearful perception of Islam is so pervasive that we now have a common term to describe the anxiety and fear experienced by non-Muslims in the face of an entire religion—Islamophobia, which emerged post 9/11. However, the term does not fully encompass the role of socio-political forces in growing and maintaining it. For example, an individual that suffers from arachnophobia probably does not have this fear reinforced by Channel 5 News constantly warning them that spiders are trying to kill them and take over their country. More likely than that, everyone who cares about this individual will encourage them to not be so fearful, to not imagine that there are spiders lurking in every corner. The opposite is true of Islamophobia. The term is composed of "phobia" and "Islam," insinuating that a fear of Islam leads "to some kind of mental illness, an involuntary revulsion of sorts when confronted with the Quran, prayer rugs, or Muslims in general …" (Kincheloe, Steinberg, & Stonebanks, 2010, p. x). Perceiving Islamophobia this way allows the claim that discrimination against Muslims in post 9/11 is an involuntary and individual act. This term can be misleading, since Islamophobia is a cultural, not individual phenomenon that is in fact reinforced by national political forces (Gottschalk & Greenberg, 2008). It is important to understand Islamophobia in the context of American culture, especially bombastic media, which ensnares the American public like a spider in her web.

Role of the Media

Teachers are uniquely positioned to reshape the cultural landscape and teach against Islamophobia. But the first step in teaching against Islamophobia is recognizing that it exists in the media and the culture at large. To understand how and why the media operates as it does, it is critical to pay attention to the role the media plays politically. Often the media plays a principal role in communicating official and unofficial state policies to the public, marking the enemy, and distracting the public from the casualties of war (Said, 2003). The media is often also responsible for cultural invasion. *Cultural invasion* represents a relationship of dominance between a superior culture that perceives another culture as inferior. The dominant culture uses overt and covert strategies to impose its values and culture onto the "inferior" others (Freire, 1970). Obviously the media serves many important functions as well, and can be an excellent tool for learning about current events happening across the world. However, teachers must learn to read the American media and culture with a critical eye so that they can recognize and point out bias to their students, giving their students the skills necessary to use media and culture as a tool, rather than become tools themselves.

Where the Media's Power Comes from: Public Pedagogy and Selective Tradition

If it is so apparent that there is bias in the media, how does the media hold so much power? The answer has to do with the fact that the media holds a status as a source of what's called *public pedagogy* within the culture. Giroux (2004) coined the term public pedagogy in which pedagogy is not limited to the social construction of knowledge and experience but happens through interactions among educators, students, texts, and institutional practices. Public pedagogy serves to teach how to think and feel about all the different people who make up a particular culture, including how to think of oneself. At the same time, public pedagogy builds power structures and establishes relationships. The media is a prime example of public pedagogy that works by constructing stories through metaphor, images, and emotion (Giroux, 2004). Public pedagogy is a form of mass education through cultural sources. It is different from selective tradition, which is the selection to transmit certain information to the public while omitting others. The media uses selective tradition to impact public perceptions of Islam and Muslims. For example, professors of education, Joe Kincheloe and Shirley Steinberg (2010) wrote about an incident with a Muslim student who, immediately after the public had been saturated with media images of 9/11, "was spat upon and called names" (2010, p. 79).

This student feared for her safety so much that she stopped attending evening classes. Kincheloe called CNN to report the anti-Muslim harassment and "the reporter laughed and told him they had more important events to cover and that, indeed, maybe these incidents should happen more often—maybe his student got what she deserved" (2010, p. 79). This reporter was selective in terms of the stories he constructed for the public. In this sense, the reporter was educating the public with what he wanted the public to know, without caring about what this means and how it might impact individual lives. While this is only one example from one reporter, there are many similar cases. Stories of discrimination against Muslims are very frequent and yet are almost never reported. When only stories that vilify Muslims are reported in the news, it enforces a lopsided dialectic and consequently, "it really took no time at all for an entire country to explode into rampant Islamophobia" (Steinberg, 2010, p. 80). The public pedagogy about Islam wove an emotionally riveting story about Muslims and terrorism, and because of the strength and pervasiveness of this story, Islamophobia in the culture was born as a result.

Reporting only selected stories, and contributing to a lopsided dialectic in the media, is an example of selective tradition in public pedagogy. For example, when comparing the media reports on two wars—the War on Terror and Vietnam—a teacher I interviewed, George observed that the reports on these two wars are completely different. This difference in reporting is to manipulate people into continuing in war. George said, "I think that the establishment has learned … how to undermine peace efforts and antiwar efforts without crushing skulls and arresting a lot of people, and you know the corporate media has a lot to do with that." George argued that the establishment learned from the Vietnam War how to use the media to maintain mass support for the war and the troops throughout the war period. He observed how the media has to become selective on what to present and what to conceal in order to maintain control over people's consciousness, which George described as being "numbed." George elaborated, saying:

> For them to say that, "Wow! No, we will actually make sure that you have a free flow of information from Operation Iraqi Freedom. We are going to embed journalists— right there with the troops so that you will know everything exactly as it was happening." Well, of course, all of those reports were censored. Every viewpoint that you get is down the barrel of a US gun or cannon. And that's reported to be balanced because a lot of journalists who are totally hamstrung in what they are allowed to report. It's just part of the sham of free-flow of information. (personal communication, June 5, 2010)

According to George, the establishment has learned how to manipulate the public through giving the illusion of freedom and using an undercover selective tradition to gain support for the War.

Muslims: The "Bad Guy"

In the media, it is especially evident how Muslims are viewed through an Islamophobic lens. Muslims are often represented by television, movies, video games, and news media as a homogenous group with violent tendencies with few positive or nuanced portrayals. The overwhelming image of Muslims in popular media today is as the bad guy, meaning that in popular media, Muslims are depicted as "crude and exaggerated," according to a 2007 report by the Islamic Human Rights Commission (Ameli, Marandi, Ahmed, Kara, & Merali, 2007). The former London mayor, Ken Livingstone, commissioned a study on the depiction of Muslims in the media and found that 91% of articles during a one-week period were negative. Only 4% of the 352 articles evaluated were positive. One particularly alarming and damaging example was a report which claimed that Christmas would be banned because it offended Muslims (The Guardian, 2007). The report states that Livingstone commented that the findings exposed the following:

> Hostile and scaremongering attitude … there are virtually no positive or balanced images of Islam being portrayed. … I think there is a demonization of Islam going on which damages community relations and creates alarm among Muslims. (The Guardian, 2007, para. 4)

The media portrays women of color in a negative light. However, Muslim women's representations in the media follow certain limited perspectives. These frames focus on Muslim women's: (a) appearance; in terms of how a Muslim woman looks and what she wears (Fakhraie, 2010), (b) victimhood; Muslim woman are often represented as victims of Muslim male's oppression and who are in need of liberation (Navarro, 2010), and (c) sameness; Muslim women are portrayed as having no personality or complexity (Navarro, 2010). In the following pages, I will analyze treatment of Muslims in American news, television, movies, and cartoons to demonstrate the pervasiveness of these stereotypes.

Movies and Television

You know the character: beard, dirty face, and a crazy intensity in their eyes. Almost immediately it becomes apparent that this man is the bad guy, and that he will do everything in his power to destroy everything good in the world. This is the Muslim/Arab villain, and he can be found in countless movies that needed an international flair to their conflict between good and evil. Unlike Buddhism, which is treated with reverence in films like Lost Horizon, Seven Years in Tibet, or Kundun, every new blockbuster seems to fan the flames of the Islamophobia fire (Gottschalk & Greenberg, 2008). This portrayal often includes traits such as cruelty, fanaticism, and violence. An example includes shows such as Homeland, which lasted for six seasons, and was based on demonizing Muslims and Arabs. The show frequently showed Arab and Muslim characters as terrorists and, disturbingly enough, associated prayer rugs and the Qu'ran (which are found in almost every Muslim home) with extremism. In Homeland's first episode of season five, Rupert Friend, who plays the character of an agent in the capital of the Islamic State, blamed the Qu'ran for ISIS's beheadings, and indicated that based on the teachings of the Qu'ran, "[Muslims are] there for one reason and one reason only; to die for the Caliphate and usher in a world without infidels. That's their strategy, and it's been that way since the 7th century" (Tapson, 2015). Even if the Muslim characters do not explicitly manifest these traits, popular television shows like 24 suggest to viewers that even "good Muslims" deserve suspicion (Nimer, 2007). In season four of the show, for example, the friendly next-door Muslim family was revealed to be a sleeper terrorist cell. The Islamic Human Rights Commission study suggests that Hollywood greatly impacts society's view of Muslims and Islam (Ameli et al., 2007). Darla, one of the Muslim American students I interviewed, referenced the Lybian terrorists in the wildly popular film, Back to the Future (1985). The connection between Arabs and Muslims with terrorists is so ubiquitous that, according to Darla, "It's like when you say 'park' people think 'grass.'" Mary told me about another film called Not Without My Daughter (1991), starring Sally Field. She said the movie "really represents Islam, Muslim men, and Iran in a bad way." The Iranian Muslim male protagonist beats his wife and child. Mary was upset at this representation of Islam, because the male dominance represented in the film "is all part of culture, not religion, and I think that people mix up religion and culture." A contemporary movie with six Oscar nominations and a box office record of $90 million in its opening weekend, American Snipper (2014), starring Bradley Cooper and Sienna Miller, degraded Muslims and Iraqis while glorifying Americans in a sensationalized way. It inspired some viewers to feel sympathy for the main character, who believed Iraqis are savages. In fact, in a report by BBC News, the movie resulted in an increase in anti-Muslim threats (BBC News, 2015). This led The American-Arab Anti-Discrimination Committee (ADC) to

request from the director of the movie, Clint Eastwood, and its leading character, Bradley Cooper, to speak out against violence towards Muslims. Although
there was no direct response from Eastwood nor Cooper, Jack Horner, picture
producer at Warner Brothers film studio, condemned violence against Muslims that may have resulted because of the movie (*BBC News*, 2015). There
are examples of movies just filling the scenes with Arabs (Steinberg, 2010)
such as *Wristcutters: A Love Story* (2006) starring Shannyn Sossamon and Patrick Fugit. In the movie an Arab cab driver who appears in an unexpected way
in the movie as a suicide bomber. This scene might be a small portion of the
movie, but its message and impact might be great in indicating that terrorists
are everywhere and cause harm unexpectedly (Steinberg, 2010). Also, *Iron
Man 3* (2013) starring Robert Downey Jr. has a scene in which a character,
Iron Patriot, travels to a factory in Pakistan and frees Muslim women wearing
niqab (face covering). This scene indicates that Muslim women are oppressed
and need liberation. While these images could be chalked up to the whims of
the Hollywood imagination, it is also apparent that the very same perception
of Muslims also exists in a pervasive way on U.S. news programs.

News Programs

In general, American news media sources do not blame other religions for the
egregious acts of a few the way Islam is so often held accountable for acts of
terrorism. Right after the Paris attack of November 13, 2015, *The Huffington
Post* published an article that criticized the coverage of a CNN anchor, John
Vause, of the attack for bias. Particularly alarming was when he asked a French
anti-Islamophobia activist, Yasser Louati, "Why is it that no one within the
Muslim community there in France knew what these guys were up to?" Louati
replied: "Sir, the Muslim community has nothing to do with these guys"
(Arana, 2015). Even though news programs are expected to be non-biased
and report the incidents objectively, it seems that news programs (even those
that pride themselves on reporting the news in an objective light) harbor bias
against Muslims and associate Muslim populations with the terrorist actions
of random individuals. Gabriel Arana, Senior Media Editor at *The Huffington
Post*, explained that there is a pattern that emerges when reporters attempt to
make sense of an event when scarce information is presented—reporters may
then fill in the missing information with "warrantless speculation" (Arana,
2015, para. 8). It is time news programs used a more balanced way to report
the news as it relates to Muslims.

Many individuals I spoke to for my interviews recognized the difference in treatment of Muslims as compared to other religions in the news. Participants of my study such as, Mark (a student) noticed a difference in the way the media treated violent acts from Christian individuals or groups. He gave the example that follows:

> Timothy McVeigh, when he blew up the federal building in Oklahoma City, you didn't see the media going up there and saying, "Christianity, these Christian terrorists," you know. Or even the IRA [Provisional Irish Republican Army] in Ireland—when the Catholics were fighting against the Protestants in the UK you didn't see the media saying "Oh, these Catholic terrorists," you know. So, it's definitely true. You see the media declared a war against Muslims. (personal communication, March 19, 2010)

Francis (a student) also noticed a difference in the way controversial issues within churches or Catholicism are discussed on the American news:

> How many home-grown terrorist have grown up in America and how many incidents that we had that are White American, they won't say that on the news. But if it was a Muslim group and like non-Christian, non-Catholic groups, they will say it and make it a big deal and make it one-sided and they won't show another side. Like, I can say how a lot of priests have been molesters but I am not going to go ahead and say that all priests are that way or I am not going to say that just, like, because the majority of serial killers are white, I am not going to say that every white middle-aged guy who has a family is a killer. (personal communication, April 1, 2010)

Muslim interviewees noticed that unlike other religious groups, when an incident happens by a Muslim, the entire Muslim population gets blamed as if they are responsible. The conservative news media has a role to play in the generalization of Muslims.

Conservative Media: Particularly Negative. Conservative American news media in particular represents Muslims and Islam especially adversely. It is not surprising to hear that conservative American political pundits such as Bill O'Reilly believe "Muslim Terrorism is the number one problem on Earth," as stated on October 24, 2014 on the Fox News Network (O'Reilly, 2014). When viewers hear O'Reilly say on CBS News program *The View* "Muslims killed us on 9/11" (October 14, 2010) or when they hear Brian Kilmeade say on Fox News' *Fox & Friends* on "All terrorists are Muslims" (October 15, 2010,) then, viewers are already primed to accept it when Presidential candidate (2016) Donald Trump call for a total ban on Muslims entering the United States. However, it is important to mention that Whoopi Goldberg, co-host of *The View*, defended Muslims and criticized O'Reilly's denunciation of all Muslims for 9/11. Goldberg yelled at O'Reilly "What religion was Mr. McVeigh? [Timothy McVeigh] Mr. McVeigh was an extremist as well, and he killed people" (Thomas, 2010, para. 7). In fact, she and Joy Behar walked out during the show to protest O'Reilly's statements against Muslims (Thomas, 2010). Goldberg and Behar's actions demonstrate that even though conservative news media exploits terrorist attacks to persistently fuel anti-Muslim hostility, there are those who stand up and say this is wrong.

Many of the interviewees specifically referenced Fox News, a conservative news media outlet from the United States, as a source for negative or erroneous information about Muslims and Islam. When educating people with the Muslim Student Association (MSA), Darla said that non-Muslims would "come up to the [information] tent and say, 'Why do you believe Muhammad is the God? You guys believe in blowing up yourselves for the 72 virgins?' Then I am like, 'No, not at all.' Where do they get this information from, Fox News?" (personal communication, April 3, 2010). Francis also believed that the negative stereotypes of her peers came predominantly from Fox News. According to her, "all the students would just repeat what they heard on the media, on Fox News, which is the worst" (personal communication, April 1, 2010).

Conservative news media often presents the far-right views of conservative officials who support anti-Muslim politics. I interviewed many of the Muslim American students following the 2011 US Congressional Hearings on "The Extent of Radicalization in the American Muslim Community and That Community's Response," called and led by Rep. Peter King (R-N.Y.), also the chairman of the House Homeland Security Committee. King had made controversial statements about Muslims, claiming the vast majority of mosques in the U.S. are run by radicals (Wolfe, 2011). Darla recalled how Fox News treated the hearings as "propaganda about how Muslims and the Sharia law will take over the world, and I am like, 'Are you serious?'" Henry also believed that the "American media … spreads anti-Muslim" sentiment. When I asked him, "Why are they doing that?" He responded, "just to get viewers. … I mean, if Justin Bieber gets his hair cut, that is their agenda" (personal communication, April 6, 2010). He mentioned conservative *Fox News* pundits Glenn Beck, who "might seem very anti-Muslim. I don't think he is. I think it is because there are 40 million idiots listening to him talk, and I think he gets paid for it." Linda, also said the following about her students:

> The kids look at the War on Terrorism as nothing that is real as portrayed today in the American media. They talk to their parents a lot and they have a lot of access to media in all different forms, as, you know … and they know what is going on from

other sources, not just Fox News. They laugh at *Fox News*. They know that's a joke, and you're not getting the right story. (personal communication, May 29, 2010)

Unfortunately, not everyone believes that these horrific messages about Muslims are "a joke," as demonstrated through the many upsetting experiences described by the Muslim American students, and others. Fortunately, there are media sources in the United States that convey a more balanced view of Muslims. Some teachers mentioned National Public Radio (NPR) as an example of more balanced media coverage. However, American media in general, and conservative media in particular, portrays Muslims through an Islamophobic lens. Whether they are merely poorly researched, or purposefully one-sided, or it is to attract more viewers for greater profit, the way conservative news media currently portrays and speaks about Muslims contribute to heightened Islamophobia in the United States culture. Another contributor is repressing Muslim voices.

News Programs: Whose Voice is Missing? Another example of selective tradition is demonstrated through blocking Muslim voices in the media. Muslim leaders repeatedly denounced ISIS and its atrocious and inhuman actions, however, conservative news media cover their ears and turn their backs and say "why aren't Muslims speaking up against ISIS?" For instance, Egypt's Al-Azhar's highest religious authority, Shawqi Allam, condemned the Islamic State, calling it "corrupt and a danger to Islam" on August 14, 2014 (Sandmeyer & Leung, 2014, para. 10). Meanwhile, Saudi Arabia's highest religious authority stated that organizations such as ISIS are the "number one enemy of Islam" (Sandmeyer & Leung, 2014, para. 19). Also, The Islamic Society of North America denounced ISIS actions and stated they "are in no way representative of what islam actually teaches" (Sandmeyer & Leung, 2014, para. 17). Muslim countries such as Turkey, international organizations such as The Arab League, and Western Muslim organizations such as Council on American Islamic Relations, The Muslim Council of Great Britain, and Muslim Public Affairs Council, all call ISIS a terrorist organization and stand for fighting against it (Sandmeyer & Leung, 2014). The only problem is that conservative news media overlooks their condemnation.

There are many frustrating examples of this happening. In fact, on August 11, ABC News' Laura Ingraham asked "if any, in the Muslim community have condemned the Islamic State" (Sandmeyer & Leung, 2014, para. 6). She is not the only one. On August 12, Sean Hannity's Fox News program had a section called "The Silence of Muslims," in which he asked "where are the Muslim leaders speaking out against the Islamic state terrorist group?" Finally, on August 21, 2014, Anna Kooiman, the Co-host of Fox News' *Fox & Friends* "claimed that 'we aren't hearing much' from Muslim countries and groups in response to the brutal acts of violence committed by the Islamic State" a week after Al-Azhar's denunciation of ISIS actions (Sandmeyer & Leung, 2014, para. 2). What Fox conservative news media wants Muslim leaders to do is to apologize for ISIS behavior. However, apologizing would mean that a group such as ISIS or al-Qaeda are part of the Muslim community and that there is a collective shared responsibility for the attacks. It is not Muslim leaders' responsibility to defend the entire Muslim population when a few individuals act irrationally in the name of a religion. This is not asked from any other religious group. Indeed, it is not a Muslim leader or country's responsibility to speak out against ISIS behaviors. Nevertheless, Muslim countries and leaders do denounce these horrible actions and disassociate themselves from these groups. Many times, they do so to let people know that these groups are committing crimes against Islam and that Muslims are not responsible for their actions.

The fact is Muslim leaders, societies, and communities denounce any violence committed by any group or individuals, however, their voices are blocked from the news media. Blocking their voices sends a message that they approve of such horrific acts or that they are not members of the community. When Muslim voices do not reach the public, Americans will not learn about the diversity of Muslim experiences and cultures, leaving many Americans vulnerable to indoctrination from corporate media and far right extremists. Mainstream American media enforces an "us versus them" mentality with flat and faulty news coverage. Allowing more Muslims airtime—Muslims from a variety of backgrounds, countries, and political dispositions—dispels the myth that Muslims are a unified bloc. In other words, there is no "them." Allowing more human diversity in general on the nightly news would also dispel the idea that there is a white, Christian "us." Just as the Muslim community is diverse, so is the American one. Permitting Muslim voices to reach Americans could work against the unbalanced conversation and develop a counter-hegemonic discourse that could provide more critical analysis of America's foreign policy, as well as reveal the imperfections of ideals such as democracy, freedom, and citizenship, especially in regards to Muslim Americans.

Even when Muslim scholars are invited to speak on television their integrity is questioned based on their religion. For example, Fox News interviewed Reza Aslan in 2013 about his book *Zealot: The Life and Times of Jesus of Nazareth*. The interviewer asked, "You are a Muslim, so why did you write a book about the founder of Christianity?" Aslan responded, "I am a scholar of religions with four degrees who also just happens to be a Muslim. ... I am not just a random Muslim who wrote a book. ... I do think it's perhaps a little bit strange that instead of debating the arguments of the book, we are debating the right of the scholar to actually write it" (*Wemple*, 2013). The interviewer seemed uninterested and unaware of the book contents, instead choosing to focus on Aslan's religious identity rather than his professional, scholarly one. Under rare occasions Muslims are invited to talk shows without their faith being the focus of the conversation. Therefore, to respond to people who ask why Muslims do not speak up against Islamophobia or to condemn Isis or Al Qaeda, there is evidence that their voices are excluded, shut down, or questioned for bias. Muslim scholars want to speak out, but often the mainstream media does not give them a chance. Maybe it is time that the media invited Muslim scholars to rectify a lopsided dialectic about terrorism and Muslims. In summary, Islam seems irrevocably tied with terrorism through the nightly news. This is also true when it comes to the print media even more innocuous-seeming things such as the Sunday funnies.

Cartoons and Caricatures

Cartoons and caricatures also foment negative stereotypes of Islam and Muslims. Though exaggerations, caricatures still "operate under the assumption that the representation physically resembles, even in an embellished manner, the person or people to whom it refers" (Gottschalk & Greenberg, 2008, p. 46). According to Peter Gottschalk, professor of religion at Wesleyan University & Gabriel Greenberg, Assistant professor of philosophy at UCLA (2008), cartoonists use caricatures to depict Muslims in a pejorative manner, often quite differently from images of Christians or Jews. Symbols of incivility and immorality such as the scimitar, long beards hanging under a big nose and full turban, or the heavily burqa-draped women with only their eyes exposed, may be in good fun, but inevitably perpetuate an erroneous yet widely accepted perspective of Islam. Negative stereotypes about Islam and Muslims create a necessary "Other" that Gottschalk and Greenberg (2008) claim bolster the Wests' self-image. These images are not taken well by most Muslims who often see these representations as discriminatory. In rare and extreme cases, radicals react violently, as was the case with shooting at the *Charlie Hebdo* office. Charlie Hebdo is a satirical weekly newspaper from France, which features cartoons, reports, and jokes. On January 7, 2015, twelve journalists were killed by terrorists who cited the portrayal of Islam and Mohammed as their reason for murder. These murders are not justified, but appear to be an extreme response to persistent Islamophobic imagery. However, and although scarce, there are some pleasant representations of Muslims.

Positive Treatment of Muslims in the Media

There are positive examples of officials and media outlets that treats Muslims positively. In his visit to a Baltimore mosque on February 3, 2016, Obama started by thanking the Muslim community for their contributions to American society while condemning the overwhelming association of Muslims with terrorism in the media. Consequently, the president urged the media to portray Muslims in more positive light. In his words: "Our television shows should have some Muslim characters that are unrelated to national security. It's not that hard to do" (Levine, 2016). Indeed, there are some TV shows and movies that show Muslims in positive light. For instance, the character Abed Nadir in the American sitcom *Community*, portrays a relatable character that is half-Palestinian, socially awkward, and well-versed in American pop culture. There is Sayid Jarrah in *Lost* who represents a past Iraqi prison guard that used methods of torture who turns against the Iraqi government after his supervisor ordered the execution of his beloved, Nadia. Finally, there is Arastoo Vaziri who appeared in the fourth season of the TV show, *Bones*. He is a dedicated Iranian Muslim and a lab assistant to Doctor Brennan, aka Bones. The TV show presents him as an empathetic person who cares for the victims' social lives (Samir, 2016). Also, it is important to mention that not all Americans accept the demonization of Muslims. For example, American Evangelical Christians petitioned Donald Trump, condemning his racist comments and religious intolerance as contrary to Christian values. In their words:

We have to make it publicly clear that Mr. Trump's racial and religious bigotry and treatment of women is morally unacceptable to us as evangelical Christians, as we attempt to model Jesus' command to "love your neighbors as yourself." (Evangelical Leaders United States, 2016, para. 12). Further, a special report by *The Washington Post* investigates the ways that Muslims merge their American identity with their Islamic faith. The report includes videos showing interviews with Muslims about their struggles and fears post 9/11, telling their stories with incidents in which they felt they were under suspicion, and sharing their opinions about radicalization. The report also features Muslim comedians who defy negative stereotypes with comedy in Georgia, Alabama and Tennessee (*The Washington Post*, 2011). Finally, in the wake of fatal shootings of two Muslim men who were walking home after praying at a mosque in New York City, social media users started a campaign #Ill-WalkWithYou hashtag offering to walk with Muslims to their mosques so that they feel safe and protected (*ABC News*, 2016). Positive social media supports Muslims and provides an alternative to the consistent bashing of Muslims, and so do media outlets abroad.

Muslims in the Media Outside of the United States

However, not all sources of media portray Muslims in a negative light. When Bridget travelled to Jordan to spend some time in an Islamic society, she was shocked by how different Jordanian media was from U.S. media:

> Living in Jordan has been different, you know. The media coverage that we get there is different from the media coverage that we get here, so I think there is not ... they don't portray Muslims as terrorists or evil people. There are a lot of good things. They talk about the bad people that represent Islam but, you know, they always correspond with, "This is only a minor percent of the people," and it doesn't generalize, you know, and it doesn't generalize that all Muslims are like them. ... (personal communication, March 24, 2010)

Other interviewees repeated this sentiment about how different American media is from the media in other countries. When Henry spoke about the media in Henry's native Pakistan as compared to the media in the United States, he said, "It is like for the media over here, there is a media over there." He perceived that each media source had its own particular slant based on geographic location or perhaps ideological perspective. But, whether it is in the United States or abroad, the media affects social marginalization of Muslims.

How Media Leads to Exclusion for Muslims in America

The public pedagogy in the media saturates the American culture with fear of Muslims and facilitates the social exclusion of Muslims from mainstream society. A Gallup Survey conducted within 2008–2011 reported that 52% of U.S. Americans do not respect Muslims. 36% indicated that the reason of disrespect is due to the Islamic religion, while 35% stated that they disrespect Muslims due to political interest. The report also shows that while 30% of Americans believed that Muslims are not treated fairly in the United States, a 48% of Muslims reported experiencing prejudice or religious discrimination, particularly in 2009, which was the highest rate in comparison to other religious groups. While it is challenging to draw direct ties between the media and views of Muslims, it is not hard to extrapolate that it may be influencing American's perceptions.

There is a correlation between Islamophobia in media and the culture and heightened discrimination against Muslims. *START* researchers conducted three studies; one experimental, and two correlational studies; that surveyed a total of 1200 college students about the correlation between negative portrayal of Muslims in the media and supporting anti-Muslim policies. They found that "exposure to news reports portraying Muslims as terrorists is significantly associated with support for military action in Muslim countries, civil restrictions for Muslim Americans and policies harming Muslims domestically and abroad" (Snaman, 2016, para. 1). The study found that consistent positive representations of Muslims result in a decline in support for policies that harm them (Snaman, 2016). In fact, *The Washington Post* article focusing on hate crimes against Muslims post 9/11 shows FBI records that compare hate crimes against Muslims prior to the 9/11 attacks which were around 30 crimes per year which increased to 500 in 2001 (Ingraham, 2015). Also, the Southern Poverty Law Center (SPLC) recorded a 2011 FBI's national hate crime report directly made this connection, stating that hate crimes against perceived Muslims doubled in 2010 to reach 160 during a time of heightened anti-Muslim propaganda (*Southern Poverty Law Center*, 2013). In 2015, right after the Bernardino shootings on December 2, 2015, 63 incidents of vandalism at mosques across the United States occurred, which tripled the number of incidents of 2014. Even Muslims who walked in parks or drove their cars got spat on (Burke, 2015). All these examples demonstrate the impact of Media representations of Muslims on their social acceptance and inclusion.

This disrespect aids the continuous exclusion of Muslims from the American community, even those who commit heroic acts. Mohammad Salman Hamdani was a Muslim hero left out of 9/11 memorial. Mohammad was walking to his job at DNA analysis lab at Rockefeller University, but when September 11 he hurried to the World Trade Center to assist police cadet. Even though, Mohammad was declared a hero by the city's police commissioner and buried with full honors from the New York Police Department, his name did not make it on the list of fallen first responders at the 9/11 Memorial in Lower Manhattan. He was only mentioned among the names of people who died on September 11, but he was not mentioned among the heroes who died to save others. His mother told the New York Times "They do not want anyone with a Muslim name to be acknowledged at ground zero with such high honors. ... They don't want someone with the name Mohammad to be up there" (Otterman, 2012).

Even Muslim students that I interviewed experienced disrespect and exclusion. The nine Muslim American students that I interviewed reported daily harassment in the streets, at the airport, at work, in general society, and even among people they considered friends. The effects of Islamophobia were perhaps most stark in airports, the iconic location where terrorists gained entry and wreaked havoc on New York City. At the airport, Mary experienced more security surveillance after 9/11, especially having an Iranian last name and arriving travelled back from Iran. The airport security officials started questioning her about her identity and the reasons why she visited Iran. She believed being an Iranian also added more tension to the situation beyond that which she would have already experienced as a Muslim, since the United States' relationship with Iran is currently tense. Similarly, Francis mentioned that after 9/11, "me and my mom we were randomly selected a couple of times when we went to Michigan a couple of years ago, that never happened before" (personal communication, April 1, 2010). Francis explained that when they were getting on a plane, the TSA "randomly selected" them for a more advanced private search. However, Francis found it hard to believe that, even though she does not travel much, they were randomly selected twice. Someone might say that these are only individual suspicions and do not provide evidence. But imagine yourself in any of these youth's shoes. If you are a Muslim, the media repeatedly says Muslims are terrorists, and you get randomly selected to be thoroughly searched at the airport in front of all people as part of a counter terrorism act. How would you feel?

Perhaps a change in airport security staff affected airport security measures. After 9/11, Naber (2008) explained that the U.S. Federal Government took charge of airport security, particularly hiring retired security and military personnel who may have exercised racism and discrimination against Muslim Americans in the name of national security. Such extreme government security measures influenced how travelers interacted with Muslims at the airport and in airplanes. A 2011 report by The Guardian indicated that people from ethnic minority groups are 42 times more likely than Whites to be carefully searched by airport security under the counter-terrorism Act. The report specifically mentioned Muslims along with Hindus, Indian Christians, and even Buddhists (White, 2011). Bridget (a student) stated that riding an airplane is definitely different after 9/11 because people showed fear towards her. "Even though they wouldn't tell me they were afraid, they would still give me looks, or they seemed a little bit nervous by me." Bridget explained, "I remember a lot of the people asking me if this religion was a cult and if they taught us to become martyrs, you know" (personal communication, March 24, 2010). She was shocked by the explicit association of Islam with extremism and martyr-dom and explained to the people she met on the airplane that every religion has extremist groups, and Islam should not be singled out.

Although the experiences of the Muslims at the airport were filled with fear and discomfort, their experiences in other places were no different. In the street, some Americans treated Muslim youth with disrespect and hostility. Heidi narrated an incident in which she was driving with her mother and a man stuck his head out and called them "camel jockies." Heidi got very upset, "I tried to get my mom to turn around and follow him because I wanted to talk to him and my mom was like, 'No, you can't talk to him'" (personal communication, March 17, 2010). Heidi wanted to explain to him that his comment offended her. In an incident while riding public transportation, Bridget felt that people sometimes avoided sitting by her or gave her weird looks. She believed this is because she was wearing the *hijab* and was associated with the aforementioned Arab/Muslim/Middle Eastern stereotypes. Sirin and Fine (2008) demonstrated Bridget's hypothesis stating that after 9/11, the media ignored the diversity among Muslim American people and ideologically constructed their identities into one racial and ethnic homogenized group through a "forced *ethnogenesis*, or creating one people out of many" (p. 59). Bonnet (2011) further stated that the media helped in fusing Arabs, Muslims, and Middle Easterners in one group and associating them with "the axis of evil that threatened America and all it stands for" (p. 49). Indeed, The Center of Hate & Extremism at California State University, San Bernardino, conducted research that found that hate crimes against American Muslims, mainly Arabs, increased by 78% in 2015. Negative media representations of Muslims aids their marginalization in society and assists offensive actions against them.

Social Exclusion Heightened for More "Muslim-looking" Individuals

The forms of harassment Muslims experienced in the street show that 9/11 and the context of the War on Terror allowed racialization of all Muslim Americans as somehow related to terrorists and terrorism. Whoever fits the media's stereotypical image of what a terrorist looks like faces more often harassment from the government and in the streets (Naber, 2008). There are specific characteristics for terrorists, and any individual fitting such a "terrorist profile" (Naber, 2008, p. 284) faces discrimination. According to Naber (2008), there are specific characteristics for terrorists as follows:

> The category "Arab /Middle Eastern/ Muslim" operated as a constructed category that lumps together several incongruous subcategories (such as Arabs and Iranians, including Christians, Jews, and Muslims, and all Muslims from Muslim majority countries, as well as persons who are perceived to be Arab, Middle Eastern, or Muslim, such as South Asians, including Sikhs and Hindus). (Naber, 2008, p. 279)

From Naber's description, the category "Arab /Middle Eastern/ Muslim" lumps together people from different ethnicities, geographies and even religions. Such a blurry profile allows for inclusion of a wide range of assumed terrorist suspects, which facilitates abuse, discrimination, and harassment against anyone who might fit the stereotype. Further, professor of Asian American Studies at University of California Davis, Sunaina Maira (2009) explained that the United States' cultural citizenship and nationalism constructs Muslim culture as anti-modern and as a threat to the American way of life, thus exposing Muslims to discrimination and harassment including workplace discrimination.

Post 9/11 witnessed an increase in workplace injustice against Muslims. Workplace discrimination filed by Muslims to the Federal Equal Employment Opportunity Commission (EEOC) more than doubled since 2004. In 2009, the EEOC received 1,490 complaints that include discharge, harassment, and terms and conditions of work (Greenhouse, 2010). The *New York Times* reported a story about Mohammad Kaleemuddin who was fired by a construction company in Houston for complaining against his supervisor and peers for using derogatory insults against him (Greenhouse, 2010). Another complaint was filed by a woman called Imane Boudlal who worked for two years as a hostess at the Storytellers Cafe at California's Disneyland, and was warned by her supervisors that if she insisted on wearing the *hijab* she would work either in the back or in the telephone room (Greenhouse, 2010). Those might seem like random incidents, however, Abed Ayoub, legal director of the American-Arab Anti-Discrimination Committee told *Salon* (2010) that he believes that rising employment discrimination are congruent with the heightened Islamophobia in society. He justified his claim by comparing employment discrimination complaints by Muslims right after 9/11 with the year before the attacks.

He stated that in 2000, the EEOC received 557 complaints by Muslims. Only two years later, in 2002, that amount almost tripled to reach 1,463. After that, complaints declined significantly and then soared up again to reach its highest peak in 2009 (Benjamin, 2010). It is important to mention that the EEOC do file lawsuits that brings justice to discriminated employees including Muslims. But, for Muslims who do not file complaints, workplace discrimination remains a challenge.

Muslim students I interviewed experienced discrimination at work—and this is most acutely felt by Muslims who look more stereotypically Islamic. For instance, Bridget worked with several government entities and she always felt she was treated differently than her colleagues. Bridget explained:

> You know, I felt I was limited to how far I could go with my career. And actually at one point, one of my bosses who was very honest with me came out and we had a long conversation and he told me, you know, you are a very bright woman and you could go so far in your career but because, you know, you are wearing a veil it is going to limit you to how far you could go, especially with government entities. (personal communication, March 24, 2010)

Bridget's experience is similar to many women wearing the *hijab*. Zine (2006) conducted a study in Toronto that surveyed 32 women on their experiences wearing the *hijab* to a job interview, and 29 out of 32 women stated that an employer commented on their *hijab* during the interview or asked them to take it off if they wanted the job. Maira (2009) agreed that work is a place in which anti-Muslim and anti-Arab discrimination intensifies. Francis, another student I interviewed, also noticed the difference in treatment between *hijab*-wearing women and other Muslim women who could blend more into American culture. Francis did not wear the *hijab* at the time of our interview. She said the following:

> For me, they don't know until they speak to me, and they might be a little bit open minded because they'll see me as, "Whatever, she is like a normal looking girl," or whatever in their view. I will probably have a better chance of making them understand my background.... (personal communication, April 1, 2010)

At this point she paused, observing me in my *hijab*, and then she continued: "While you [Randa], they will probably look at you and that's it. They have this image or opinion about you already without speaking to you." It is worth asking: Where does this image come from? The evidence seems to point universally to the media and culture at large.

Although Muslim males might not wear religious symbols such as the *hijab*, they might still face discriminatory treatment at their work place, as demonstrated through the examples above. The male Muslim students I interviewed also experienced this. Wayne explained that 9/11 severely damaged his flea market business and customers treated him more negatively when they found out he was Muslim. He said, "Sometimes you get the racist and the kind of red-neck like, 'Oh, you are Muslim,' you know, like, 'Go and take your business somewhere else.' So, I see that being a problem" (personal communication, April 11, 2010). Wayne recognized the Islamophobia of some Americans who shopped at his stall in the market, and to protect himself and his business, changed his name in the market place so that people would not associate him with the Arabs/Muslims/Middle Easterners perceived to be terrorists. Not all Americans are discriminatory in the public sphere—there are many who are very kind. For example, during the month of Ramadan, Wayne lets people know he is a Muslim and fasting so they would not offer him food. He usually finds empathy, especially when he does not drink during hot days of the summer.

Still, discrimination at the work place is a common experience for Muslims whose religious identity is known to their colleagues or customers, but this discrimination is especially potent when the Muslim youth wear physical religious identifiers. Many Americans are kind, but the problem with the overwhelming Islamophobia in public pedagogy is that it teaches Americans that it is acceptable to be unkind to Muslims. The law and the media signal that Muslims are a threat and to be feared. As a result, Muslim American youth and other Muslims nationwide share experiences of discriminatory interactions at the hands of some Americans in U.S. culture—for example, at the airport, in the street, and at work.

Legal Influences on the Perception of Muslims

How did Islamophobia in the media influence a discriminatory environment that permitted the development of laws that socially exclude Muslims? Through affirming societal values and social norms of inclusion, exclusion, and social sanctions, the law enforces representations and accusations made by the media (Benabou & Tirole, 2011). In many ways, legal control of Muslims is a natural development of the fear and anxiety many Americans feel about Islam and its practitioners. Sarah Ahmed (2004) does a wonderful job explaining how emotions such as fear impact political support for certain laws. Fear starts with existing stereotypes, which grow through repetition from outside, such as from sources like the media, and also inside, such as within our own minds (Ahmed, 2004). Exaggerated fear of a particular kind of person leads to enough political groundswell to pass legislation that "protects" one population against another, often to the extreme detriment of the "'othered' population" (Ahmed, 2004; Steinberg, 2010). Through the repetition of stereotypes, the "other" becomes fixed as a threat, thus justifying discriminatory laws leveled against that other. Terrorists are portrayed as unpredictable and subversive—there could be a sleeper cell in your neighborhood, there could be a violent fundamentalist in your calculus class, and there could be a terrorist waiting in line behind you at the grocery store. The American public has been told that anyone who looks like a terrorist has a potential to be one. Ahmed (2004) argued that this causes greater anxiety than having a fixed enemy, and also justifies extensive defensive measures to protect from these unknowns.

Such fear allows illogical security measures, such as detaining people for the possibility of them being a terrorist, or to spy on all people for the possibility of one being a terrorist, and so on. For instance, Aristide Zolberg (2002), late professor of political science at the New School for Social Research, reported that an estimated 1,147 people have been detained between 9/11 and November 2001, many of whom "were picked up based on tips or were people of Middle Eastern or South Asian descent who had been stopped for traffic violations or for acting suspiciously" (as cited in Ahmed, 2004, p. 75). The fear of terrorism also paved the way for the construction of Guantanamo Bay, where detainees were legally tortured through methods such as 50,000-volt shock belts and waterboarding. Violation of basic human rights like habeas corpus, the right to protection from torture, and commitment to international law will forever change the way the world sees the United States (Stiglitz, 2004). There is a correlation between international human rights law and international humanitarian law.

Another outcome of Islamophobia in the media and culture is on America's humanitarian laws. International Humanitarian Law emerged as a branch of international law one of its goals is regulating the conduct of wars and armed conflict by restricting the methods and resources for combatants and protecting those not participating in the war. However, deciding who is a combatant and who is not has been blurred since 9/11, when all Muslims have been propagated as terrorist/militant/combatant. This makes the decision to provide international humanitarian aid subjective and under the mercy of those who see past the propaganda. For instance, people displaced because of war or escaping any other life-threatening situation could be from any country, religion, or ethnicity across the world. However, some people receive more help and support from the United States than others. The appearance of those seeking asylum may affect the likelihood that they will be able to find a home in the U.S. or any other Western nation. For example, *The Independent* reported that Poland refused to accept a single Syrian refugee out of fear of terrorism (Broomfield, 2016). Asylum seekers from Syria are often associated with potential terrorist threats in the American media, thus leading to less political support for opening America's doors to "your tired, your poor, your huddled masses yearning to breathe free" (Lazarus, 1883) as the quote so proudly boasts on the Statue of Liberty. Presidential candidates, Hillary Clinton and Donald Trump used the case of the Syrian refugees to serve their campaigns (Sakuma, 2016). While Clinton insisted "we cannot be shutting the doors to people in need" (para. 12), Trump maintained that all Muslims, including Syrian refugees should be banned (para. 13), Instead he suggested helping them in Syria by creating "a safe zone, get a lot of sand … put them there, you build it out, you have security, create a little bit of an environment until they go to their homes" (para. 13). Also, the United States pledged to accept 10,000 Syrian refugees and has accepted only 1,285 because many state governors opposed Syrian immigration for fear of terrorism. In this case, fear plays an important role in national and international legislation. It is important to understand how the public pedagogy of 9/11 and the War on Terror constructed by the media and enforced by the law influence the United States culture and consequently the social interactions experienced by Muslims.

How Islamophobia in the Culture Impacts Schools

For some, Islamophobia in the media has also directly impacted the school environment, steeping it in fear, disrespect, and closed-mindedness. Schools are not isolated institutions; they are social institutions affected by the media. Islamophobia from the media has filtered down to the educational system. Joe Kincheloe and Shirley Steinberg (2004) wrote a book, *The Miseducation of the West: How Schools and the Media Distort Our Understanding of the Islamic World*. Their main argument is how both the media and educational institutions contribute to further misinformation about Islam and Muslims. For instance, they gave the example of a textbook—*World Culture* by Petrovich, Roberts, and Roberts—showing a picture of Muslim men praying with guns next to them. They argued that selecting such a picture out of all the other available pictures of Muslims praying suggests that Muslims are violent and should be feared. Additionally, educator, author, and Newsweek magazine editor Gilbert T. Sewall (2003) surveyed frequently used world history textbooks in middle and high schools to analyze their contents about Islam, Muslims, and the history of the Middle East. He found that they are related to terms defined by officials in society. For instance, Sewall (2003) noted that a high school textbook published by Glencoe, *The Human Experience*, described jihad as: "holy struggle to bring Islam to other lands" (p. 278). This definition comes closer to that provided by the Library of Congress' glossary as holy war, which the Council on Islamic Education referred to as a distortion and misrepresentation (Sewall, 2003). Instead, Council on Islamic Education defines jihad as "any spiritual, moral or physical struggle in the cause of God, which can take many forms. In personal spheres, efforts such as obtaining an education, trying to quit smoking, or controlling one's temper are forms of jihad" (Sewall, 2003, para. 17). The textbooks defined the term based on U.S. officials' definition instead of researching what the term, which is in Arabic, actually means to the people who use it. Some of the pictures and information in textbooks are directly taken from media sources. For example, *The American Vision Modern Times*, Student Edition, by Glencoe McGraw-Hill (2010) includes a map entitled "Major terrorist attacks involving Al-Qaeda, 1993–2006" (p. 810). This map has National Geographic logo on it. Also, Osama bin Laden's picture inserted onto the map in the textbook originally comes from a Time Magazine cover image of 2001. These are just a few demonstrations of how the media filters down to textbooks. Some teachers are uncritical of the media and use textbooks without critical inspection of the material.

Though the Muslim students interviewed saw Islamophobic bias in the media and experienced it in the culture at large, many of their peers and teachers within the American school system not only failed to recognize it, but actually propagated it due to the public pedagogy reproduced by the media and law, and buttressed by the banking educational models of the American school system. In other words, what many students and teachers heard on the news is what they repeated in the classroom. For example, Mark observed that the way teachers spoke about Islam "is kind of like what you see on Fox News, basically, but in a classroom setting" (personal communication, March, 19, 2010). Though Francis noticed her classmates "[were] wanting to learn more," there was "a lot of ignorance just because of one event [9/11], because of the media" which "blamed it on us [Muslims]." Francis felt that "all the students would just repeat what they heard on the media, on Fox News ..." (personal communication, April 1, 2010). Heidi described the "stupid kids" who harassed her in middle school as people that "didn't care about anything besides what was really going on in the media," which meant "they weren't as educated" (personal communication, March, 17, 2010). The media is the most obvious example of the influence of public pedagogy on the school system. Representations of Muslims in the media are filtered down to the school system and circulated back out in society demonstrating a reciprocal flow of cultural knowledge and politics between school and society.

As an ideological entity, the educational system is involved in the process of building students' identities as well as restructuring notions of citizenship, belonging, and an enemy. Specifically, the classroom is a site where stereotypes about different groups are confirmed and reproduced (Kincheloe & Steinberg, 2004). For instance, stereotypes that Muslims are terrorists and an enemy of the United States are fostered in a classroom that supports an Islamophobic mentality (Kincheloe & Steinberg, 2004). In such a classroom, critical debates and discussions about Islamophobia and discrimination are avoided and a curriculum that enforces stereotypes about Muslims is likely to exist (Zine, 2004). As a result of this public pedagogy and a banking education model, Muslim students are likely to have been exposed to harassment and violence by their peers and teachers. Even when the discrimination is not directly leveled by the teachers, administration, and other school staff members, there is often an environment of permissiveness in regards to Islamophobia. For example, Sirin and Fine (2008) interviewed a Muslim American student who had complained to school staff that a peer was verbally abusing her. She was met with indifference and a laissez-faire attitude. This impacted the Muslim student's sense of safety at school. When a teacher fails to question the Islamophobia in public pedagogy, and does not utilize critical thinking in their classrooms, this often leads to a hostile environment against Muslim students.

On the other hand, when a teacher realizes and acknowledges the public pedagogy of Islamophobia in the media, she/he is more likely to be supportive of Muslim students. For example, the teachers who defended Heidi (a student.) behaved in a supportive way. "They would read the newspaper on occasions, like, all the teachers, they knew what was going on and they were very nice to me and they tried to help me out through this time" (personal communication, March 17, 2010). How could the teachers reading the newspapers "know what was going on" and the students paying attention to the media be just "stupid kids," according to Heidi? What was different about the public pedagogy that these teachers were exposed to? As a conjecture, perhaps the teachers were conducting more research into what is really happening, and reading other sources of news rather than mainstream, conservative

American media. The difference, according to Heidi, was that the students "didn't know much about access to good knowledge or real truth" (personal communication, March 17, 2010). Instead, Heidi believed the students listened to the sort of media that was generally Islamophobic. The teachers in this instance were certainly being helpful and supportive, but were they actually teaching against Islamophobia? These supportive actions certainly were helpful for one individual student, but did the teachers make a broader impact on the opinions and beliefs of the school children? How can teachers start realizing that what they teach in the classroom can influence public pedagogy?

Islamophobia often leads to intolerance and perhaps even violence within the school system. *The Huffington Post* published a blog about Islamophobic bullying in schools with inscriptions by teachers and students in a middle school yearbook that targeted Muslim students. Among the inscriptions, one by a teacher that stated: "You boys were so much fun on the 8th grade trip! Thanks for not bombing anything while we were there!"(Abdelkader, 2011, para. 1). While, this yearbook's inscriptions might have been done as a joke, why should a middle school child endure such offenses? The mother of the student took her complaints to the school's principal who assured her she would take action against the teacher. Also, she allowed the mother to conduct a cultural sensitivity training about Arabs and Muslims which was taken well by the school community (Abdelkader, 2011). However, when a teacher tries to counter Islamophobia like in George's (a teacher I interviewed) situation, some parents do not like it. For example, while teaching U.S. history advanced placement courses, George noticed significant intolerance towards his anti-Islamophobic perspective, particularly from military families who often dis-enrolled their children from his class:

George:	I had one student who was the daughter of a Colonel and she dis-enrolled from my class because she didn't like the approach that we were taking in my class.
Me:	Did you have any parents come up to you and tell you, "What are you teaching my kid?"
George:	Yes ... two to three times I had parents dis-enroll them. Twice it was after a chance of having spoken to the parents and just saying, "We respect your opinion but we want our kid out of here." And they were, of course military families. (personal communication, June 5, 2010)

Aggression was also prevalent in George's school, fueled by Islamophobia. George reported some startling behavior on behalf of a few students at his high school, with some aggression even directed at teachers:

There were some ROTC students who were not as educated as they are trained, ok. Which is the military program in our high school. There were some reported incidents of verbal abuse towards Muslim students but the school tried to make the faculty aware of the things that were going on and as far as I know it never got to the point of a physical confrontation. The worst side was of some verbal abuse and I have seen some things written on the bathroom wall … especially the boys restroom. And they didn't just target Muslims, they targeted France for their opposition of the Iraq War and they targeted teachers [anti-war] bumper stickers, so there were some backlash. (personal communication, June 5, 2010)

The problem with students who are trained in the Reserve Officers' Training Corps (ROTC) program and those who are children of people in the army is that they could become closed-minded about the War on Terror through public pedagogy and banking education. They may believe so fiercely in the ideas presented in media, law, and the classroom, that when alternatives are presented (such as France's opposition to the war, or the personal opinions of teachers) they may act violently to defend these learned perspectives. Unfortunately, an intolerant and permissive environment can result in destructive outcomes such as writing insults on bathroom walls, harassing Muslim students, or defacing teacher property. Ignorance facilitates aggression.

How Ignorance Creates Space for the Acceptance of Islamophobia

But why are these public pedagogies acceptable to people? What leads some people to question the status quo, and others to accept it? Some believe ignorance about history and culture creates mental space among an American public for a discriminatory and bigoted public pedagogy. Linda, one of the high school teachers I interviewed in New Mexico, said the following:

Ignorance, I mean it is something that Americans aren't comfortable with in general, they are not familiar with [Islam], and I think it may just be education. I never taught World History, but I know that, over the years, when you teach World History, you teach Western Civilization, you don't teach Eastern Civilization as much. It's gotten better, but the parents of my children had Western Civilization, and I think, until we understand as a nation, history of the world, we are so bigoted and biased I guess to look at something different. I mean, people say the most absurd things in news programs now about Muslims or about the War on Terror, and there are ignorant people out there who believe everything in the news. That needs to change—I mean, the portrayal of not just Muslims, but of African people, the portrayal of people all over the world. They are so stereotyped. So if you are a Muslim, you must be a terrorist,

because it was Muslims who did this or that or the other and so the only way to help
that is education. (Linda, personal communication, May 29, 2010)

The gaps in education about history and non-Western culture lead to some
Americans connecting the dots with images and ideas generated from a lopsided dialectic. The images and conclusions they draw from a lopsided dialectic do not paint a pretty picture of Muslims or Islam.

Fear of Islam, or Islamophobia, is evident in the public pedagogy spread by
the media, law, and American culture through representations of Muslims in
the news, television, movies, and politics, as well as treatment of Muslims at
schools. It is also evident how this fear indelibly impacts Muslim Americans,
teachers, and the school environment. This fear spills out in society, affecting
treatment of Muslim students at the airport, the street, work, school, and the
American society at large. However, because culture is fluid and school and
society influence each other in a reciprocal manner, it is not only possible but
urgently necessary that school become a place where Islamophobia is questioned, and ultimately history and culture more deeply understood.

Conclusion

The most pervasive image aired on U.S. televisions and other news media
sources links Muslims and Arabs to terrorism. The danger of these images lies
in their unrestricted permeability in homes, schools, and minds, seeping in
like lethal gasses, and leaving lasting effects on consumers who breathe them
in. Once ingested, these images pave the road for acceptance of harsh views
and actions that sustain wars and discriminatory policies. This fear and anxiety of Muslims has a name—it is called Islamophobia.

Muslims are often represented by television, movies, video games, and news
media as a homogenous group with violent inclinations. Muslim women are
portrayed as oppressed by their religion and culture. In comparison to other religions such as Christianity or Buddhism, Islam is seen in a more negative light.
Even video games encourage youth to play at religious genocide, a prime example of how wide and deep the roots of Islamophobia branch into American culture. With such pervasive depictions it comes as no surprise that political figures,
such as Donald Trump, suggest banning Muslim immigrants to wild applause.

Unlike media sources in other countries that portray Muslims in a positive
light, the news media in the United States, particularly conservative sources,
are consistent in their negative representations of Muslims. The result is a

reproduction of Islamophobia. As the primary source of public pedagogy, the media teaches its consumers how to think about themselves, and the world around them. Through only selecting to broadcast reports of Muslim violence and blocking stories Muslim victimhood, the media enforces a one-sided ideology. Clearly, selective tradition is not restricted to textbooks, it is widespread in the media. Eventually, with the culture steeped in Islamophobia, laws are passed which confirm a public pedagogy that excludes and discriminates against Muslims. For example, the fear of terrorism granted permission for human rights abuses that would have never become allowable otherwise such as torture, unlawful detention, and disregard for international humanitarian law. The fear of terrorism also made American's question helping those seeking asylum from nations perceived as terrorist hotbeds, such as Syria. Those are just a few examples of the impact of Islamophobia spread through the media's public pedagogy.

Muslim American youth experienced the impact of Islamophobia first-hand through hurtful encounters with the American public in the street, at work, and at the airport. The similarity between how Muslims were treated in school and society demonstrates the permeability between the two, and also proves the importance of teachers' responsibility to rectify the lopsided dialectic. When a teacher fails to evaluate these issues critically, this is likely to result in an intolerant classroom environment emotionally and physically abusive towards Muslim students. Indeed, media plays a role in generating Islamophobic attitudes in society that filter down to schools. However, Islamophobia in the media assists an imperialist project.

References

Abdelkader, E. (2011, December 24). Islamophobic bullying in our schools. *The Huffington Post*. Retrieved October 13, 2016 from http://www.huffingtonpost.com/engy-abdelkader/islamophobia-in-schools_b_1002293.html

Ahmed, S. (2004). *The cultural politics of emotion*. New York, NY: Routledge.

Ameli, S. R., Marandi, S. M., Ahmed, S., Kara, S., & Merali, A. (2007, February 16). The British media and Muslim representation: The ideology of demonization. *Islamic Human Rights Commission*. Retrieved October 13, 2016 from http://www.ihrc.org.uk/publications/reports/5679-the-british-media-and-muslim-representation-the-ideology-of-demonisation

American Sniper Film 'Behind Rise in Anti-Muslim Threats'. (2015, January 25). *BBC News*. Retrieved October 11, 2016 from http://www.bbc.com/news/entertainment-arts-30972690

Arana, G. (2015, November 18). Islamophobic media coverage is out of control. It needs to stop. *The Huffington Post*. Retrieved October 11, 2016 from http://www.huffingtonpost.com/entry/islamophobia-mainstream-media-paris-terrorist-attacks_us_564cb277e4b08c74b7339984

Benabou, R., & Tirole, J. (2011, November). Laws and norms. *The National Bureau of Economic Research*. Retrieved October 11, 2016 from http://www.nber.org/papers/w17579

Benjamin, M. (2010, September 8). Job discrimination claims by Muslims on the rise. *Salon*. Retrieved October 11, 2016 from http://www.salon.com/2010/09/08/muslim_employment_discrimination/

Bonnet, S. W. (2011). Educating Muslim American Youth in post 9/11 era: A critical review of policy. *High School Journal, 95*(1), 46–55.

Broomfield, M. (2016, May 9). Poland refuses to take a single refugee because of 'security' fears. *Independent*. Retrieved October 11, 2016 from http://www.independent.co.uk/news/world/europe/poland-refuses-to-take-a-single-refugee-because-of-security-fears-a7020076.html

Burke, D. (2015, December 11). Threats, harassment, vandalism at Mosques reach record high. *CNN*. Retrieved September 14, 2016 from http://www.nytimes.com/2010/09/24/business/24muslim.html?pagewanted=all&_r=0

Donald Trump Urges Ban on Muslims Coming to U.S. (2015, December 8). *BBC News*. Retrieved December 11, 2016 from http://www.bbc.com/news/world-us-canada-35035190

Fakhraie, F. (2010, August 30). Opinion: The media is obsessed with how Muslim women look. *CNN*. Retrieved December 11, 2016 from http://www.cnn.com/2010/OPINION/08/30/muslim.women.media/index.html fix indents

FBI: Bias Crimes Against Muslims Remain at High Levels. (2013, February 27). *Southern Poverty Law Center (SPLC)*. Retrieved October 11, 2016 from https://www.splcenter.org/fighting-hate/intelligence-report/2013/fbi-bias-crimes-against-muslims-remain-high-levels

Freire, P. (1970). *Pedagogy of the oppressed*. New York, NY: Herder & Herder.

Giroux, H. A. (2004, March). Cultural Studies, Public Pedagogy, and the Responsibility of Intellectuals. *Communication and Critical/Cultural Studies, 1*(1), 59–29. Retrieved from http://www.public.iastate.edu/~drrussel/www548/giroux-respofintells.pdf

Glencoe McGraw-Hill. (2010). *The American vision modern times, student edition*. Columbus, OH: Author.

Gottschalk, P., & Greenberg, G. (2008). *Islamophobia: Making Muslims the enemy*. Lanham, MD: Rowman & Littlefield.

Greenhouse, S. (2010, September 23). Muslims report rising discrimination at work. *The New York Times*. Retrieved September 14, 2016 from http://www.nytimes.com/2010/09/24/business/24muslim.html?pagewanted=all&_r=2

Ingraham, C. (2015, February 11). Anti-Muslim hate crimes are still five times more common today than before 9/11. *John Hopkins School of Advanced International Studies*. Retrieved October 13, 2016 from https://www.washingtonpost.com/news/wonk/wp/2015/02/11/anti-muslim-hate-crimes-are-still-five-times-more-common-today-than-before-911/

Islamophobia: Understanding Anti-Muslim Sentiment in the West. (2011). *Gallup*. Retrieved October 11, 2016 from http://www.gallup.com/poll/157082/islamophobia-understanding-anti-muslim-sentiment-west.aspx

Kincheloe, J. L., & Steinberg, S. R. (2004). *The miseducation of the west: How schools and the media distort our understanding of the Islamic world*. Westport, CT: Praeger Publishers.

Kincheloe, J. L., & Steinberg, S. R. (2010). Why teach against Islamophobia? Striking the empire back. In J. L. Kincheloe, S. R. Steinberg, & C. D. Stonebanks (Eds.), *Teaching against Islamophobia* (pp. 3–29). New York, NY: Peter Lang Publishing.

Kincheloe, J. L., Steinberg, S. R., & Stonebanks, C. D. (Eds.). (2010). *Teaching against Islamophobia*. New York, NY: Peter Lang Publishing.

Lazarus, E. (Artist). (1883). *The New Colossus: Poem by Emma Lazarus*. [Painting]. Liberty Island, New York; Statue of Liberty.

Levine, S. (2016, December 13). Obama: Muslims on TV deserve to be portrayed as more than just terrorists. *The Huffington Post*. Retrieved February 3, 2016 from http://www.huffingtonpost.com/entry/obama-muslims-tv_us_56b2573ce4b01d80b244d44d

Lieutenant General William G. "Jerry" Boykin (Ret.). (n.d.). *Southern Poverty Law Center (SPLC)*. Retrieved October 13, 2016 from https://www.splcenter.org/fighting-hate/extremist-files/individual/lieutenant-general-william-g-"jerry"-boykin-ret

Maira, S. (2009). *Missing: youth, citizenship, and empire after 9/11*. Durham, NC: Duke University Press.

Naber, N. (2008). "Look, Mohamed the terrorist is coming!" Cultural racism, nation-based racism and the intersectionality of oppression after 9/11. In N. Naber & A. Jamal (Eds.), *Race and Arab Americans before and after 9/11: From invisible citizens to visible subjects* (pp. 276–305). Syracuse, NY: Syracuse University Press.

Navarro, L. (2010, Fall). Islamophobia and sexism: Muslim women in the western mass media. *Human Architecture Journal of the Sociology of Self-Knowledge*, 8(2), 95–114. Retrieved October 11, 2016 from http://www.okcir.com/Articles%20VIII%202/Navarro-FM.pdf

Nimer, M. (2007). *Islamophobia and Anti-Americanism: Causes and remedi*. Beltsville, MD: Amana Publications.

O'Reilly, B. (2014, October 24). Bill O'Reilly: More ISIS-inspired terrorist. *Fox News*. Retrieved October 11, 2016 from http://www.foxnews.com/transcript/2014/10/24/bill-oreilly-more-isis-inspired-terrorist/

Otterman, S. (2012, January 1). Obscuring a Muslim name, and an American's sacrifice. *The New York Times*. Retrieved October 11, 2016 from http://www.nytimes.com/2012/01/02/nyregion/sept-11-memorial-obscures-a-police-cadets-bravery.html?_r=0

Press Association. (2007, November 14). Study shows 'demonisation' of Muslims. *The Guardian*. Retrieved October 11, 2016 from http://www.theguardian.com/media/2007/nov/14/pressandpublishing.religion

Said, E. (2003, July 24). Imperial Perspectives. In *Znet*. Retrieved March 28, 2012, from http://www.zcommunications.org/imperial-perspectives-by-edward-said

Sakuma, A. (2016, April 7). The U.S. is way behind its goal of accepting 10,000 Syrian refugees. *NBC News*. Retrieved October 11, 2016 from http://www.nbcnews.com/storyline/syrias-suffering-families/u-s-way-behind-its-goal-accepting-10-000-syrian-n552521

Saletan, W. (2015, December 11). Ted Cruz's shameful Anti-Muslim rhetoric. *Slate*. Retrieved October 11, 2016 from http://www.slate.com/articles/news_and_politics/politics/2015/12/ted_cruz_s_latest_anti_muslim_rhetoric_is_beyond_shameful.html

Samir, M. (2016, February 4). 5 "Good" Arab & Muslim characters in Hollywood pop culture. *The Glocal*. Retrieved October 11, 2016 from http://www.theglocal.com/articles/565/5-good-arab-and-muslim-characters-in-hollywood-pop-culture

Sandmeyer, E., & Leung, M. (2014, August 21). Muslim leaders have roundly denounced Islamic state, but conservative media won't tell you that. *Media Matters for America*. Retrieved October 11, 2016 from http://mediamatters.org/research/2014/08/21/muslim-leaders-have-roundly-denounced-islamic-s/200498

Sewall, G. T. (2003). Islam and the textbooks: A report of the American textbook council. *The Middle East Quarterly, 10*(3), 69–78. Retrieved October 11, 2016 from http://www.meforum.org/559/islam-and-the-textbooks

Sirin, S., & Fine, M. (2008). *Muslim American youth: Understanding hyphenated identities through multiple methods*: New York, NY: New York University Press.

Snaman, V. (2016, March 2). News media affects how Muslims are perceived, treated. *Start: National Consortium for the Study of Terrorism and Responses to Terrorism*. Retrieved October 13, 2016 from http://www.start.umd.edu/news/news-media-affects-how-muslims-are-perceived-treated

Steinberg, S. (2010). Islamophobia: The viewed and the viewers. In J. L. Kincheloe, S. R. Steinberg, & C. D. Stonebanks (Eds.), *Teaching against Islamophobia* (pp. 79–99). New York, NY: Peter Lang Publishing.

Stiglitz, J. (2004, March 5). Criticism of neoliberalism: Interview with Joseph Stiglitz. *Portland Independent Media Center*. Retrieved October 11, 2016 from http://portland.indymedia.org/en/2004/03/282123.shtml

Tapson, M. (2015, October 7). 'Homeland' speech tells it like it is about ISIS. *Truth Revolt*. Retrieved October 7, 2016 from http://www.truthrevolt.org/news/homeland-speech-tells-it-it-about-isis

Thomas, D. (2010, October 5). Bill O'Reilly on "the view": "Muslims killed us on 9/11" [Video]; Co-hosts walk off. *CBS News*. Retrieved October 11, 2016 from http://www.cbsnews.com/news/bill-oreilly-on-the-view-muslims-killed-us-on-9-11-video-co-hosts-walk-off/

Under Suspicion: Muslims in America. (2011). *The Washington Post*. Retrieved October 13, 2016 from https://www.washingtonpost.com/muslims/

#IllWalkWithYou Campaign Kicks Off on Social Media In Support of US Muslims after Fatal Shooting. (2016, August 14). *ABC News*. Retrieved October 13, 2016 from http://www.abc.net.au/news/2016-08-14/illwalkwithyou-trends-in-support-of-muslims-after-fatal-shooting/7733042

Wemple, E. (2013, July 29). Fox News must apologize to Reza Aslan. In *The Washington Post*. Retrieved September 5, 2017, from https://www.washingtonpost.com/blogs/erik-wemple/wp/2013/07/29/fox-news-must-apologize-to-reza-aslan/?utm_term=.0fe5214c00c1

White, M. (2011, May 24). Airport security checks: More offensive to some than to others. *The Guardian*. Retrieved October 11, 2016 from https://www.theguardian.com/politics/blog/2011/may/24/airport-security-checks-terrorism-act

Wolfe, S. (2011, March 10). Statement of Chairman Peter T. King: "The Extent of Radicalization in the American Muslim Community and that Community's Response". In *The*

House Committee on Homeland Security. Retrieved September 5, 2017, from https://homeland.house.gov/files/03-10-11%20Final%20King%20Opening%20Statement_0.pdf

Zine, J. (2004). Anti-Islamophobia education as transformative pedagogy: Reflections from the education frontlines. *The American Journal of Islamic Social Sciences, 21*(3), 110–118.

Zine, J. (2006). *Canadian Islamic schools: Unraveling the politics of faith, gender, knowledge, and identity.* Ontario: University of Toronto Press Incorporated.

· 7 ·

ISLAMOPHOBIA AND WHAT IT MIGHT BE HIDING FROM YOU

What we have discussed thus far is the existence of Islamophobia on the surface level. But what lies underneath are strong and firm roots. There is a history to Islamophobia that is not included in the conversation. There is also an upsetting reality about why and by whom these negative stereotypes are used. Burying this history and the ulterior motives obfuscates political and economic components, resulting in a lopsided dialectic. We need to understand why Islamophobia is presented and fomented by the culture—why is it a tool being used? What is it distracting us from and who is benefiting from it?

In large part, fear of Islam is wielded for political and economic power on behalf of global elites, and at the expense of all. However those especially impacted are, of course, Muslim individuals themselves. For teachers interested in teaching in a balanced and holistic way, it is important to dig deeper than the surface, and to not allow the conventional narrative about Islamophobia be the only one discussed and analyzed. Teachers who wish to develop critical thinking among their students must themselves take a second look, and encourage their students to do the same.

History of Seeing Muslims as the "Bad Guy"

Fear of Muslims is not just an involuntary or individual experience, it is an ideology with historical precedent. Through this ideology, Muslims are portrayed and perceived as violent terrorists who are disloyal American citizens (Maira, 2009). Said (2003) described these representations, saying:

> Several generations of Americans have come to see the Arab world mainly as a dangerous place, where terrorism and religious fanaticism are spawned, and where a gratuitous anti-Americanism is mischievously inculcated in the young by badly-intentioned clerics who are anti-democratic and virulently anti-Semitic. Ignorance is directly translated into knowledge in such cases. (p. 3)

There is a historical precedent for Islamophobia—even before 9/11—yet the creation of this fear comes from a history of a skewed perspective about Islam and the Arab world. During these past few generations of which Said speaks, certain facts are constantly repeated and other facts in the history are lost, another example of what Apple (2004) defines as selective tradition. Another challenge is the separation of historical events, and an inability to see the connections between them. This kind of thinking was demonstrated by George's students, as "they were inclined to dismiss all that as, well, 'That's past history, that is not part of what we are dealing with now, okay'" (personal communication, June 5, 2010). A lack of exposure to other sides of history precludes many Americans to believing hateful and disparaging rhetoric about Muslims in present-day.

It is critical to uncover the historical precedent of Islamophobia, because the "Us vs Them" rhetoric has strong and deep roots. Marr (2006) attributes this to a complex historical relationship of "othering" Islam. He calls these processes *Islamicism* and *Orientalism*, both of which have led to modern-day Islamophobia. *Orientalism*, defined in the seminal 1978 book of the same name by scholar Edward Said, criticizes the West's patronizing perceptions and fictional depictions of "the Orient"—people and places in Asia, North Africa, and the Middle East. Though Said absolved the United States of this phenomenon, Marr points out obvious American examples of "othering" Islam—what he calls Islamicism. Islamophobia takes Islamicism one step further and adds a fear-based response to Islam and Muslims that results in suspicion, rejection, and avoidance (Haque, 2004), often leading to policies that reshape the structure of Muslim citizenship in countries where Islam is not the dominant religion.

Islamicism was very common among American missionaries. For example, during the 1800s, Protestant Americans were sent on missions to the former Ottoman Empire. Their hope was to convert the inhabitants and reclaim land previously under Christian rule. Faced with the disappointment of their own inability to convert Muslims, many Protestant Americans interpreted the Islamic world through a perspective that reflected their own imagination about Muslims in relation to America's global dominance (Marr, 2006). Professor of History at Rice University, Ussama Makdisi stated the Protestants rejected Islam as a legitimate faith entirely, viewing the Islamic world as a realm of dark destruction. According to these missionaries, the curse of Islam had been divinely decreed to punish Christians who incorporated foreign influences into their religious practices. Consequently, the fall of Islam became one of the principal hopes and goals of Protestant evangelical in early U.S. history (Makdisi, 2008). Hatred of Islam is clearly not a new phenomenon. It also was not strictly a religious rivalry, but often a political one.

Hatred of other nation-states was a hallmark of the United States, and many other countries, as they fought over resources and boundary lines. Professor of American Studies at University of North Carolina, Timothy Marr, argued the United States often defined itself as a civilized nation through comparisons with other, more "barbaric" ones (Marr, 2006). Negative cultural images of Muslims circulated during the colonial period, often portraying them as barbaric, despotic and undemocratic. For example, a short piece of fiction called the "Algerian Spy" told a heavy-handed story about a character named Mehemed who is a terrible husband and father. Mehemed develops a fascination and passion for American democracy, leading to his conversion to Christianity. The book showed a character whose personality traits were bad when he was a Muslim, and good when he converted to Christianity and developed a political taste for democracy. This is an example of how Muslim inferiority served a role in asserting American identity and superiority.

Muslim women's bodies have often served as another battleground over which the United States has staked its claims of moral and political higher grounds. The West is portrayed as a place where women are liberated while "the Orient" traps and oppresses them. Linda Steet (2000) analyzed representations of Arab and Muslim women in National Geographic from 1888 to 1988. She identified two main representations, namely the dancing prostitute girl and the veiled primitive woman. Oversimplified and more related to imagination than reality, Steet (2000) claimed such representations feed negative stereotypes about Islam, negate the diversity of lived experiences of Muslim and Arab women, and justify Western intervention in the Arab world. Indeed, by the nineteenth century, colonialism and Christian missionaries' activities in the Middle East became the lens through which the West viewed Muslim women. The image of Muslim women in need of liberation served as one of the justifications of the Western colonization, and often supplements justifications for present-day wars on the Middle East. For instance, a *Brown Political Review* article states that Laura Bush indicated in a radio address to the nation on November of 2001 that "the fight against terrorism is also a fight for the rights and dignity of women" (Akyol, 2014, para. 1). Right after her speech, Bush included in his War against terrorism, a goal to liberate women from Taliban and spread democracy in the Middle East (Akyol, 2014, para. 1). This indeed convinced the American people that the War on Terror is a war of liberation and freedom and consequently led to Americans support for the wars. Even today, take for example how France regulates Muslim women's clothing from the ban of the burqa to the recent French ban of Muslim women's full-body swimsuits on French beaches. These instances point out that the need for controlling Muslim women's bodies disguised as a necessity of liberation.

Political Motivations for Muslim Stereotypes in the Twentieth Century

By the late twentieth century, America adapted old stereotypes into new methods for justifying political involvement in Islamic countries. Political and economic reasons convinced the U.S. to financially support proxy wars in Central America, Africa, and the Middle East. The United States' Cold War tactics led directly to the creation of terrorist cells now deemed national enemies. For example, during the Reagan administration, the CIA and Pakistan cooperated to recruit, train and arm the Afghan Mujahideen, a group of radically anti-communist Muslims mainly from Afghanistan to fight the Soviet Union in Afghanistan (Holmes & Dixon, 2001). Recruited and funded by the CIA, Osama bin Laden built "The Khost complex" that housed sophisticated military equipment, a training facility, and a modified center for al mujahedeen. The CIA's goal was to create a guerrilla unit. Mamdani (2004) explained that after the mission was accomplished and al mujahedeen won the proxy war against the Soviets, individuals in the group found that they were trapped; they were exiled, often wanted by their countries, and with a long list of enemies at home and abroad. What started as a marriage of convenience became a bitter divorce. In the aftermath, Osama bin Laden formed the al Qaeda organization. In Mamdani's (2004) words:

Al-Qaeda was a transnational movement whose violence was unrestrained by any form of law. Al-Qaeda members, originally recruited from dozens of countries around the world, found they had no home to return to when the jihad ended. John Cooley gives the example of North African recruits, many of whom "feared to return" and "stayed in the postwar training program for future terrorists." (p. 177)

Mamdani (2004) insisted that, "the source of privatized and globalized terrorism today is a true ideological child of Reagan's crusade against the evil empire" (p. 177). Thus, what is now one of the most notorious and dangerous terrorism cells in the world was born through U.S. interventions in the Middle East.

The United States has also been instrumental in toppling stable, democratically elected governments in the Middle East when it served the nation financially and politically. For example, the Middle East became significantly important to the United States during the Cold War because of its oil supply (Marr, 2006). During World War II, the United States consumed a significant amount of oil. It became clear that national oil reserves would be insufficient to fuel a potentially long and protracted war with the Soviet Union. This also coincided with the American automobile boom. The United States, convinced of the national security and social necessity of procuring oil provisions abroad, increased their dependence on oil from the Middle East. However, this increasing dependence coincided with Arab nationalist movements (such as in Iran) and the creation of the State of Israel, which led to an embittered Arab-Israeli conflict. For example in 1953, the United States orchestrated an overthrow along with the United Kingdom of the democratically elected Prime Minister Mohammad Mosaddegh of Iran under the name "Operation Ajax." The U.S. and U.K. handed the government over to the monarch Mohammad Reza Pahlavi, who promised to give both the United States and the United Kingdom better terms of access of Iranian Petroleum, than those given by the Mosaddegh government. Prior to the rise of the Mosaddegh administration, Iranian petroleum was controlled predominantly by British corporations. The Mosaddegh government had sought to limit the control of the U.S. and the U.K. of Iranian oil reserves through nationalization of the industry, something neither of these countries appreciated. Toppling Mosaddegh meant supporting the subsequent monarchical dictatorship, which promised to ensure the interests of Western nations. This case and many others demonstrate how United States' involvement in predominantly Muslim countries benefits corporate interests at the expense of local civilians. It also demonstrates that democracy is often only a cover for other interests.

Pan-nationalist movements in the Middle East were also considered a national security concern in the United States. Often this was because these pan-nationalist movements sought to end colonialist and imperialist relationships with the West, and American foreign policy in the region revealed a strong desire to acquire greater control over these nations' natural resources (Byrne, 2013; Kemp & Harkavy, 1997). In other words, maintaining access to cheap oil was not only a financial necessity; it was integral to the United States retaining their status as a military powerhouse, especially during the Cold War. Any threat to this was perceived as a threat to the United States' global military dominance. To this end, the United States would do almost anything to maintain control over these precious natural resources, including taking in unexpected bedfellows.

One of those unexpected bedfellows were Islamic guerilla groups. During the Cold War, the CIA armed and trained many such guerilla groups in their blind fervor to weed out communism, including in the Middle East. The slow and simmering end of the Cold War meant many of these guerilla groups were left abandoned on the tattered battlegrounds over which democracy and communism clashed in the Middle East, while Americans gained a tighter grasp over the oil reserves in the Persian Gulf. After the fall of the Berlin wall in 1989, communism posed less of a perceived threat to U.S. national security, however, as one of the major oil-consuming countries, the social need for reserves only grew. Clashes over oil during the Gulf War with Saddam Hussein led to the creation of a new national enemy. Fear of the Soviet Union's communism was replaced with Islam.

There is a connection between the Cold War and the War on Terror. Andrew J. Bacevich, a visiting fellow at Notre Dame's Kroc Institute for International Peace Studies explained that between 1940s and 1980s, when the United States waged the Cold War against Communism because of its denial of God, it found great support and consensus among its citizens. Through using similar religious rhetoric and confirming that Christians, Muslims, and Jews all share the same God, the United States was able to persuade al mujahedeen to fight and win over the disbelieving Soviets. In this, the United States found that religion was the best theme through which to wage its global dominance. As a result, "what Americans in the 1950s knew as McCarthyism has reappeared in the form of Boykinism" (Bacevich, 2012, para. 17). Bacevich used the term Boykinism to refer to deputy undersecretary of defense for intelligence, William G. ("Jerry") Boykin's uninformed ways of explaining religious threats. Post 9/11, the United States used religion once more, but this time using a divisive rhetoric that separated Muslims from Christians and Jews in the God that they worship. This divisive rhetoric helped to launch a war for the sake of religion pinning Christians who are on the side of God against Muslims who worshiped the devil. Former Iraq ambassador Edward Peck said the following on NBC on January 16, 1991 to describe the Gulf War conflict:

> Where we in the West tend to think of our New Testament heritage, where you turn the other cheek and you let bygones be bygones and forgive and forget, the people of the Middle East are the people of the Old Testament, if you will, if the Muslims will let me say that, where there's much more of an eye for an eye and a tooth for a tooth and you don't forget and you don't forgive and you carry on the vendetta and the struggle long after people in the West would be prepared to say all right, it's over, let's not worry about it any longer. (Naureckas, 2001, para. 19)

Embedding a religious purpose in the War on Terror has been used before in the Cold War and is proved to be an excellent strategy to gain Christian Americans' support for the war.

Who Benefits from Fear of Muslims in the Post-9/11 World?

When two hijacked planes crashed into the twin towers in New York City, the American perception of Islam only worsened. However, the collective anger and sadness which spilled over after the horrific attacks was directed in a particular way to benefit many global socio-political elites, and the anger and sadness was also fomented in many regards to further the success of these individuals and their associates. Post-9/11, as New York City and the rest of the nation grieved, U.S. citizens were bombarded with a series of messages that instilled a great and urgent sense of fear. There were color-coded terrorism alerts and fear of weapons of mass destruction (WMDs) in the hands of evil men. On March 17, 2006, *Democracy Now's* Amy Goodman interviewed Michael Gordon, *The New York Times* Chief Military Correspondent, regarding his pre-war reporting on (WMDs). Gordon cited anonymous administrative officials saying that Saddam Hussein was attempting to acquire aluminum tubes designed to enrich uranium. In the journalists' minds, this could only mean one thing—a weapon of mass destruction. "The first sign of a 'smoking gun,'" they wrote, "may be a mushroom cloud" (Goodman, 2006, para. 20). The claim that Hussein was searching for aluminum tubes was actually made by the Bush administration, with no supportive evidence. In other words, The

New York Times quoted an unsubstantiated Bush administration claim about WMDs. The Bush Administration then cited the *New York Times* to validate their claim. This tall tale ended up becoming the backbone of the United States argument for going to war against Iraq.

A righteous mentality made the stakes seem even higher than they actually were, and helped give credence to and energy behind socio-political changes that benefited many elites. The rhetoric used by the media, former President George W. Bush, and other politicians focused on religious metaphors of good versus evil (Mamdani, 2004). For instance, on November 9th, Bush said: "America faces an evil and a determined enemy" (*Magniloquence against Evil*, n.d.). The next day, on November 10th he said: "We know that evil is real, but good will prevail against it. This is the teaching of many faiths, and in that assurance we gain strength for a long journey" (*Magniloquence against Evil*, n.d.). Then, on November 12th, 2001, Bush said:

> It is also a reminder of the great purpose of our great land, and that is to rid this world of evil and terror. The evil ones have roused a might nation, a mighty land. And for however long it takes, I am determined that we will prevail. (*Magniloquence against Evil*, n.d.)

President Bush was not the only one to stress on good vs. bad rhetoric, his administration specifically deputy undersecretary of defense for intelligence, William G. Boykin, repeatedly remarked that Islamic values are inferior to Christian ones (Bacevich, 2012). Those are just a few among many examples of how Bush administration infused religious terms to make the war appear to be a religious one. Embedded within this rhetoric are echoes of the Crusades and other holy wars (Maira, 2009). This "cultural talk" (Mamdani, 2002) linked religion to politics and reframed terrorism as a common characteristic of Muslim culture. Mahmoud Mamdani, who coined the term *cultural talk*, defines it as a way of seeing and talking about a culture as fixed and unchangeable over time, as well as inferior when compared to the superiority of others. But beneath these stereotypes was a desire to leverage these unfair beliefs for political gain. For, a perception of Islam as indelibly tied with terrorism encourages "collective discipline and punishment" (Mamdani, 2002, p. 767). Explaining events like the War on Terror through a cultural lens diverts the discussion from analyzing it politically, historically, or economically (Mamdani, 2002). Consequently, launching a war against entire nations such as Afghanistan, or Iraq or any other Muslim nation becomes justified since the war is seen to be against the Muslim culture, which is portrayed as having a political agenda of destroying the West. It also becomes easier for the United States to justify political and economic interventions, and sanctions in these nations, for to leave these cultures to their own devises could spell imminent doom for the rest of the world (Maira, 2009). Uncovering the deep roots of Islamophobia sheds light on historical negative beliefs about Muslims buried in a one-sided debate and worsened over time through a contentious Arab–Western relationship.

What is clear about current Islamophobic sentiment is that it serves a particular purpose and role in American culture. From what we have discussed thus far it seems clear that Islamophobia achieves the goal of unifying American citizens' fear behind policies that reshape the structure of their citizenship, and discriminate against Muslims on a local and a global scale (Maira, 2009). Based on such an observation, Islamophobia could be seen as "part of a rational system of power and domination that manifests as individual, ideological, and systemic forms of discrimination and oppression" (Zine, 2004, p. 113). When comparing Islamophobia to other systems of discrimination such as racism, Islamophobia is a form of racialization of the religion of Islam that supports a system of discrimination based on the intersection of religion, race, social class, and in many cases gender. Alan Johnson (2001) said that Islamophobia is xenophobia and racism packaged in religious terms. Thinking of Islamophobia as a rational system—whether racial or religious or gendered—allows us to see the different parts of the system at work, and helps people shift the focus from an individual aversion to a systemic force. Islamophobia is a system that discriminates against Muslim Americans and Muslims overseas, and ultimately serves the goals and desires of those behind an imperialistic force within the United States.

American Imperialism and Islamophobia

The War on Terror is no different than previous acts of military invention for financial and political gain on behalf of the United States, yet the colonial undertones are so well-packaged that many Americans accept the prospect of an un-ending war without the blink of an eye. Many scholars have argued that the military interventions in post 9/11 are part of an *imperial project* (Kincheloe & Steinberg, 2004; Maira, 2009; McLaren, 2005; Said, 2003), that is supported by an imperial perspective that sees the colonized people as inferior who lack culture and civilization. According to Said (2003):

> The great modern empires have never been held together only by military power but by what activates that power, puts it to use and then reinforces it with daily practices of domination, conviction, and authority. The key element is imperial perspective,

that way of looking at a distant foreign reality by subordinating it to one's gaze, con-structing its history from one's own point of view, seeing its people as subjects whose fate is to be decided not by them but by what distant administrators think is best for them. From such willful perspectives actual ideas develop, including the theory that imperialism is a benign and necessary thing. (p. 1)

Analyzing Arab and Muslim societies through a one-dimensional orientalist lens has indeed justified past and present colonization and imperialism. Like other empires, the United States tells its people and the world that "it has a mission certainly not to plunder and control but to educate and liberate the peoples and places it rules directly or indirectly" (Said, 2003, p. 1). For example, when Tim Russert asked Dick Cheney about the Iraq war on NBC's *Meet the Press* on March 16, 2003, "Do you think the American people are prepared for a long, costly, and bloody battle with significant American casualties?" Cheney responded: "My belief is, we will, in fact be greeted as liberators" (NBC News, 2003). Still, Said (2003) argued:

… these ideas are not shared by the people who live there, whose views are in many cases directly opposite. Nevertheless, this hasn't prevented the whole apparatus of American information, policy, and decision-making about the Arab/Islamic world from imposing its perspectives not just on Arabs and Muslims but on Americans, whose sources of information about the Arabs and Islam are woefully, indeed tragi-cally, inadequate. (p. 2)

According to Said, the United States spiked the Imperialism punch with Islamophobia, and now most everyone is drinking the Kool-Aid.

But can the United States be considered an imperialist nation? Edward Said defined the term imperialism as "the practice, the theory, and the atti-tudes of a dominating metropolitan center ruling a distant territory" (Said, 2003, p. 9). Post-Marxist philosophers Michael Hardt and Antonio Negri (2000) stated that the United States is not considered imperialist since it is unlike earlier forms of European imperialism that established colonies and direct dominance of other nations; instead, the United States exercises its dominance from a distance through global economic, militant, and political networks and hegemonic power. Maira (2009) stated that the United States uses the strategy of "non-colonial imperial expansion" (p. 4) as a form of "open door imperialism" (p. 4) in order to administer its global, economic, and polit-ical expansion while avoiding the scrutiny now felt by directly imperialistic nations. This may allow the United States imperialism to fly under the radar (Kaplan, 2005) under the guise of humanitarian intervention which obscures "the settler colonial roots of nation-state" (Maira, 2009, p. 51). In the case of the War on Terror, the United States masks its imperialistic goals by using the rhetoric of democracy and freedom to justify neo-colonial occupations; for example, the War on Terror was framed as a "war for democracy" or a "war for freedom" (Maira, 2009, p. 52). This is an example of putting lipstick on a pig. Unfortunately, a pig is still a pig no matter how you try to dress is up. It is becoming more and more apparent to theorists, politicians, and educators alike that there is evidence of imperialism beneath the Islamophobic veneer.

When the 110-story World Trade Center tumbled to the ground, the fire was barely out before war profiteers came swooping in. September 11 helped in reorganizing and restructuring dominance and subordinate relationships on the local, national, regional, and international level (Apple, 2004). With the expansion of global capitalism, neo-liberal ideology is imposed as the best means to transform and regulate the global economy (Fairclough, 2003). Neo-liberalism is used to restructure relationships between institutions on a local and global scale to facilitate the expansion of U.S.-driven imperialism and global economic dominance. The fear of Islam and Muslims served as a cover for an economic and political restructuring that continues to this day.

Because of this sense of impending doom, the American public agreed very quickly after the 9/11 attacks to pay well over $5 trillion dollars for a war of choice, torture hundreds of innocent people at Guantanamo Bay, and forfeit basic human rights for American citizens. Some, such as Naomi Klein (2007), would call this "disaster capitalism," in which man-made crises such as 9/11 are manipulated by corporations to create opportunities to achieve far-reaching sociopolitical and economic goals. The disaster of September 11 allowed the privatization of sectors in society that were not privatized during the 80s or the 90s such as security, combat, and reconstruction (Klein, 2007). The fear of terrorism and the War on Terror yielded huge economic gains not only for huge corporations but also for over 85,000 private firms (McLaren, 2005). For many, the war was good for business.

But it was not just certain businesses that boomed during wartime—war is often a crucial driver for economic growth, especially in capitalistic nations such as the United States. Historian and political scientist Jacques R. Pauwels (2003) argued that United States economic system mainly depends on Wars. The United States only discovered the high revenue of wars after World War II. During the 1920s, there was high industrial productivity of merchandise such as Ford automobiles that saturated the market with vehicles and assembly lines that many people could not afford to purchase. The result was an overproduction and supply of vehicles that was more than the demand of the market. This and many other products that faced a similar fate caused the great depression in which many factories closed down, people were laid off work, and jobs were scarce. The depression then was a result of overproduction of goods. The depression only ended because of World War II, when the United States was able to utilize the surplus of goods and factories in the production of war equipment.

World War II and the booming war industry revived the United States economy and created jobs for and increased the salaries of many Americans. However, the ones that benefited the most from the war were around 2,000 corporations that made in the years between 1942 and 1945 a net profit that was 40% higher than during 1936–1939. Among such companies were corporations called "war hogs" such as Ford and IBM. IBM increased its annual sales in 1940–2945 from $46 to $140 million dollars, making immense profits because of war-related orders. For instance, IBM punch card technology was used by both the United States and Nazi Germany to document and manage operations within their camps. Critiques of IBM's activities with Nazi Germany government often include mentioning it being complicit in the Holocaust (Black, 2002). The increase was made possible when the state ordered billions of dollars of military equipment, did not control the price, and did not tax the profits (Pauwels, 2003). Deregulation of the market emerged as a necessary policy in relation to war profits.

Wars generate money. Once corporations discovered the immense amount of money that wars generated, there became a constant need for wars to achieve such profits once more. International relations specialist, Aminata M. Kone, wrote in *Inquiries Journal* that the wars make the rich of America richer, particularly those in the military-industrial complex (Kone, 2013). After World War II, military spending in the United States became the highest in the world at 41% in 2011, right after Russia at eight percent and China at four percent (Kone, 2013, para. 1). This military expansion in the United States that grew from World War II onward to the War on Terror changed its end goals from being a means to stabilize the global economy and to serve the interests of national security to becoming an end in itself and a means to serve the interests of a few global elites who developed in wealth and power enough to influence the decision making of the United States' foreign policy (Kone, 2013, para. 1). The loyalty of these elites center around their own wealth and greed for more power.

Global elites use the War on Terror and fear of Muslims as a method for distracting the American public from the fact that these few individuals and corporations are benefiting significantly, and consequently regular Americans are losing. Among those global elites according to Lily Dane, Centre for Research on Globalization, are the arms producing corporations whose business include arms sales, advisory, planes, vehicles and weapons (Dane, 2015, para. 16). The top ten arms producers in the world include companies that are Western-European, but, still, the United States arms corporations dominate the arms production industry. According to Dane, of "the top 100 arms-producing companies, 39 are based in the United States, and U.S. companies accounted for more than 58% of total arms sales among the top 100 U.S." (Dane, 2015, para. 16). On the other hand, Western European arms companies "accounted for just 28% of the total top 100 arms sales" (Dane, 2015, para. 16). U.S. arms producing corporations make enormous profits.

Among the top U.S. arms-producing corporations and the sales they made in 2013 are as follows:

- United Technologies which made Arms sales of $11.9 billion and a profit of $5.7 billion
- General Dynamics which made sales of $18.7 billion and a profit of $2.4 billion
- Northrop Grumman with arms sales of $20.2 billion and a profit of $2 billion
- Raytheon with arm sales of $29.9 billion and a profit $2 billion
- Boeing with arm sales of $30.7 billion and a profit $4.6 billion
- and finally Lockheed Martin with arm sales of $35.5 billion and a profit of $3 billion. (Dane, 2015, para. 17)

These corporations enjoy deep ties within the United States government that facilitate their work. They are even involved in politics and involved in lobbying in the 2014 presidential elections including candidates, parties, and committees among others (Dane, 2015). Lockheed Martin contributed to the 2016 presidential cycle with a total of $2,313,250 in which 37% to Democrats, and 63% to Republicans (*Center for Responsive Politics*, 2016). As a defense aerospace contractors, contributing to both parties ensures government connections in case any of the party's candidates won the presidency.

The arms industry is not the only one benefiting financially from the War on Terror. In fact, some companies make a living by defaming Muslims. Former editor at AlterNet, Alex Kane (2013), wrote that 9/11 attacks facilitated privatizing America's national security apparatus. He cited an article in *The Washington Post* that stated that in 2010 almost 70% of the national security budget went towards private contractors who made around six billion dollars of profit a year out of fighting terrorism. *The Washington Post* article stated that although these firms are hidden from the American public, their investigations found around 1,931 firms nation-wide that make money out of Americans' fear of terrorism. (Kane, 2013). Who would have imagined that some companies make money out of fear?

Companies of fear are specialized in many areas that promise to protect American citizens from terrorism. The range of their expertise varies between making sure that Americans are safe at airports by using full body scanners, to providing trainings about terrorists who could attack at any time, to launching their experts who are able to decode Islam and analyze Islamists threat messages. These corporations according to Kane (2013) are The Chertoff Group, headed by the former director of the National Security Agency, Michael Hayden. *The Huffington Post* reported that this firm made a profit of $118 million dollars between 2009 and 2010 for selling 300 Rapiscan machines (full body scanners) to the TSA right after the failed terrorist attempt on Christmas day in 2010 to blow up an airplane with a bomb in his underwear. The second firm is Booz Allen Hamilton, a private intelligence contractor in which Edward Snowden worked and leaked the scandalous NSA surveillance documents. This firm's vice-president is the former director of national intelligence (who became replaced by the former director of Booz Allen) and according to the New York Times employs thousands who analyze the massive amount of data government agencies collect for the NSA every day. The third is Science Applications International Corporation (SAIC) based in California. The firm specializes in producing manuals and trainings on combatting terrorist threats including training for a national Weapons of Mass Destruction (WMD) situation, military installation, or a special facility, among others. The firm's CEO is John P. Jumper, previous Air Force general and it made a net revenue of $525 million in 2012 (Kane, 2013). Forth, Center for Counterintelligence and Security Studies that provide their so called experts on Islam to analyze Islamists' threats for federal agencies and law enforcement involved in the War on Terror. Fifth in line, is another firm, the Center for Counterintelligence and Security Studies that provides Islamophobic training and made billions of dollars through U.S. Homeland Security grant programs. The firm trained over 67,000 people, including government officials. For instance, "a five-day course for government employees on the 'Global Jihadist Threat Doctrine' costs $39,280." (Kane, 2013, para. 21). It is no surprise that the company pushes an anti-Muslim ideology since it financially lives off of it. Another company that lives off of defaming Muslims is called Security

Solutions International in Miami. The president is Henry Morgenstern, an Israeli-U.S. citizen, who uses Israeli security trainers to prepare over 700 law enforcement agencies on counter-terrorism efforts, including Massachusetts Bay Transportation Authority and the Department of Homeland Security. They hold conferences that cost a fee of $400 for each attendee and usually contain anti-Muslim graphics and statements. A key-note speaker in one of these conferences was Steve Emerson, a journalist and fake pundit on national security, terrorism, and Islamic extremism. They have over 15,000 subscribers and a yearly subscription fee of $35 (Kane, 2013). Fear companies and arms industry work together to financially benefit from Americans' fear of terrorism.

This huge Islamophobic arms industry is made possible by slandering Muslims in the media. It turns out that corporation pay money to buy airtime. In 2011, *The Center for American Progress* published a study called "Fear Incorporated" in which they listed corporations such as

- Donors Capital Fund
- Richard Mellon Scaife Foundation
- Lynde and Harry Bradley Foundation
- Newoton and Rochelle Becker Foundation and Newoton and Rochelle Becker Charitable Trust
- Russell Berrie Foundation
- Anchorage Charitable Fund
- William Family Fund
- and the Fairbrook Foundation

All of these organizations collectively paid $42 million to buy airtime to support 8 Islamophobic networks and promote "TV Hoppers," who make money out of delivering anti-Muslim sentiments such as David Yerushalmi, Steven Emerson, Daniel Pipes, Frank Gafney, and Robert Spencer (Ali et al., 2011, p. 1). The hateful think tank against Islam assists the arms business.

These egregious acts were not limited to the private sector, but were common among Western national governments. According to the Bureau of Investigative Journalism, the Pentagon itself paid $540 million to a U.K. public relations firm, Bell Pottinger, to make fake terrorist videos of al Qaeda right after the U.S. invasion of Iraq to use in a secret propaganda campaign used to promote "the 'democratic elections' for the [Iraqi] administration before moving on to more lucrative psychological and information operations" (RT, 2016, para. 5). The PR firm reported its achievements to the CIA, the National Security Council and the Pentagon (RT, 2016). And just like

George W. Bush posed with a fake turkey in Baghdad on Thanksgiving to propagate a positive image of the U.S. invasion (Klein, 2007), the PR crew faked "short TV segments made in the style of Arabic news networks and fake insurgent videos" (Black & Fielding-Smith, 2016, para. 2) and placed them in homes that were raided afterwards (RT, 2016). The videos were picked up at different locations in Iran, Syria, and the United States to make it seem like there is a trail. The article stated that the Pentagon confirmed using the PR firm under the Information Operations Task Force (IOTF). The article suggests that since the law prohibits the use of propaganda against its own population, they hired the external firm.

How does all this relate to education? Imagine that public pedagogy about Muslims is controlled by non-experts who purposefully lie and defame Muslims to serve the economic interests of arms production corporations and contracted national security firms. These corporations control foreign policy, the government, and national rhetoric about the War on Terror. They take fake pictures and videos and lie about historical events and locations that become included in the United States history books and part of our students' education.

But the United States is making a killing in other, more literal ways, too. The result of the War on Terror is not only that corporations made and continue to make billions, widening the gap even further between rich and poor. The result of this War is that many people have lost their lives, families, and all their worldly possessions. People like you or me, who merely wanted to live out their lives in peace. The only difference is that they prayed in a different way to their god. And what's even worse is that this information is missing from the media. Their lives are not depicted as valuable because they are simply not depicted. As if it is not news worthy when an innocent Muslim or an Arab dies, as if they are not humans, as if it is acceptable to terrorize them and their families. For example, many more Iraqis and Afghanis have died than American troops in battle. An estimated 2,165 American soldiers have died in Afghanistan (Wihbey, 2013), and 4,486 American soldiers died in Iraq (Goodman, 2014). These numbers represent 6,651 soldier fatalities total. I mentioned this information before, but it is worth repeating for its importance, that in a new Public Library of Science Medicine Journal (PLOS) survey, led by public health expert Amy Hagopian of the University of Washington in Seattle, around 405,000 civilian Iraqi deaths are attributable to the war and occupation in Iraq. More than 60% of these deaths were the direct result of shootings, bombings, airstrikes, or other violence, according to the study. This number does not include those who died fleeing the violence, or those that died while in exile (Morin, 2013). In Afghanistan, the number of civilian deaths could be as high as 20,000, according to *The Guardian* (Rasmussen, 2015). This is a total of 425,000 civilian deaths in Iraq and Afghanistan over the past 13 years because of American-led air and land strikes. The rough estimate of civilian deaths in Afghanistan and Iraq is 62 times greater than the total number of losses sustained by U.S. military troops. The sheer human loss and the fact that so few Americans know about it, or care to know about it, is indicative of a negative perception of Muslim life and the persistence of a crooked discourse.

While terrorism is often portrayed as an effort of a radicalized religious group to steal American freedom, this flat and noncritical portrayal of terrorism does more to support covert imperialist efforts and foster Islamophobia rather than expand and complete the uneven discussion. After 9/11, many media sources hysterically called for war without providing a coherent account of what had happened. Chief among the details absent from many media source accounts is the fact that the terrorists are not nation-state actors, and that attacking sovereign nations in retaliation may not be an example of tit for tat. Critical scholars question such approach in regards to the respect for democracy, while right-wing groups call this un-American. Canadian Critical Studies scholar Peter McLaren (2005) attributed the War on Terror to an imperialist capitalist project, or "imperialist war of terror" (p. 214). Investigating the United States historical accounts of foreign policy reveals that funding and training Islamic fundamentalists has been long embedded in U.S. foreign policy (McLaren, 2005). Despite this information, McLaren (2005) warned us not to assume that the U.S. policies were the direct cause of the attacks of 9/11, but rather the agency of the individuals responsible. His argument is based on the idea that terrorism is not a natural reaction to US foreign policy. Rather, the US economic and geopolitical policies are only some among some other factors that contribute to creating an environment ripe for terrorism (McLaren, 2005). But certainly, attempting to spread democracy through military assaults can't help the situation. Is it truly democracy if it is achieved with the barrel of a gun pressed firmly to the forehead? As such, it is easy to see that "the taproot of terrorism surely lies in the fertile soil of imperialism" (McLaren, 2005, p. 231). Terrorism and imperialism are married till death do they part.

What Causes Terrorism?

While terrorism is a horrific and egregious act, the desperation and hatred necessary for a small group of people to take extreme measures such as these becomes more understandable in light of the history of imperialism and violent disrespect visited upon them. This in no way justifies the actions. A woman who murders her husband after having been raped and abused by her husband for years must still stand trial. However, her choices must be viewed in context and not merely as a random act separate from the toxic environment in which she lived. It is with this mindset that we must ask ourselves why and how 9/11 and other terrorist acts happen. McLaren (2005) asserted that there are multiple causations for 9/11. "While U.S. imperialism clearly contributes to the conditions that are likely to foster terrorism, the actual causes of terrorism are conjunctural: they are a multiple and complex articulation of forces and relations rooted in globalized capitalism" (McLaren, 2005, p. 234). One explanation given by McLaren (2005) is that terrorism associated with Muslim groups is an adaptation to global capitalism. He argued that political movements under the guise of Islam are "motivated by the self-interest of the capitalist class of each country" (2005, p. 233). He further argued that in some cases these movements emerge as a reaction to the failure of upper classes of many countries to provide basic services such as social welfare, and education to its impoverished masses. There is a view that terrorism is the weapon of the weak. Since terrorists are not typically representative of a nation-state, they lack the might and power to engage in wars, and therefore use methods such as suicide bombings and other means to engage in warfare with organizations, institutions, or countries with whom they have a bone to pick (as cited in McLaren, 2005). But, is terrorism defined based on the actions or the actors?

Who Gets to Determine What Terrorism Is?

But who gets to define what true terrorism is? The online Merriam-Webster dictionary defines terrorism as "the use of violent acts to frighten the people in an area as a way of trying to achieve a political goal." Perhaps the hundreds of thousands of innocent civilians in Afghanistan or Iraq killed in the crosshairs of an American made gun would feel that they are on the receiving end of terror. As Chomsky (2001) wrote, "Like other means of violence, it's primarily a weapon of the strong, overwhelmingly" (p. 11). Chomsky is, of course, describing the feeling of terror that in fact, all humans are capable of feeling. A feeling experienced not only by those whose lives are shattered by suicide bombers in a street car, but those whose entire neighborhoods or cities are decimated by a drone. Yet, it seems that terrorism is something that is only done against the United States and other Western nations. However, terrorism as a noun, in its most common usage in American culture, and is often recognized as "a weapon of the weak because the strong also control the doctrinal systems and their terror doesn't count as terror" (Chomsky, 2001, p. 11). Some scholars such as Eqbal Ahmad (1998) made a similar point that "we are to feel the terror of those groups, which are officially disapproved. We are to applaud the terror of those groups of whom officials do approve" (p. 3). In response, McLaren (2005) pointed out the double standard of the United States that condemns other countries for violating human rights violence and acts of terror when it houses, educates, and graduates thousands of the most notorious world butchers. For example, The Western Hemisphere Institute for Security Cooperation of Georgia trained more than 60,000 Latin American soldiers and police officers who are torturers, mass murderers, dictators, and state terrorists. McLaren (2005) argued that "if the United States really believes that supporting terrorists makes you as guilty as the terrorists themselves, then it had to put on trial most of its military and political leadership over the last handful of administrations—and more" (p. 235). If we apply the definition of terrorism by Merriam Webster to current events, then all terrorist acts that frighten people to achieve political agenda should be evaluated by the same rulebook whether they are committed by the United States military or by terrorist organizations based in Afghanistan.

How Schools Perpetuate or Uncover Noncritical Discussions about Islamophobia

What is the stance of schools on Islamophobia and terrorism? Schools have served and continue to serve as important sites where Islamophobia is leveraged as an excuse for imperialistic actions. According to Bourdieu (1998), schools help universalize neo-liberal ideology and reproduce subjects who conform to a specific style of life required for the transformation process and expansion of neo-liberal capitalism. In that sense, schools reproduce dominant subjects, laborers, and consumers in neo-liberal capitalism. Mark, among other participants felt shocked by the US quick reaction in response to the event of 9/11. He said:

> It kind of very quickly changed from we are concerned about what happened to people—to we are angry and we need to do something about it. That was the kind of the reaction you saw; a lot of people, you know, going from concern and passion to anger and wanting to take some kind of revenge. That happened very quickly, propably within a couple of weeks when president Bush started giving speeches saying

"these people did it, we need to go get them, and we are going to take revenge against these people." He was refering to the people of Afghanistan basically. Now, without any proof actually but with just manipulating the emotions of the people of the United States, and so alot of people at school they kind of fell into this and were saying things like: "Oh, yeah we want to go and enlist in the army" and stuff like that. (personal communication, March 19, 2010)

While teachers need not agree with all the different points on this argument, it is important to not prioritize certain viewpoints while sweeping others under the rug. In order to have a healthy, democratic debate that will prepare youth for the complex future they inherit, it is critical to engage students in discussions that pose problems rather than turn students into blind receptors of pre-packaged information.

Why should teachers care? What's at stake if they do not take action? Teachers must understand that schools are social institutions directly linked to society. As public pedagogy such as the media and the law inform content knowledge in the classroom, in a reciprocal way, knowledge that emanates from the classroom circles back into society. Therefore, whether teachers acknowledge it or not, they play an important role in public pedagogy and must choose between enforcing the unidimensional dialogue or rectifying it.

Part of the problem with the disproportionate dialectic is that it foregrounds Islamophobia and almost completely erases other aspects of the conversation. Foregrounding Islamophobia focuses on Muslims as the problem that needs to be fixed; a terrorist to be targeted and fought. Such an imbalanced discourse has caused hatred and division in society, splitting American citizens into "Us versus Them" along religious and racial lines, and thus weakening the pluralistic fabric of the United States. Islamophobia negatively affects Americans' views of Muslims and promotes hateful actions that enforce hostility. Also, Muslim Americans, like others, are influenced by Islamophobic public pedagogy and thus are absorbing who they are as Muslims and the history of their ancestors from biased sources, which leads to their negative self-identity (Erikson, 1968). The development of unhealthy identities at an individual level can lead to the development of an unhealthy collective identity at the societal level.

Identity crisis is only one aspect of the problem. Islamophobia has exposed Muslims to increased discrimination that varies from verbal assaults and disrespect to vandalism, physical abuse, and even oppressive laws. Anti-Muslim aggression has already increased in the US since 2001 and continues to rise with the anti-Muslim slurs from 2016 presidential candidates such as Donald

Trump. Trump has suggested a ban on all Muslims. The problem with Trump's words is that if he's elected, his words may become law, thus expanding the division in society even more. Foregrounding Islamophobia has already justified the establishment of laws that directly discriminate against Muslims such as religious and ethnic profiling, airport security, and workplace prejudice. If the unequal dialogue persists, such laws will continue to single Muslims out for their ethnic or religious identity.

Even though such laws initially emerged to counter the Muslim terrorist threat and protect American "freedom," these laws not only took away freedoms, they also targeted many law-abiding citizens. For instance, many Americans do not know that the United States government secretly collected records of U.S. citizens' international telephone calls since 1992 to track down drug trafficking activities. According to an investigative reporter with *USA Today*, Brad Heath, this work of gathering and analyzing billions of calls provided a blueprint for the post-9/11 National Security Agency Spying program (Heath, 2015). The NSA and other laws have corroded and perverted core American values of human rights and justice. For example, the War on Terror has targeted not only terrorists but caused significant collateral damage. Yet, fear has numbed many American citizens to care about or question the death toll of innocent people in Muslim countries. This dehumanization of Muslims leads to the dehumanization of American society since the absence of humanity "marks not only those whose humanity has been stolen, but also (though in a different way) those who have stolen it" (Freire, 1970, p. 44). Due to the Islamophobic skewed argument, many Americans are willing to sacrifice fundamental values of human rights and justice, the very essence of humanity, to protect themselves from unreasonable fears.

I do not mean to say that it is irrational to fear terrorists; of course such fear is justified, to a degree. What I am against is constant fear and anxiety that paralyzes the United States as a nation. Irrational fear is an impediment against progress in society since there will be no prosperity or creativity in a culture of fear. For example, during our interview, one of the high school teachers I interviewed, Linda said, "So I will probably get fired one day," immediately after she shared her personal opinion with me about the widespread ignorance about Muslims. Linda explained that such ignorance is due to Eurocentrism—an inability to acknowledge that there are other people (besides Europeans) who had civilizations that contributed to humanity. Such arrogance and ignorance leads to bigotry and fear. This bigotry and fear is so strong that some teachers, like Linda, do not feel safe criticizing it and, in fact, fear they may lose their jobs for not conforming. What does this fear then say about the contemporary school environment and the possibility of teaching about current events? And what would happen to democracy if such fear persists in society? Linda's fear to even speak with me (a Muslim American woman) does not only reflect the fear of difference at that particular school but also signals a fear established at a systemic, societal level. This fear leads to heightened militarism and security in society and the literal and figurative hardening and emptying of schools (De Lissovoy, 2008) into strict banking educational models. Dewey (1916) and other educators who care about social progress would argue that schools are supposed to be safe spaces in which teachers facilitate dialogue about what's happening in society so that all may share their opinions and ideas. Similarly, Kincheloe and Steinberg (2004) argued that if educators understood that the American society is a pluralistic one and capitalize on the different ways of knowing everyone brings to the classroom, such an approach to difference could be a powerful tool of social transformation.

However, if we, teachers, allow irrational fear to control what we teach in the classroom, including enforcing a cockeyed debate, we will raise a generation of school children who are unable to think critically, and therefore unable to fully contribute in a meaningful and thoughtful way to civic society. Although Freire did not specifically speak about Islamophobia or 9/11 and the War on Terror, he spoke about a banking model of education that indoctrinates students to accept and even normalize oppression and one-dimensional views without questioning. The end result of this, according to Freire, is obedience rather than civic engagement. The one-sided dialogue of 9/11 and the War on Terror enhances the banking model. Such a dialectic fails to analyze the social, political and economic context and therefore fails to encourage civic actions and social improvements.

For instance, the lopsided examination almost never addresses imperialism as part of the conversation about 9/11 and the War on Terror. Discussing other aspects of the dialectic such as imperialism shows that there are other reasons for the War on Terror other than to fight Muslim terrorists, such as the economic benefits of an elite over the more expendable members of the global citizenry. Giroux (2016) argued that these elites cared only about increasing their wealth and power over the expense of the most vulnerable people in society including "low-income groups, the elderly, minorities of color, the unemployed, the homeless, immigrants, and any others whom the ruling class considers disposable" (Giroux, 2016, p. 21). In truth, expanding the logic about 9/11 and the War on

Terror to include other aspects such as imperialism does not only change the rhetoric and perceptions about Muslims as possible victims in the War on Terror, but also sheds light on marginalized peoples everywhere and calls attention to another form of global terrorism—which is, essentially, unbounded greed.

Showing other aspects of the conversation will help the American public to refuse simplistic explanations to complex current events and to make moral choices based on a holistic understanding. As George, one of the teachers I interviewed, said: "You have to dig deeper than just the rhetoric of politicians and look for a variety of causes." The goal of this chapter was to do just that.

Conclusion

The next time you see a veiled woman on television, or a Muslim person wielding a gun, as yourself—what are the purposes of this image? Islamophobia serves a purpose in more ways than one, and it is not always, or often, to protect American "freedom." Pre-9/11, fear of Islam served as an ideology that facilitated historical colonialism in Muslim lands. Post-9/11, Islamophobia continues to aid an imperialist project, while pretending this imperialistic project does not exist. Through foregrounding Islamophobia, the public quickly and easily gives their consent to violent actions that, unfortunately, lead to great profit for some. The loss of life, liberty, and property caused by war and political and economic restructuring are far more disturbing because many Americans do not know or care to know about them—as if lives of people who are different did not matter.

Teachers must know what's at stake. Knowledge flows between school and society; the knowledge that goes out comes back in. Therefore, whether teachers are aware of it or not, they do play a role in educating society and they have to choose whether to enforce an unbalanced discourse or repair it. Due to Islamophobia, Americans have permitted violations of human rights and loss of freedoms, thus, a denigration of what is held most dear—democracy. Shedding light on Islamophobia strengthens democracy. It is a sign of strength to highlight the most undesirable parts of a culture and ask fellow citizens to join you in helping to fix them. Including as many perspectives as possible in the analysis of 9/11 and the War on Terror expands students' abilities to think critically and empathize with all people. After all, allowing multiple voices to speak is what democracy is about. As educators, it is not necessary to agree or disagree with any one aspect of the dialogue, but it is important to address each contributing factor in this complex situation, and allow students to determine for themselves what they believe. From a balanced and holistic view teachers can contribute to increasing the value of diverse thought, thereby achieving intellectual freedom for students, humanization of Muslims, and a restoration of democracy within American society. The following chapter discusses in greater detail how teachers can apply critical dialectical pedagogy so that the classroom can serve as a site for this kind of transformation.

References

Ahmad, E. (1998, October 12). Terrorism—Theirs and ours. *A presentation at the University of Colorado, Boulder*. Retrieved September 28, 2016 from http://www.sangam.org/ANALYSIS/Ahmad.htm

Akyol, N. (2014, December 9). Liberation through war: The paradox facing Middle Eastern women. *Brown Political Review*. Retrieved October 12, 2016 from http://www.brownpolitical-review.org/2014/12/liberation-through-war-the-paradox-facing-middle-eastern-women/

Ali, W., Clifton, E., Duss, M., Fang, L., Keyes, S., & Shakir, F. (2011, August 26). Fear, Inc. The Roots of the Islamophobia Network in America. *Center for American Progress*. Retrieved October 7, 2016 from https://www.americanprogress.org/issues/religion/report/2011/08/26/10165/fear-inc/

Apple, M. (2004). *Ideology and curriculum*. New York, NY: Routledge Falmer.

Bacevich, A. (2012, September 25). Is Islamophobia the new mccarthyism. *Mother Jones*. Retrieved October 12, 2016 from http://www.motherjones.com/politics/2012/09/jerry-boykin-islam-andrew-bacevich

Black, C., & Fielding-Smith, A. (2016, October 2). Latest investigation fake news and false flags: How the Pentagon paid a British PR firm $500M for top secret Iraq propaganda. *The Bureau of Investigation Journalism*. Retrieved October 12, 2016 from http://labs.thebureau-investigates.com/fake-news-and-false-flags/

Black, E. (2002). *IBM and the Holocaust: The strategic alliance between Nazi Germany and America's most powerful corporation*. New York, NY: Three Rivers Press.

Bourdieu, P. (1998, December). Utopia of endless exploitation: The essence of neoliberalism. What is neoliberalism? A programme for destroying collective structures that may impede the pure market logic. *Le Monde Diplomatique*. Retrieved March 25, 2012 from http://mondediplo.com/1998/12/08bourdieu

Byrne, M. (2013, August 19). CIA admits it was behind Iran's coup. *Foreign Policy*. Retrieved July 11, 2015 from http://foreignpolicy.com/2013/08/19/cia-admits-it-was-behind-irans-coup/

Chomsky, N. (2001, October 24). The new war against terror. *Counterpunch*. Retrieved September 28, 2016 from http://www.counterpunch.org/2001/10/24/the-new-war-against-terror/

Dane, L. (2015, March 25). Blood money: These companies and people make billions of dollars from war. *Centre for Research on Globalization*. Retrieved October 7, 2016 from http://www.globalresearch.ca/blood-money-these-companies-and-people-make-billions-of-dollars-from-war/5438657

De Lissovoy, N. (2008). *Power, crisis, and education for liberation: Rethinking critical pedagogy.* New York, NY: Palgrave Macmillan.

Dewey, J. (1916). *Democracy and education: An introduction to the philosophy of education.* New York, NY: The Free Press.

Erikson, E. H. (1968). *Identity: Youth and crisis.* New York, NY: W. W. Norton.

Fairclough, N. (2003). *Analyzing discourse: Textual analysis for social research.* New York, NY: Routledge.

Freire, P. (1970). *Pedagogy of the oppressed.* New York, NY: Herder & Herder.

Giroux, H. (2016). *America's addiction to terrorism.* New York, NY: Monthly Review Press.

Goodman, A. (Interviewer), & Gordon, M. (Interviewee). (2006, March 17). New York Times Chief Military correspondent Michael Gordon defends pre-war report in on WMDs. *Democracy Now!* Retrieved October 11, 2016 from http://www.democracynow. org/2006/3/17/new_york_times_chief_military_correspondent

Goodman, H. A. (2014, September 17). 4,486 American soldiers have died in Iraq. President Obama is continuing a pointless and deadly quagmire. *The Huffington Post.* Retrieved October 11, 2016 from http://www.huffingtonpost.com/h-a-goodman/4486-american-soldiers-ha_b_5834592.html

Haque, A. (2004). Islamophobia in North America: Confronting the menace. In B. Van Driel (Ed.), *Islamophobia in educational settings* (pp. 1–19). London: Trentham House.

Hardt, M., & Negri, A. (2000). *Multitude: War and democracy in the age of empire.* New York, NY: Penguin Books.

Heath, B. (2015, April 8). U.S. secretly tracked billions of calls for decades. *USA Today.* Retrieved October 11, 2016 from http://www.usatoday.com/story/news/2015/04/07/dea-bulk-telephone-surveillance-operation/70808616/

Holmes, D., & Dixon, N. (2001). *Behind the US war in Afghanistan.* Chippendale: Resistance Books.

Johnson, A. (2011, March 6). The Idea of 'Islamophobia'. In *World Affairs.* Retrieved September 3, 2017, from http://www.worldaffairsjournal.org/blog/alan-johnson/idea-%E2%80%98islamophobia%E2%80%99

Kane, A. (2013, August 16). 5 companies that make money by keeping Americans terrified of terror attacks: A massive industry profits off the government-induced fear of terrorism. *Alternet.* Retrieved October 8, 2016 from http://www.alternet.org/civil-liberties/5-companies-make-money-keeping-americans-terrified-terror-attacks

Kaplan, A. (2005). "Where is Guantanamo?" Legal borderlands: Law and the construction of American borders. *Special Issue of American Quarterly, 57*(3), 831–858.

Kemp, G., & Harkavy, R. (1997). Strategic geography and the changing Middle East: Concepts, definitions, and parameters. *Arab Culture and Civilization.* Retrieved October 8, 2016 from http://acc.teachmideast.org/texts.php?module_id=4&reading_id=120&sequence=19

Kincheloe, J. L., & Steinberg, S. R. (2004). *The miseducation of the West: How schools and the media distort our understanding of the Islamic world.* Westport, CT: Praeger Publishers.

Klein, N. (2007). *The shock doctrine: The rise of disaster capitalism.* New York, NY: Henry Holt & Company.

Kone, A. M. (2013). The military-industrial complex in the United States: Evolution and expansion from World War II to the war on terror. *Inquiries*. Retrieved October 8, 2016 from http://www.inquiriesjournal.com/articles/749/the-military-industrial-complex-in-the-united-states-evolution-and-expansion-from-world-war-ii-to-the-war-on-terror

Lockheed Martin. (2016). *Center for responsive politics: Influence & lobbying*. Retrieved October 12, 2016 from https://www.opensecrets.org/pacs/lookup2.php?strID=C00303024

Maira, S. (2009). *Missing: Youth, citizenship, and empire after 9/11*. Durham, NC: Duke University Press.

Makdisi, U. (2008). *Artillery of heaven: American Missionaries and the failed conversion of the Middle East*. New York, NY: Cornell University.

Mamdani, M. (2002). Good Muslim, Bad Muslim: A political perspective on culture and terrorism. *American Anthropological Association*. Retrieved September 29, 2016 from http://jan.ucc.nau.edu/sj6/mamdanigoodmuslimbadmuslim.pdf

Mamdani, M. (2004). *Good Muslim, bad Muslim: America, the Cold War, and the roots of terror*. New York, NY: Random House.

Marr, T. (2006). *The cultural roots of American Islamicism*. Cambridge: Cambridge University Press.

McLaren, P. (2005). *Capitalists and conquerors: A critical pedagogy against empire*. New York, NY: Rowman & Littlefield.

Morin, M. (2013, October 15). Study estimates nearly 500,000 Iraqis died in war. *Los Angeles Times*. Retrieved September 29, 2016 from http://articles.latimes.com/2013/oct/15/world/la-fg-iraq-war-deaths-20131016

Naureckas, J. (2001, April 1). Gulf war coverage: The worst censorship was at home. *FAIR: Fairness & Accuracy in Reporting*. Retrieved September 29, 2016 from http://fair.org/extra/gulf-war-coverage/

Pauwels, J. R. (2003, April 30). Why America needs war. *Centre for Research on Globalization*. Retrieved October 8, 2016 from http://www.globalresearch.ca/why-america-needs-war/5328631

Pentagon Paid PR Firm $540mn To Make Fake Terrorist Videos. (2016, October 2). *RT: Question More*. Retrieved October 8, 2016 from https://www.rt.com/usa/361385-pentagon-pr-firm-terrorist-videos/

Rasmussen, S. E. (2015, February 18). Afghan civilian deaths hit record high. *The Guardian*. Retrieved October 11, 2016 from http://www.theguardian.com/world/2015/feb/18/afghan-civilian-deaths-record-high

Said, E. (2003). *Culture and imperialism*. New York, NY: Vintage Books.

Steet, L. (2000). *Veils and daggers: A century of the National Geographic's representations of the Arab world*. Philadelphia, PA: Temple University Press.

The War on Evil—President George W. Bush's Insights on Evil. (n.d.). *Magniloquence against War*. Retrieved October 13, 2016 from http://irregulartimes.com/evilwar.html

Transcript for September 14: Guest: Dick Cheney, Vice President–Tim Russert, Moderator. (2003, March 16). *NBC News: Meet the Press*. Retrieved October 12, 2016 from http://www.nbcnews.com/id/3080244/#.V_5di4WcHIV

Wihbey, J. (2013, October 22). U.S. military casualties and the costs of war: Iraq, Afghanistan and post-9/11 conflicts. *Journalists Resource: Research on Today's New Topics*. Retrieved October 13, 2016 from http://journalistsresource.org/studies/government/security-military/us-military-casualty-statistics-costs-war-iraq-afghanistan-post-911

Zine, J. (2004). Anti-Islamophobia education as transformative pedagogy: Reflections from the education frontlines. *The American Journal of Islamic Social Sciences*, 21(3), 110–118.

· 8 ·

SOLUTIONS IN CRITICAL DIALECTICAL PEDAGOGY (CDP)

> I am interested in seeing this research, for sure, and I guess I want to say thanks
> for the opportunity to reflect a little bit, and I will make changes in my teachings
> based on that. It is a great topic. I want my students to walk away with a better
> understanding of the current world and the tensions involved and the tolerance
> we need to show one another, so that means I need to focus on doing it.
> —Patrick [teacher], personal communication (May 30, 2010)

Through our conversation and the fact that the interview provided a much needed opportunity for reflection, Patrick, a high school teacher I interviewed in New Mexico, recognized the need to work on his pedagogy of teaching about 9/11 and the War on Terror in his classroom. Teachers need an opportunity for reflection to realize how important it is to teach about these topics in a critical way. This book provides that opportunity, but also helps teachers tackle the all-important question of what now?

There are many reasons why it is challenging for teachers to teach about 9/11 and the War on Terror. The skewed perspective of 9/11 and the War on Terror presented through the public pedagogy of the media, politics, laws, and textbooks upholds a one-sided perspective that associates Muslims with terrorism and antagonism against the United States. These ideas support an imperialist perspective that dominates the American culture. This results in support for wars overseas that kill Muslims and destroy their societies, as well as backing for laws in the United States that discriminate against Muslims. Unfortunately, because of this hostile environment many Muslim American students question their identities, citizenship and sense of belonging in the United States. The skewed conversation generates textbooks and curriculum that support simplistic explanations for complex issues, and to teach against this dialectic may feel like fighting against society, especially since some teachers may encounter backlash from the school administration, parents, or even students for presenting alternative perspectives. This may give teachers who want to teach about these topics a sense of alienation, fear, and isolation. However, teachers can and must try to counter these intolerant and alienating discourses, despite the fact that it may be an unpopular choice and perhaps even an uphill battle. The War on Terror is woven into the fabric of Americans' lives; therefore teaching about it in a critical way is crucial to achieving a nuanced understanding of the past and present.

Despite the critical nature of these topics, many teachers struggle to teach these topics in a critical way. But, it is possible for them and all teachers to improve and to push back. Within education are the seeds of hope. Many scholars criticize oppressive forces in the school system that restrict teachers' efforts towards social justice, yet such scholars also believe in the transformative power of education and the role of teachers in this process (Apple, 2013; Freire, 1970; Leo, Giroux, McClennen, & Saltman, 2013). I, too, am one of these scholars. I believe that even within a challenging system, individual teachers can encourage deep reflection among their students and serve as one of the most important catalysts for change. If the lopsided dialectic persists, democracy will suffer. However, when teachers encourage a holistic dialectic inside their classrooms, this will inevitably impact society for the better.

In order to facilitate this process, this chapter provides a discussion of a new methodology for teaching, as well as concrete lesson plans that teachers can use in their classrooms. Consider this the teacher tool-kit chapter with strategies for countering ignorance, stereotyping, and cruelty. Through these methods and strategies, teachers can begin to remove the lenses through which students perceive the world, and ask them to report, with their own eyes, what they really see.

All the teachers interviewed for the purposes of this book demonstrated a desire and commitment to learning how they could improve their pedagogies of 9/11 and the War on Terror. Therefore, this chapter is dedicated to these teachers and all teachers who care about engaging their students in critical education. Using a Critical Dialectical Pedagogy framework, I will highlight teaching suggestions based on my own work as an educator, strategies gleaned from other seasoned teachers and theorists, as well as suggestions expressed by interviewed teachers and students.

What Teachers Can Do: Use Critical Dialectical Pedagogy

In order to facilitate an intellectually tolerant environment, humanization of Muslims, and restoration of democracy in society, teachers need to implement a pedagogy that re-inflates this lopsided dialectic. Using dialectics is the art of investigating or discussing the truth. If we think of the holistic dialectic as a sphere that represents all diverse perspectives of an event, a lopsided dialectic would be a sphere missing parts or perspectives. We can use Critical Dialectical Pedagogy (CDP) to restore wholeness to the dialogue.

Critical dialectical pedagogy is a version of critical pedagogy that focuses on teaching current events in a holistic way, paired with practical applications for the classroom. Critical Dialectical Pedagogy builds on the work of theorists and professionals dedicated to critical pedagogy. Critical Dialectical Pedagogy shares the same focus as critical pedagogy; it is opposed to one-sided and uncritical educational models that result in obedience rather than civic engagement as demonstrated in Freire's (1970) banking model of education. Instead, CDP supports a "problem-posing" education (Freire, 1970) that empowers students with intellectual skills and a sense of agency with which to recognize oppression within society, interrogate systems of domination and inequality, and take action to make improvements (Freire, 1970). Freire and other critical pedagogues have built excellent methodologies for teaching critical thinking within the classroom that are certainly useful and applicable.

Differences between CDP and Problem-Posing Education

There are, however, multiple differences between Freire's theory of problem posing educational models and CDP. Critical Dialectical Pedagogy distinguishes itself from Freire's theories in that it is not limited to a binary of experiences and perspectives of oppressor versus oppressed or banking education versus problem-posing education. It acknowledges the existence of polar opposites, but stresses that most individuals and methodologies fall somewhere along the spectrum. Specifically, CDP recognizes that most teachers are neither problem-posing nor banking pedagogues. This means that if a teacher has not yet succeeded in mastering a problem-posing educational model, they should not feel frustrated or unmotivated. Instead, teachers must understand that with constant reflection and training, they can improve. As long as teachers identify an end goal, then they can work towards achieving it. Critical Dialectical Pedagogy seeks to be more compassionate towards educators and the processes necessary for developing critical pedagogy that truly liberates its participants.

The idea of dialectics is important because it emphasizes how teachers can facilitate critical thinking for themselves and their students. I borrowed the concept of dialectics from Socrates' (470–399 B.C.) dialectic method. I define dialectics as a method of reasoning used to explore the truth through dialogue (Nikulin, 2010). Plotinus (204–270 A.D.) argued that by using dialectics, we are able to dialogue about the following:

> Everything by means of reasoning, *logos*, about what everything is, how it differs from other things and what it has in common, and to what kind of things it belongs and where it stands among those things, and if it is, what it is, and how many existing things of this kind there are, and again how many are non-existent. It discusses what is good and what is not good, and the things that are considered under what is good and its opposite, and what is eternal and what not eternal, providing knowledge about everything, not opinion. (as cited in Nikulin, 2010, p. 46)

In other words, dialectics is a process through which we deeply consider the world around us. Through asking logical questions and by engaging in the process of dialogue, gaps in logic will become apparent. In some cases, participants might reach a final agreement on a topic and this, in Socrates' opinion, represents the truth. It is important to understand, though, that dialectics is different from a debate, as debate typically only involves two opposing views, while dialectics strives to represent multiple views; two, three, or a hundred. The main goal in a debate is typically to win an argument, whereas the main goal of dialectics is to collectively discover the truth. Also, dialectics is different from rhetoric since rhetoric also has persuasion of an audience at its center regardless of whether or not the person sincerely believes in what they argue. Dialectics stands out from both debate and rhetoric in its objective: to find the truth. Among the followers of Socrates, Aristotle (384–322 B.C.), believed that dialogue is best when its participants are rational, respect themselves and others, and agree that the goal is the search for the truth and therefore are willing to listen and accept reason even when they are wrong. If you think about it, in a democratic society that cherishes pluralism, there should always be a multiplicity of opinions. When former President Abraham Lincoln assembled his cabinet, he put together many of his former competitors for the White House in what Doris Kearns Goodwin, his biographer, deemed "a team of rivals" (Goodwin, 2006). Three of these men were Attorney General Edward Bates, Secretary of the Treasury Salmon P. Chase, and Secretary of State William H. Seward. Lincoln selected these men to serve in his administration because he knew they would share their own opinions and beliefs rather than acquiescing to everything Lincoln said. In other words, Lincoln understood that building the foundations of a strong democracy was easier to do if many hands pitched in. My idea of using dialectics here is to develop a new meaning of reality through dialogue among diverse perspectives for the purpose of making better inclusive decisions to benefit the entire society, not just its elites.

Another difference between CDP and Freire's theory of critical pedagogy is that CDP advocates for transformation in small steps from the ground up, whereas Freire calls for a revolution. Critical Dialectical Pedagogy does not put the full burden of transformation and humanization on the shoulders of the oppressed, either. Instead, a central idea in CDP is that people in positions of some influence and power, such as teachers, can work within the system towards a restoration of democracy. By using a problem-posing model of education with dialectics as a process at its center, teachers can develop pedagogies that impact change.

Though Freire mentioned the role of outside institutions (such as the media) in influencing school and society in a theoretical way, he does not mention how teachers can analyze and utilize these factors within the classroom. Dialectics across sociocultural, historic, and political discourses help teachers and students understand an issue on a macro level. For example, when discussing current events such as 9/11 and the War on Terror, other influences such as neoliberalism, history, the media and public pedagogy should be brought into the dialogue in addition to religion to fully understand the events and their aftermath.

Freire analyzed current events through the way he described the role of the media as a means of propaganda in service of the oppressor. However, he did not particularly focus on current events. On the other hand, CDP specifically focuses on addressing current events as a requirement to understanding reality and analyzing the world of oppression to subvert it. The definition of current events here is what is happening in society, not just what is being reported in the news. For example, on September 6, 2016, Native Americans of North Dakota protested and filed a lawsuit to stop an oil pipeline from going into their land and river. This event was aired by *Democracy Now* and not covered by any of the main news media until sometime later. The news often includes specific voices to the exclusion of others, so teaching current events in a critical way does not mean parroting what the talking heads on the television say. Focusing on current events means featuring the voices and perspectives of all members of society, including marginalized populations. By defining current events in this way, teachers see the need to gather nontraditional resources to make sure that all voices are heard.

Finally, Freire's theory was mainly philosophical and did not address specifically how to achieve intellectual liberation through education, while the capstone of CDP is the development of practical classroom applications that teachers can use to that end. Specifically, CDP consists of helping teachers develop their classroom management skills and exposing teachers to more holistic dialectics of 9/11 and the War on Terror paired with actionable lesson plans for sharing this content with students.

First Things First: Developing Critical Thinking Skills with CDP

To begin, this chapter will discuss ways to help teachers develop into critical thinkers. A key component of critical dialectical pedagogy is helping teachers develop their critical thinking skills. Freire mentioned five areas in which teachers must focus their energies in order to effectively develop into problem-posing teachers. These include the following:

1. Facilitating dialogue
2. Understanding reality
3. Minimizing hierarchy
4. Developing praxis (which Freire defines as action plus reflection)
5. Encouraging students to be agents of history rather than mere observers of it

Critical Dialectical Pedagogy, however, builds upon Freire's theories by considering practical applications for them and taking Freire's concept of dialogue one step further and asking teachers to master the art of dialectics, which is a capstone of the CDP method. The following paragraphs will demonstrate to teachers and professors of education how to (a) master dialectics, (b) unveil reality, (c) minimize hierarchy, (d) develop praxis, and (e) encourage students to be agents of history. All of these elements must work towards expanding the lopsided dialectic. Educators and teachers can apply the following key components of CDP in their classrooms. The ideas included here can be tailored for either a teacher preparation classroom or a high school classroom to enhance democratic education among both soon-to-be teachers and high school students.

Step 1: Mastering Dialectics

So many of the Muslim students that I interviewed felt that just a little bit of conversation here and there could have greatly changed their high school experiences, as well as their peers' understanding of the world. This first section—Mastering Dialectics—explains how teachers can cultivate deep and respectful conversation within their classrooms. In many ways, students feel as though there are certain topics that are taboo—as Francis, one of the students I interviewed, put it, 9/11 and the War on Terror were "topics you can't talk about." How can teachers make sure that students feel comfortable bringing up these more edgy, yet extremely critical, topics of conversation? The answer lies in training teachers and students in dialectics. Since this is the foundation upon which the rest of CDP is built, this section will be longer and more in-depth.

Utilizing dialectics will require that the teacher go through stages of personal development, learn to craft an arc of dialogue, teach towards multiple intelligences, hone their classroom management skills, and spend lots of time practicing. But first, it may be useful to consider the words dialogue, dialectic, and discussion. Dialogue is derived from two Greek words *dia-*, meaning "through," and *-logos*, "the meaning of the word." When put together, dialogue etymologically means going through a process of collectively generating new meanings to understand the world. This is different from a discussion in that the suffix *dis-* means apart, away, divided. So a discussion may often look like everyone standing firm and separate in their own beliefs about a topic, and sparring with these individual opinions in a conversation. It is important for teachers and students to understand the difference between the intent of discussion and dialogue so that they can be clear on the end goal of the conversation; is it to hold a discussion through which to hear a survey of students' divided opinions or to go deeper and facilitate a dialectical dialogue through which to collectively discover new meanings. It may be useful for teachers to teach this to their students in a few ways. First, teachers can ask students to recount a time when they had an enjoyable conversation with people who did not necessarily share their views about a controversial topic—ask the students, What about it was enjoyable? How was this conversation different from other controversial conversations that you have had, that were not enjoyable? Then, teachers can present a short lecture the differences between debate/discussion and dialogue, explaining how dialogue:

1. Is an exchange of ideas and experiences that is so effective and highly-charged that participants cannot help but be changed by.
2. Requires the suspension of one's opinions in order to truly listen to the opinions of another.
3. Obliges all participants to remain in the dialogue, even when one's beliefs are challenged.
4. Necessitates participation from all.
5. In the best-case scenario, can result in divergent views converging.

Reminding students that the whole point of sharing their beliefs as a group is to reach a new social consciousness changes the goal from winning an argument, to more fully understanding the world around them through listening to one another. Understanding this, however, is a process for the student and the teacher.

These processes require going through stages of development. Development of the teacher is different from developing the arc of the dialogue or mastering the art of dialectics. For example, a teacher needs to develop the skill set necessary to facilitate dialectics. Wellesley College has an excellent resource about the skills, or what they call the *attending behaviors* required to facilitate these dialogues (Bradford, n.d.). For Wellesley College, there are three key attending behaviors. Those are: use of eye contact, use of body language, and use of discretion. The authors suggest that when it comes to good eye contact, teachers should look at the individual that speaks, but be careful not to stare and make that individual uncomfortable. Body language is a bit more complicated, but extremely crucial. Think back to a challenging conversation in which you were either a participant or a facilitator. Did you notice anyone in the group physically closing off their bodies, putting their arms over their chest and ducking their head down? This person removes themselves from the conversation with this nonverbal cue. As a facilitator, it is important both to demonstrate an open, at-ease posture, and also pay attention to the nonverbal cues of the participants around you. For more shy individuals, they made need more smiles and nods to coax them into speaking. For more talkative individuals that monopolize the conversation, they made need a nonverbal cue from you that it is time to cede the floor to someone else. Use of discretion is another complicated idea. Essentially, teachers must learn to allow the dialogue to take its natural course, while also encouraging the flow to continue when it seems to stagnate. This involves allowing topics to fully develop before introducing a new one. It also involves occasionally paraphrasing what has been said, especially if the content was not entirely clear to you or to the group. However, the danger with paraphrasing is that sometimes a teacher may do it too often. The dialogue should not turn into a conversation between the class on one end, and the teacher on the other. As much as possible, the facilitator should allow the conversation to evolve without sharing their own opinions. A teacher can use their discretion to either spur more dialogue or end the dialogue by asking open or closed questions. Open questions cannot be answered with a simple yes or no, whereas closed questions can. An example of an open questions is "Why do you think terrorists attacked the World Trade Center?" and an example of a closed question is "Did the terrorists attack the World Trade Center because they hate our freedom?" Both techniques are useful, depending on the goals of the facilitator. Developing these skills is an on-going process for the teacher, and no one is perfect. However, if you pay attention to these skills and consciously working to improve them, you will notice a difference in the quality of the dialogue you are able to facilitate in the classroom. Besides developing these skills, however, teachers also need to think about how they are developing an arc of the dialogue.

To develop the arc of the dialogue, or the different emotional stages of the dialogue, a teacher, as the facilitator, should deeply understand the topic and how to progress to more profound emotional and intellectual stages. First and foremost, through sufficient knowledge of the topic, teachers will be able to provide enough content information for students so that they may understand the topic of conversation enough to have an opinion. Secondly, teachers must understand how to build the conversation slowly. For example, it does not make sense to ask students something like "Why does racism still exist?" as the bell is still ringing between class periods. Students need time to "warm-up," in a sense, to the discussion. Therefore, it is recommended that teachers start with an easy question to build trust and then add levels of emotional difficulty and intellectual complexity as the discussion progresses. Mastering the art of dialectics require teachers' knowledge of the type of questions that generate particular levels of engagement.

A Bloom's Taxonomy query model would be a great resource for teachers to design questions based on the level of cognitive and emotional achievement. *A Taxonomy for Learning, Teaching, and Assessing: A Revision of Bloom's Taxonomy of Educational Objectives*, Complete Edition by Lorin W. Anderson and David R. Krathwohl (2000) is a great resource. Bloom categorized based on different levels of thinking which range from lower to higher. Krawthwohl and Anderson modified these categories to help teachers understand them and implement them in a standards-based curriculum. These levels are: (a) remember (b) understand, (c) apply, (d) analyze, (e) evaluate, and (f) create. The following are examples of useful verbs to use when constructing the question, sample questions, and potential activities and products, based on Krawthwohl and Anderson's revision to Bloom, as well as activities and questions and activities devised by Australian educators Joan Dalton and David Smith (1986). Many of the sample activities and products do not involve dialogue. However, it is important to remember that engaging in these activities may provide time and space for the student to reflect on their understanding of the topic, as well as allow them to connect emotionally to it, thus preparing them for a deeper and richer conversation.

Remember. In this stage, students are retrieving relevant information. Useful verbs for teachers asking questions in this stage might be: (a) tell, (b) list, (c) describe), (d) relate, (e) locate, (f) write, (g) state, (h) name. All of these verbs elicit the knowledge of the student. Some sample questions include: (a) What happened after ...?, (b) How many ...?, (c) Who was it that ...?, (d) Describe what happened at ...?, (e) Who spoke to ...? (f) Which is true or false ...? Some potential activities include (a) making a list of the main events, (b) making a timeline of events, (c) or making a facts chart. All of these activities will allow students to collectively express their knowledge on any given topic.

Understand. Once students express their knowledge, students are ready to construct meaning based on the information they recalled. Useful verbs for teachers asking questions in this stage might be: (a) explain, (b) interpret, (c) outline, (d) discuss, (e) distinguish, (f) predict, (g) restate, (h) translate, (i) compare, (j) describe. Some sample questions include: (a) Can you write in your own words ...?, (b) Can you write a brief outline?, (c) What was the main idea ...?, (d) What differences exist between ...?, (e) Can you provide a definition for ...? Some potential activities this stage include: (a) Cutting out and drawing pictures to show a particular event, (b) illustrating what you think the main idea was, (c) Write a summary report of an event.

Apply. At this stage, students carry out their knowledge in a particular procedure. Useful verbs to use when crafting questions in this stage include: (a) solve, (b) show, (c) use, (d) illustrate, (e) construct, (f) complete, (g) examine. Sample questions include: (a) Do you know another instance where ...?,

(b) Could this have happened in ...?, (c) What factors would you change if ...?, (d) Can you apply the method used to some experience of your own ...?, (e) From the information given, can you develop a set of instructions about ...? Some Potential activities in this stage include: (a) Making a scrapbook about the area of study, (b) Write a textbook about [fill in the blank] for others.

Analyze. Students are now ready to dissect the information to determine how all the separate parts relate to one another and to a broader structure or purpose. Some useful verbs include: (a) analyze, (b) distinguish, (c) examine, (d) integrate, (e) organize, (f) differentiate, (g) categorize, (h) separate, (i) deconstruct. Sample questions include: (a) Which events could have happened ...?, (b) What do you see as other possible outcomes?, (c) How is ... similar to ...?, (d) Can you distinguish between ...?, (e) What were some of the motives behind ...? Some possible activities include (a) Making a family tree to demonstrate relationships between people, events, etc., (b) Review a film, book, etc., (c) Write an opinion essay with a thesis and relevant support.

Evaluate. At this stage, students make judgments based on what they have learned and experienced thus far. Useful verbs for questions include: (a) detect, (b) check, (c) monitor, (d) test, (e) critique, (f) judge. Some questions teachers can use include: (a) What elements of this process would you critique ...?, (b) given what you know, how would you judge ...?, (c) in what ways should we monitor this situation? Activities students can do at this stage include: (a) creating a pro and con list, (b) host a trial with judge and jury, (c) evaluate a particular person, policy, or situation with a report card of their own creation.

Create. At this stage, students are more proactive and put what they have learned together in a design of their own imagination. Useful verbs when creating questions include: (a) create, (b) invent, (c) compose, (d) plan, (e) construct, (f) design, (g) imagine, (h) propose, (i) devise, (j) formulate. Sample questions include: (a) Can you design a ... to ...?, (b) devise a possible solution to ...?, (c) if you had access to all resources, how would you deal with ...?, (d) can you create new and unusual uses for ...?, (e) can you develop a proposal which would ...? Possible activities include: (a) inventing a machine to do a specific task, (b) writing a letter to an editor, politician, the President, etc., with an idea about how to resolve a particular issue, (c) designing, planning, and implementing an event as a class to address a particular issue.

Through using Bloom's taxonomy as a basis for steadily building more complex intellectual and emotional development, students will be prepared to fully invest their hearts and minds at each stage. As you may have noticed, many of the activities listed above involve using different skills and abilities. This deserves further attention, for developing activities that engage different aspects of the brain and body will help students really connect with the material.

In other words, teachers should support the multiple intelligence and learning styles of the students. Multiple Intelligences theory by Howard Gardner (2011) taps on the different and overlapping intelligences that students might have including the following: (a) linguistic, (b) logical-mathematical, (c) spatial, (d) bodily-kinesthetic, (e) musical, (f) interpersonal, (g) intrapersonal, and (h) naturalist. Learning about multiple intelligences allows teachers to develop lesson plans and classroom activities while incorporating various learning styles. Much like the lopsided dialectic of 9/11 leads to misunderstanding, developing activities without considering multiple intelligences excludes many voices, experiences, and learning approaches and results in a lack of cognitive and emotional development for many students. *Frames of Mind: The Theory of Multiple Intelligences* by Howard Gardner (2011) and *Multiple Intelligences in the Classroom*, 3rd Edition by Thomas Armstrong (2009) are good resources.

Multiple intelligence activities can be brought into the classroom in a variety of ways. Examples of how to bring linguistic intelligences into the classroom include: (a) asking students to write a poem, short story, diary of a person or character you have studied, (b) listen to an interview, or (c) dialogue. Examples of how to bring logical-mathematical learning styles into the classroom include: (a) create a mystery that students need to solve based on clues and evidence, (b) develop a grading rubric for a policy, person, event, or (c) conduct experiments in the classroom such as different classroom management methods, or discussion techniques, or teaching techniques, and have students develop methods for evaluating the efficacy of these methods themselves. Teachers can incorporate spatial learning through (a) picture language—teachers can lay out certain photographs or pictures on the floor and ask students which one resonates most with them based on a particular question or criteria, (b) showing television or movie clips, (c) bringing physical artifacts or models that students can touch or hold. Speaking of touching or holding, bodily-kinesthetic learners may enjoy (a) not only touching or holding things, but making things, (b) role-playing, which can be especially useful for demonstrating appropriate dialogue behavior, (c) trust-building activities, such as having a blind-folded individual led through verbal cues by another individual who does not have a blindfold on. Musical learners show sensitivity to rhythm and sound, and not just that of music. Examples of ways to help these individuals learn include: (a) incorporating meditative silence into the day, (b) creating songs or rhythms to memorize information, (c) playing certain kinds, such as classical music or songs without lyrics, during certain times of the day. Interpersonal learners grow and develop through connection with others and may enjoy (a) large group discussions, (b) small group discussions, (c) interviewing an individual who has experience with a particular historical or social event being discussed in the classroom. Intrapersonal learners tend to be more shy and introverted and may enjoy (a) keeping a diary of their thoughts on a particular subject, (b) quiet time in the classroom for reading and other activities, (c) anonymous reflection—teachers can have students write down their thoughts and ideas on a piece of paper and turn it in to the teacher, where the teacher can then read these thoughts and ideas aloud to the class without anyone knowing whose thoughts and ideas they are. Naturalists may enjoy (a) observing the natural and social world around them, (b) seeing the connections between historical and social changes and issues, and the natural world, (c) documenting changes and metamorphoses over time. Using these examples of as a jumping-off point, teachers will notice that all students become more engaged since the activities are interesting and diverse. In this way, the teacher or facilitator develops dialectical activities—activities which create space for diverse individuals. To truly develop these skills, teachers must practice, practice, and practice.

Dialectics is the capstone of CDP and must be daily included in the classroom. However, there are many challenges faced by teachers, especially new teachers, as they attempt to build dialectics into the classroom. One of the largest issues that many teachers mention, including Patrick, one of the teachers interviewed in New Mexico, is a lack of respect among students for one another. Consequently, a principle element in CDP is helping teachers develop stronger classroom management skills, through which teachers may foster respectful and inquisitive classroom environments conducive to dialectical dialogue. This was not always an easy process for the teachers I interviewed, such as Patrick:

> When you're obviously working against what students have heard at home and or in media that may not be as reputable, let's say unbiased, so we are trying to dispel myths or misunderstandings. So trying to disassociate Al Qaeda, say, from Saddam Hussein. There is always this misunderstanding that we are in Iraq because of the attacks of September 11, and so as an example of trying to bring more clarity to the issue, so you end up ... and then having it discussed in a respectful way that you don't end up with any kind of slurs or disrespectful speech, recognizing that it's probably going to

happen and then responding to it appropriately so that it doesn't necessarily kind of squash everybody but that you at least stand up for respectful discussion and tolerance and understanding of people. So dispelling myths, dealing with how do you have a discussion with people on a topic that brings up a lot of passion and has, I think, a root of discrimination and what I think and racism involved. (Patrick, personal communication, May 30, 2010)

In Patrick's classroom, racial slurs were "probably going to happen," yet he struggled with how to respond to these comments because he did not want to also "squash everybody" for having their opinions. The solution for Patrick and other teachers is to prepare the classroom setting for dialogue. One of the best ways to do so is by setting ground rules at the beginning of the school year. Ground rules lay out a series of expected behaviors for classroom conduct. These rules can be established by the teacher, or students, or both. In my experience, students are more likely to follow these rules if they take an active role in creating them. Here are a few sample ground rules, based off of the Carnegie Mellon University's Eberly Center for Teaching Excellence (n.d.). They include:

- Show respect for others by using their preferred names and pronouns
- Listen and do not interrupt
- Do not generalize about groups of people, and never ask another person to speak as a representative of a group
- What is said in class, stays in the class
- Critique ideas, not people
- Use "I" statements instead of "we" or "you" statements
- Open your mind and expect to learn something new or change your opinion
- Step up and step back: if you are shy or quiet, push yourself to speak and if you are more outspoken, push yourself to listen
- Support your arguments with evidence
- If you are offended or hurt by something that was said, acknowledge it immediately
- Frustrated with patterns you see in the class discussion? Bring them to the attention to the teacher.

Ground rules work best when set at the beginning of the course. The teacher or facilitator must explain why they are important to the students (for example, to ensure that all voices are heard, or to create a safe environment in which students feel comfortable expressing their opinions and feelings, etc.).

During the first day of class, you can divide the students into small groups. Each group can brainstorm ground rules for 10 minutes. Afterwards, write down some ideas generated by each group. From there, students vote by raising hands on whether or not they would like to include the rules suggested. To make students feel that the discussion rules are permanent, once all the rules are voted on and finalized, you can invite volunteers to develop a poster with the rules. Hang the rules in the classroom. You could also have all students sign the poster, kind of like a contract. Next, you and the students need to determine an appropriate "punishment" for breaking any of the ground rules. A few ideas of punishments include: (a) marking down participation grades, (b) making students sing a song of their choice, (c) having a jar of pennies that, when totally filled, means the students receive some kind of reward, but when students disregard the ground rules, pennies are removed. It will be helpful to review the ground rules before beginning any discussion. The teacher must be the referee. In some highly functioning groups, students and participants can take turns being the referee, themselves. It is very important that, regardless of who enforces them, the ground rules are followed.

If even once a teacher lets some participants get away with being disrespectful of others, that participant will shut down and blame the teacher for not maintaining safety. This then breaks the carefully built trust and the willingness to be open is lost. And how should a teacher respond if the teacher realizes that he or she failed to uphold a rule? Depending on the nature or seriousness of the failure, the teacher can respond accordingly. For example, if there is one student who constantly interrupts others, and the teacher does not rein that student in, perhaps the next day before beginning class discussion the teacher can apologize for this mistake and ask that all students listen quietly and respectfully while others are speaking. This time around, it will be extremely important for the teacher to actually hold students accountable for this behavior. However, if a teacher allows a student to make generalizations about groups (even groups with which they belong) during a class discussion, this could lead to a very emotionally unsafe environment for others. A teacher's method of apology will have to match the severity of their failure. Perhaps the teacher, like Patrick (one of the teachers I interviewed), did not want to "squash" anyone's feelings. Still, this is not acceptable. The teacher may feel free to demonstrate a bit of their thinking and vulnerability to the students— perhaps by explaining that their desire to not hurt anyone's feelings prevented them from stepping in, but that after some reflection they have realized this was the wrong course of action. The teacher will then need to explain why this kind of behavior is counter-productive to the goals of the dialogue, and what kinds of punishment will be in store for those who break this rule. Again, after this apology, the teacher will have to be extremely careful to follow through. If the teacher loses the trust of their students too many times, it will be challenging to regain it. This is why one of the foundational elements of setting successful ground rules is modeling the appropriate behavior to students.

The second recommendation in classroom management is modeling for students how to behave and interact during dialectics. In reflecting on his own struggles with holding dialogues in his classroom, Patrick made the following suggestions: "… number one is modeling it. I think it is very important, any type of behavioral change or any kind of respect that you expect from students, you have to model it yourself." Modeling is the best strategy to teach students how to participate in a dialogue. Displaying behaviors such as the following will allow students to mimic the teachers' actions and will lead to enhancing dialectical thinking and facilitate a democratic classroom environment: (a) respect, (b) trust, (c) active listening, (d) understanding, (e) tolerance, and (f) reasonableness. For example, during a dialogue, if a student says something like, "I am afraid of Muslims because all of the terrorist attacks we see on T.V.," a teacher can paraphrase in respectful terms what this student has said very respectfully. The teacher could respond by saying the following:

> Thank you for sharing your feelings. The threat of terrorism is a very real and scary thing. However, most Muslims are not terrorists, and it can be very scary for them for you to associate their religion with acts of violence. Remember how in our ground rules we all agreed to not make generalizations of groups? [at this point the teacher can decide if there needs to be some kind of punishment for the student] Now, what I hear you saying is that you are scared because of the images you see on T.V., and I think that is an excellent point. Can you explain to us a little further what exactly you mean by that?

In this way, the teacher immediately and forcefully responds to the disrespectful speech, but gives the student an opportunity to feel like they still are a contributing member of the discussion.

Part of modeling also includes teachers showing their human side, the side of them that exists outside of the classroom. Sharing their passions, goals, and other life pursuits in a positive way can encourage students to share more of themselves personally, and demonstrate the diversity of experiences and values present in the classroom, hopefully leading to greater appreciation of this diversity (Kohl, n.d.). I personally show my students my computer graphic artwork to demonstrate to them my passions and encourage students to share with me their own hobbies and personal development goals. Modeling also includes sharing stories about times when one has felt scared or confused, especially if we ask students to share their experiences with similar situations. This reciprocal vulnerability allows all involved to go deeper, share more. Laughing with students, smiling often, sitting next to them, encouraging them, attending events they invite us to or writing letters in their support all serve to demonstrate that the teacher is personally invested in the student. In all cases, showing our human side connects us teachers with our students on a personal level, which fosters a safe classroom environment based on respect, collaboration, and community building.

Dialectics must involve participants with diverse opinions. Otherwise, if all members agree on the same issue, the conversation cannot be considered dialectical. However, to truly participate in a dialectic, all participants must be willing to share their perspectives, become open to new knowledge, and be flexible with their ideas upon learning new information. When peers share their experiences in a classroom setting, theories at this point become less abstract. Instead, this might connect concepts to lived experiences and show practical application of theories, leading participants to new realizations. In this case, dialogue has the potential to encourage understanding of different perspectives and empathy with others. Mastering dialectics can help teachers sail with their students on an emotional and intellectual journey through minimization of the choppiness often present in classrooms that do not prioritize diversity of thought.

Step 2: Unveiling Reality

> When you teach AP, you want them to be successful on this test at the end of the year, so you can't spend too much time on the detail sometimes. (Linda, personal communication, May 29, 2010)

Many teachers, including Linda, prioritize teaching for students' success on state exams. But this might mean excluding discussion of current events (i.e., reality) and other topics not included in the exam. For many teachers, this is a great source of frustration. You probably have tons of great ideas of other ways to teach your students, yet, because of time constraints, there are so few minutes during the class period to actually utilize any of them. However, through savvy organization, a critical teacher can incorporate educating students about the world around them.

A critical teacher sees that his or her role as a member of society is to educate themselves not only about subject matters such as math, science, language arts, and social studies, but also about the systems and structures of power that sustain inequality. Freire (1970) and other pioneers in critical pedagogy have argued that the educational system plays an important role in the reproduction of inequality in society. Cultural and ideological mechanisms at schools reproduce inequality through re-creation and distribution of cultural capital, selective tradition, and cultural and ideological hegemony. In order to understand how schools reproduce and distribute cultural capital, teachers must analyze the systems of schools and the ways they reproduce hegemony, ideology, and selective tradition in relation to one another in the current context of a post-9/11 world (Apple, 2004). All the activities and recommendations in this chapter are designed to help teachers rethink these terms and draw connections between them towards unraveling reality. The next few paragraphs will be devoted to teachers of education who seek to develop critical awareness of reality among their students.

For teachers and professors of education: in your Diversity in the Classroom courses, Inclusion in Education courses, or Social Justice and Education courses, the following tools and strategies may be useful to you. For example, professors of education could have their students, soon-to-be teachers, read part of Linda Steet's (2000) book, *Veils and Daggers: A Century of National Geographic's Representation of the Arab World*, in which she analyzes the biased presentation of Arab people in *National Geographic* for the past 100 years since the magazine began in the late 1800s. Before reading the book, ask soon-to-be teachers to reflect on what they think about when they hear the words "veils" and "daggers" in association with the Middle East? What do these symbols represent? After reading the book, reflect again on what they think of veils and daggers? Is the representation of the Arab world in the book different from what they had originally thought, and why do they think so? Do they believe the perceptions of the author of the book, or their original perceptions, or are they now somewhere in the middle, and why? How might these historic representations of the Arab world have influenced the soon-to-be teachers understanding of present-day Arab societies? How might these representations of Muslim women lead to hegemony? Professors of education could also have their students reflect on what they think about Muslim women's *hijab*. Professors can ask their students: What does this religious symbol represent?

Through deep questioning of assumptions, professors and students of education can begin the life-long process of evaluating perceptions. However, for a classroom to unravel reality together, students and teachers must be comfortable enough with one another to collaboratively and reciprocally question the ideas and biases within themselves. As such, teachers must be trained to establish non-hierarchical relationships with students.

For high school teachers hoping to develop critical awareness of reality among their students, the above technique could be modified to suit their classroom, or other, slightly easier methods could be used. For example, high school students could watch the video, "Listening to the Voices from the Hijabi World" (Winokur, 2016). After watching the video, have students reflect again on what they think of the *hijab*. Ask students if their ideas about Muslim women changed after watching the video? If yes, in what ways; if no, why not? How might new understandings of Muslim women influence the soon-to-be teachers' understanding of present-day Muslim societies? How might this new knowledge affect their perceptions of and relationship with their Muslim students? Creating opportunities for students to check their assumptions by looking at the world through a different lens is critical for both professors of education, as well as high school teachers.

Step 3: Minimizing Hierarchy

While teachers can and should keep some power as the head of the classroom, especially when it comes to refereeing ground rules, it is important that teachers do not wield their power in a dictatorial way. As Freire once said, truly liberational pedagogies are dialogical, and subvert the teacher-student hierarchy, so that not only do students learn from their teachers, but so do teachers learn from their students. Delivering a one sided-lecture, or talking down to students because of their alternative ideas or backgrounds, or treating students as empty receptors needing to be filled with the teacher's knowledge are not traits of a critical teacher. Instead, a critical teacher tries to do the following: (a) understand students' backgrounds with an eye of openness, respect and curiosity (b) value all their students equally, (c) facilitate discussions that appreciate all students' opinions, and (d) look for ways for deep collaboration among and with students, ways that dissolve the teacher-student hierarchy while at the same time maintaining respect among all participants. These underlying values will guide the teacher's actions, some examples of which are given in the following paragraph.

Key to enacting the underlying values mentioned above is through collaborating with students, as if on the same team. For example, teachers can start every curricular unit or theme with a survey through which they can learn about students' prior knowledge and areas of curiosity about the topic. This will help teachers to design human-centered curriculum and classroom activities based on students' prior knowledge and interests. In the questionnaire, teachers can ask questions such as: "What do you know about (this topic)?" or "What would you like to learn about (this topic)?" By asking such questions, the teacher treats students not as empty receptors, but as individuals with background knowledge. This contributes to a respectful relationship between the teacher and students, and encourages students' interest in a topic and in learning. Students will often feel that they are co-developing the curriculum, thereby nourishing their own self-directed curiosities. The teacher could collect student questionnaires with their suggestions of topics and methods, and input the data in a graph. Teachers can then bring the graph to class for analysis. Students can critically reflect on their answers and take votes on which topics to include in the curriculum. The votes could be calculated by students either raising their hands or through a survey based on the Likert scale stating each topic and asking students to select a response of either "strongly agree, agree, neutral, disagree, or strongly disagree." Based on the results of the votes, the teacher will develop the curriculum. This facilitates a democratic classroom environment, and demonstrates that the teacher is not all-knowing and all-powerful, but rather a facilitator of an egalitarian space. This breaks down the classroom hierarchy and helps students feel that they work together with the teacher in the pursuit of knowledge. Collaborating with students to achieve critical thinking requires establishing a nonhierarchical classroom environment. In turn, a nonhierarchical relationship between teachers and students supports the development of a safe space in which all can evaluate their own actions, and the actions of others in what Freire would call praxis.

Step 4: Focusing on Praxis (Reflection + Action)

Many teachers demonstrate elements of problem-posing or banking education, but the question they need to figure out is to what end do they teach? Banking education resists dialogue, inhibits creativity, and prevents people from recognizing oppression, and therefore results in students incapable of understanding the world or transforming it. On the other hand, problem-posing education encourages dialogue, "bases itself on creativity and stimulates true reflection and action upon reality" (Freire, 1970, p. 84) and therefore, results in an understanding of the world and people's agency in transforming it. Its gains are felt not only by a privileged few but by the entire society. When a teacher awakens to a more critical method of teaching, they may often develop objectives that go beyond teaching rote memorization and regurgitation of subject matter topics. As teachers move along the spectrum from uncritical to critical, their motivations for teaching may likely change.

Part of encouraging this shift is the development of praxis, the process of reflection and action. Professors training future teachers must encourage this process, and there are many ways to do so. For example, inspired by John Dewey's (2015) *My Pedagogic Creed*, students studying to become teachers could write a three to five page reflective paper examining the theories and beliefs they hold that influence their pedagogic practices and, in turn, shape society. The goal of the paper would be to help soon-to-be-teachers reflect on the influence of their beliefs about the role of education and schools on their teaching, students' learning, and curriculum choices, and to discover their role in impacting society through their teaching. The reflective paper should address the following issues: (a) what is education?, (b) what is school?, (c) what is the curriculum?, (d) what is teaching?, (e) what is learning?, (f) what is assessment?, (g) why do I personally teach?, (h) how does what I teach impact society and social progress? Once these students become teachers, it is useful to conduct this activity once a year. It is best if teachers keep their responses to these questions in a Word document so that they might compare how their philosophies change over the years, and why.

Most teachers go through a process of organic development in which they demonstrate an acquirement of technical skills. The development of techniques such as efficiency in using classroom time and materials, compelling and informative lectures, and effective assessment methods and strategies, often develop organically over the years. However, "good teaching cannot be reduced to techniques" but rather "good teaching comes from the identity and integrity of the teacher" (Palmer, 2007, p. 10). To teach beyond technique requires self-awareness, and strength of character. Dewey (1916) for instance, insisted that the role of education is to develop students' social and psychological skills in addition to demonstrating to students how they can utilize their own skills, ability, and role in society to potentially address social problems (1916). In that sense, how can a teacher guide students to realize their abilities and their role in the world without understanding their own inner selves? Freire (1998) insisted that, "I cannot be a teacher if I do not perceive with ever greater clarity that my practice demands of me a definition about where I stand" (p. 93). To lead students in bettering themselves and society not only requires self-knowledge, but also integrity (Palmer, 2007). To have integrity means to have morals and take actions based on these morals when one encounters challenging life events. When the self is "inwardly integrated," the teacher is "able to make the outward connections on which good teaching depends" (Palmer, 2007, p. 16). When teachers understand themselves and decide to teach based on their principles and with a sense of integrity, they will move beyond mere technique to finding ways to use their power as an educator to encourage change within society.

Training teachers to have better self-awareness and integrity is an important step in developing critical teachers. Some examples of methods for doing so are having teachers-to-be read Chapter 3 of Erich Fromm's (1990) *Man For Himself* about the five types of character, which he describes as an individual's relationship with the world: (a) The Receptive Orientation; which depends upon and constantly needs support from others, The Exploitive Orientation; a character willing to manipulate others to obtain what it wants, (b) The Hoarding Orientation; cares about gathering material possessions and cares less about people, (c) The Marketing Orientation; evaluates relationships based on what they can get in exchange, (d) and The Productive Orientation; a character able to channel all its energies and feelings (including negative ones) into productive work. All of these "orientations" represent aspects of identity that are created through choice. Future teachers could fill out a Fromm's orientation test online to understand the characteristics that define each orientation. This self-awareness of their personalities can support the individual in developing greater self-awareness on their teaching.

Self-awareness of one's teaching can often be spurred through analysis of books, television, and movies about teachers. Teachers can then evaluate the characters in the books and films based on their level of integrity. Some great novels include: *Goodbye, Mr. Chips* by James Hilton (2013) or *Three Cups of Tea* by Greg Mortenson and David Oliver Relin (2007). Movies that might spur some great thought among teachers include: *Stand and Deliver* (1988), *Dangerous Minds* (1995), and *Chalk* (2007). Then students in the education course could analyze and categorize the characters of the teachers in the novels or movies based on Fromm's models by answering the question: What type of character does the teacher fall under? They could then compare their analysis of the characters and write a reflective paper about which character they feel is similar to their own. The other aspect of the analysis includes evaluating teacher integrity using the following leading questions: (a) do the teachers in the movies or novels have morals?, (b) have the teachers in the movies or books encountered situations that challenged their integrity?, (c) have they done something against their principles?, (d) how have they handled it?, (e) were the teachers honest, or have they lied?, (f) have they betrayed anyone?, (g) have they taken something that belonged to someone else?, (h) how have they treated strangers or people different from themselves?, (i) if the teachers disagreed with someone, how have they treated them?, (j) have they done something that upheld their principles despite the unpopularity of this decision?, (k) how have teachers in the movie or novel earned someone's trust? Afterward, soon-to-be teachers can answer the questions themselves and then write a reflective paper comparing the morals of the teachers in the movies and novels with their own by adding a reflection to the following question: What would you have done differently in a similar situation? Why? Evaluating praxis should not be limited to self-reflection, or evaluating those who are educators, but should extend to the world. The following paragraph explains how teachers and students can evaluate praxis of what they see around them.

It is especially important to evaluate the praxis of others by observing and analyzing the words and deeds of people and institutions in power. This is an important element of critical dialectical pedagogy (CDP) and should become an objective for critical teachers because it helps unveil the credibility and sincerity of public figures and the public policies and institutions that are created by these individuals. Analyzing the words and deeds of politicians and policies in the War on Terror help teachers look for different motives than those explicitly stated. Through questioning underlying assumptions and assessing how much individuals or institutions words do or do not align with their actions, teachers and students unveil the world around them, reflect upon oppressive elements within the situation, and act based on a new understanding of reality. For example, George seemed wary of politicians and political motives in the War on Terror, and advised his students to listen to political figures with trepidation, saying the following:

> Hopefully students come out of such an experience with the wariness of listening to politicians and a concern for trying to probe further any time a politician tries to make—offer a simple explanation for a complex event or complex problem, and to be weary of such analysis. ... They are not just there to inform, they are there to call people to action, or to call them to inaction, perhaps, from dealing with civil liberties and Constitutional guarantees.... (personal communication, June 5, 2010)

There are many ways students can be trained to evaluate praxis. For example, Bill and Cain co-interrogated with students the praxis of powerful institutions through a close read of the Constitution and an analysis of Supreme Court decisions. Students left Bill and Cain's class able to argue and defend their opinions. Another project that engages students in evaluating the praxis of people and institutions in power is to evaluate the alignment, or lack thereof, between words and deeds among public figures. Specifically, soon-to-be teachers or high school students could be divided into groups, and each group could research a politician from one of four different parties. Some examples include: Hillary Clinton from the Democratic party, Donald Trump from the Republican Party, Jill Stein from the Green Party, and Gary Johnson from the Libertarian Party. Have students research the consistency between the views and actions of these politicians and whose political views have contributed to the creation of laws. If there are laws, regulations, etc. that have been passed through the encouragement of these political figures, ask soon-to-be teachers to analyze the effects of these laws. As a class, compare and contrast the findings and analyze which politicians were consistent in their views and actions, which politicians' views were successful in being transformed into law, and some of the consequences of legislating such views. Finally, ask students to write a reflective piece on what they learned from the findings and how an inconsistency between words and actions in a political figure such as the President of the United States might impact American society? Are there any circumstances in which inconsistency between words and actions in a political figure would be justified? Praxis starts with reflecting upon the character and integrity of the individual and society, and it often leads to new realizations, including one's potential to change their situation and society.

Step 5: Teachers Helping Students to Realize That They Are the Agents of History

When people develop a new worldview through unveiling reality, often they feel inspired to change their actions to follow suit. There are teachers of education at teacher-training colleges and universities who think of their students as vessels to be filled with information provided by the teacher, then to be dumped onto school exams and re-filled again by the next unit. On the other hand, there are teachers who believe in the abilities of their students—who are, in fact, our future teachers—to become writers of history and agents of change. The first methodology would result in irresponsible teacher-citizens who are unaware of reality and their place and contributions to the world, while the second methodology results in responsible teacher-citizens who better their communities and classrooms. If the teacher wants to prepare new teachers for the school and the world, and the hope that they might make both better, those who train future teachers must help these young adults realize their power.

It is important to encourage students to share their opinions and beliefs on a broader stage than the classroom. For example, encouraging students or soon-to-be-teachers to participate in city-wide or regional Slam Poetry events in which they can share their personal and political beliefs, or to volunteer with organizations that support a cause or issue they care about. In my own "Diversity in the United States" course, I engage my students in a forum that they plan, organize, and lead called "Knowledge to Action: Where Do We Go from Here?" Leveraging the public speaking skills we developed in my classroom, students facilitate the same reflection and dialogue among their peers. One semester, students presented on five local organizations—Kids Food Basket, Salvation Army, Metron of Lamont Nursing Home, God's Kitchen, and Holland Rescue Mission—connecting class readings to the work of social organizations. This methodology encourages students to connect research to real world issues, see issues from multiple perspectives, and communicate, therefore equipping them to both continue learning autonomously, and apply their knowledge for the better of society. Other ideas to help students learn by doing include visiting a refugee camp. There are no camps in New Mexico since Governor, Susana Martinez was among those non-accepting Syrian refugees in their states. However, there is a refugee camp in Grand Rapids with Bethany Christian Services. By visiting the refugee camp, students could observe the living conditions, interview refugees about their stories, and volunteer to help refugees. In my Gender Studies course, I noticed that my students felt disturbed by the fact that Michigan is the second state in sex trafficking of minors in the United States. Consequently, the students collaborated with local organization such as The Manasseh Project, Women At Risk International, and International Justice Mission to plan and organize an event called "Educate to Save: Stopping West Michigan Sex Traffic." The students even wrote a letter to the governor of Michigan, Rick Snyder, to let him know we are following the progress of the government's procedures in handling the issue. All of these are clear examples of how teachers can demonstrate to their students the importance and efficacy of personal involvement in the making and shaping of history.

Conclusion

Many teachers including the ones in this study realize the importance as well as the difficulty of teaching about current events such as 9/11 and the War on

Terror. Nevertheless, they also expressed their thirst for new and more critical ways to teach about these topics. Teachers face limited time in the school year and the pressure to equip students with information included in state exams. This chapter is tailored specifically to address these challenges. Teachers need to know, however, that without risk, nothing will be accomplished. As Mohamed Ali once said: "He who is not courageous enough to take risks will accomplish nothing in life." Teachers who participated in this study were willing to take the risk of potential backlash for talking to a Muslim educator about how to improve the cultural sensitivity of their pedagogy for the betterment of society. The question is, will you join them?

To change things for the better requires self-reflection on what a person can do to succeed in accomplishing their goals. Once the actions are identified, then it becomes clear, if not always easy, how to work to fix them. In regards to teachers who hope to teach critically about 9/11 and the War on Terror, the lopsided dialectic that is overwhelmingly pervasive makes it hard for many teachers, including those who consider themselves critical, to understand reality and teach against faulty public pedagogy. Consequently, the path of least resistance sometimes seems like the safest way to go. But upholding the lopsided dialectic and strengthening Islamophobia is not safe because it leads to intolerance in the classroom, dehumanization of Muslims, and ultimately destruction of true democratic values in society.

But it is never too late to change. The fight for democracy is happening now and we, critical pedagogues, need teachers to join our efforts. I suggest Critical Dialectical Pedagogy (CDP) as the best solution for teachers to counter the lopsided dialectic in regards to 9/11 and the War on Terror. CDP is part of a diverse web of teaching methods used by critical pedagogues to develop critical thinking skills among their students. CDP is most useful for teachers who recognize the unfair stereotyping visited upon Muslim students, Muslim American citizens, and Muslims across the globe, and seeks to rectify it. By avoiding binary-style thinking, CDP calls for embracing a dialectical pedagogy that commends diversity and complexity through examining all logical perspectives on a current event. Critical Dialectical Pedagogy focuses on current events—in terms of what is happening in society, not just what's hot on the news—as a means to understand reality. Through calling upon the power of teachers everywhere, CDP posits that through small steps, teachers can and will contribute to a renovation of true democratic values in society.

Teachers need to develop three aspects of their teaching; (1) the art of dialectics, (2) critical skills, and (3) lesson plans that incorporate CDP while also meeting state standards. Mastering the art of dialectics requires classroom management skills, dialogue facilitation, a clear understanding that the end goal of the conversation is a collective pursuit of truth. To become critical themselves, teachers must focus their energy to improve upon four areas— unveiling the truth, diminishing hierarchy, developing praxis, and recognizing that individuals are agents of history rather than mere viewers of it. Finally, teachers must apply these critical thinking and dialectical skills to the classroom. That is why the next chapter provides actionable lesson plans to help teachers jump-start their teaching on current events such as 9/11 and the War on Terror in a critical way within the broader state standards benchmarks.

References

Anderson, L. W., & Krathwohl, D. R. (Eds.). (2000). *A taxonomy for learning, teaching, and assessing: A revision of bloom's taxonomy of educational objectives* (abridged edition). Hoboken, NJ: Pearson.

Apple, M. (2004). *Ideology and curriculum.* New York, NY: Routledge Falmer.

Apple, M. (2013). *Can education change society?* New York, NY: Routledge.

Armstrong, T. (2009). *Multiple intelligences in the classroom* (3rd ed.). Alexandria, VA: Association for Supervision & Curriculum Development.

Bradford, L. P. (n.d.). Before we can have a discussion about facilitating, we must first have an understanding of the dialogue process. *Wellesley College.* Retrieved October 14, 2016 from http://www.wellesley.edu/religiouslife/resources/east/publication/diversitykit/dialogue/facilitatorsguide#YSUjzspybhK95X2b.97

Dalton, J., & Smith, D. (1986). *Extending children's special abilities: Strategies for primary classrooms.* Melbourne: Melbourne Curriculum Branch, Schools Division.

Dewey, J. (1916). *Democracy and education: An introduction to the philosophy of education.* New York, NY: The Free Press.

Dewey, J. (2015). *My pedagogic creed.* New York, NY: Scholar's Choice.

Eberly Center for Teaching Excellence: Ground Rules. (n.d.). *Carnegie Mellon University.* Retrieved September 29, 2016 from https://www.cmu.edu/teaching/solveproblem/strat-dontparticipate/groundrules.pdf

Freire, P. (1970). *Pedagogy of the oppressed.* New York, NY: Herder & Herder.

Freire, P. (1998). *Pedagogy of freedom: Ethics, democracy, and civic courage.* Lanham, MD: Rowman & Littlefield.

Fromm, E. (1990). *Man for himself: An inquiry into the psychology of ethics.* New York, NY: Henry Holt & Company.

Gardner, H. (2011). *Frames of mind: The theory of multiple intelligences.* New York, NY: Basic Books.

Goodwin, D. K. (2006). *Team of rivals: The political genius of Abraham Lincoln.* New York, NY: Simon & Schuster.

Hilton, J. (2013). *Goodbye Mr Chips.* Create Space Independent Publishing Platform.

Kohl, S. (n.d.). Modeling positive behavior in the classroom. *National Education Association (NEA).* Retrieved September 29, 2016 from http://www.nea.org/tools/52062.htm#1

Leo, J. R., Giroux, H. A., McClennen, S. A., & Saltman, K. J. (2013). *Neoliberalism, education, and terrorism: Contemporary dialogues.* London: Paradigm Publishers.

Menéndez, R. (Director), & Musca, T. (Producer). (1988). *Stand and deliver* [Motion picture].

Mortenson, G., & Relin, D. O. (2007). *Three cups of tea: One man's mission to promote peace—one school at a time.* New York, NY: Penguin Books.

Nikulin, D. (2010). *Dialectic and dialogue.* Stanford, CA: Stanford University Press.

Palmer, P. J. (2007). *The courage to teach: Exploring the inner landscape of a teacher's life.* San Francisco, CA: Jossey-Bass.

Schremmer, T. (Actor), & Akel, M. (Director). (2007). *Chalk* [Motion picture].

Smith, J. N. (Director), & Pfeiffer, M. (Actor). (1995). *Dangerous minds* [Motion picture].

Steet, L. (2000). *Veils and daggers: A century of the National Geographic's representations of the Arab world.* Philadelphia, PA: Temple University Press.

Winokur, J. (2016, August 8). Listening to the voices from Hijabi World. *The New York Times.* Retrieved September 29, 2016 from http://lens.blogs.nytimes.com/2016/08/08/listening-to-the-voices-from-hijabi-world/?_r=0

· 9 ·

THINKING CRITICALLY IS NOT ENOUGH

Through training future teachers how to master dialectics, unveil reality, minimize hierarchy, study praxis, and demonstrate that students can be agents of change, these future teachers will be equipped to teach in a critical and thoughtful way. However, in order to rectify the lopsided dialectic about 9/11 and the War on Terror, it is not enough to merely teach in a critical way. The teacher must also strategically address the uneven conversation itself with smart, well-planned, and dialectical lessons and activities. It is important to remember that it is not just dialogue that needs to be dialectical, but also methods of instruction (such as experiential learning, role-playing, and engaging multiple intelligences), as well as dialectical resources (movies, books, etc.). The following section of this chapter proposes actionable lesson plans teachers can use to achieve a more holistic conversation in their classrooms specifically about 9/11 and the War on Terror.

The activities provided in this section fulfill New Mexico's state standards, and likely meet state standards across the United States. State Standards are often vague, but teachers should not feel frustrated because such ambiguity allows for great flexibility. For instance, most of the lesson plan suggested in the following section fit under sub-categories 9G & 9J for benchmark I-C of grade 9–22 NM social studies standards. The Benchmarks read: "International developments following World War II, the Cold War, and post-Cold War, to include" and the two sub-categories read: "national security in the changing world order"; and "new threats to peace" ("Social Studies Standards Grade 9–22," 2009). Though these are New Mexico state standards, teachers can often tweak the activities to meet standards of their own states.

Lesson Plans to Dialectically Teach about Current Events

A major part of CDP is considering the practical application of critical pedagogy theory. The next section in this chapter tackles that major question—what can teachers actually do to make a difference? The answer is to teach, for embedded within this noble profession there are so many opportunities for change, and changing people's minds. Exposing teachers and students to more holistic dialectics of 9/11 and the War on Terror includes the following: (a) through greater knowledge of Muslims, (b) media analysis, (c) economic analysis, (d) textual analysis, (e) historical analysis, (f) legal analysis, and (g) deep self-reflection. Paired with actionable lesson plans for sharing this content with students, teachers can teach more critically about these current events and support the development of democratic values. All it takes is a little research and a willingness to believe in the power of provocation for stirring up assumptions for re-examination. For that purpose, the following section will walk through some lesson plans teachers and education professors can use to increase understanding both within high school classrooms, and a college-level setting where future teachers receive their training.

Greater Knowledge of Muslims

A key component to CDP is greater knowledge of Muslims through which teachers and high school students must learn about the diversity of Muslim societies, be exposed to the real teachings of Islam, and connect with positive examples of Muslims either in society or in their communities. Many Muslim American students believed that Americans who have no contact with Muslims develop negative perceptions about them. For example, Mary insisted that educated Americans don't think that Muslims are terrorists, "especially if they know Muslims or have Muslim friends or have encountered Muslims, they would definitely not talk like that about Muslims." Similarly, Linda remarked that, "we don't have enough contact with Muslim people." She also told me that since teachers "don't teach Eastern civilization as much," Islam and Muslims end up becoming "something that Americans aren't comfortable with ..." The following section will provide some ideas for how to improve this situation. If a teacher doesn't have any Muslim students in his or her classroom, perhaps they could find one in another classroom and ask the student to come and speak openly to his or her class.

Learn about the Teachings of Islam. It is impossible for anyone have an informed opinion about 9/11 and the War on Terror as it relates to Muslims, if they have no idea what Islam is all about. Therefore, teaching students and teachers about Islam is key, and there are many ways to do this. For example, I learned from Bridget, one of the Muslim American students I interviewed, that there is a teacher's institute called Dar Al Islam in New Mexico that sponsors the attendance of non-Muslims in an Islam Education workshop for two weeks in the summer. Interested teachers may apply online. The institute pays teachers to attend this training as a way to educate Americans about basic Islam and defy misconceptions.

There are some general religious beliefs that teachers can share with students. For example, Muslims believe that Allah is the only god and Prophet Mohammed is his messenger. Islam has 4 basic tenets—Doctrines, Rituals, Ethics and Legislation—which govern spiritual and daily life. Islamic Doctrine is built on the belief that there is only one god worthy of worship, Allah. Islamic Doctrine also specifies belief in the Qu'ran, the day of Judgment, and the Qadar (Allah's divine decree). The Rituals include the daily prayers, fasting, giving alms, and pilgrimage. Islamic Ethics encourage high moral character, such as treating oneself, people, animals, and the natural environment with kindness and love. The Sharia'a law (Islamic Legislation) includes laws and regulations that govern the individual and the society in an Islamic community. In non-Muslim societies, Islamic adherents follow local government laws unless asked to do un-Islamic activities from which they should then refrain without causing disorder. The following paragraphs will go into greater detail about other aspects of Muslims lives and the truth about what Islam expects of its adherents.

Intercultural Exchange between Muslims and Students: Classroom Visits and Interviews. Teachers can invite Muslim students, leaders, or community members to come and talk to their classroom about Islam and Muslims. Students may ask such questions as to how negative representations affect these Muslim speakers, or the repercussions of 9/11 security policies on their lives. Additionally, students may ask the Muslim Americans how 9/11 has impacted their sense of belonging. It would be important to prep students with a basic understanding of the controversies surrounding the Patriot Act. Students could also interview Muslim Americans and write a biographical sketch or report.

Finally, if there are no Muslims available near you to speak about their personal experiences, the transcripts of this book are an excellent resource. Another useful classroom tool for prompting these dialogues are the, "What Would You Do? Anti-Muslim Harassment" YouTube videos and the ABC News story, "Would You Stop Muslim Discrimination?" These videos feature actors who pretend to discriminate against Muslims and Muslim Americans, recording the reactions of people around them.

Connect with your State or City Islamic Center. There are men and women dedicated to educating non-Muslims about Islam nationally and locally. This shows that Muslims are humans just like everyone else, and offers a sharp counterpoint to the negative media representations of Muslims. The reasons behind the contradiction between the reality of Muslims' lived experiences and the often negative and one-sided media portrayals need to be discussed within the classroom.

Teach Students that Muslims and Arabs are Different. Once teachers learn more about Islam, they can begin to dispel some common myths among their students. One of the most pervasive myths is that Arabs and Muslims are the same. An Arab speaks Arabic, lives in an Arabic speaking country, and upholds Arabic culture, according to the Arab League. The Arab World consists of 22 countries in the Middle East and North Africa including Egypt, Somalia, and Sudan. Most Arabs are Muslim (90%, in fact), but not all Muslims are Arabs. At least 92% of Muslims are Asian or African, according to a Pew Center Research Report (2012). Only 0.3% of the worlds' Muslim population live in North, South, and Central America. The social category "Muslim American" emerged only over the past few decades, rising to greater prominence post-9/11 (Sirin & Fine, 2008).

There are a variety of tools teachers can use in the classroom to educate students about the difference between Arabs and Muslims. First, it is helpful to begin by surveying the class to see what they think the differences are between the two. Ask students, "Are Muslims and Arabs the same? If not, what differentiates Muslims and Arabs?" To learn the truth, there is an engaging, funny, and high school age appropriate 2-minute clip on YouTube on the ADDtv channel called "What You Need to Know About Arabs vs. Muslims" (2012). Teachers could also pass out an article from *Muslim Voices*, called "Arabs and Islam: Are All Arabs Muslims?" This article, written by graduate student in the School of Journalism at Indiana University, Rosemary Pennington (2008), is a quick and simple read about the differences that teachers can easily incorporate into their classrooms. Teachers can then ask their students: Is the difference between a European and a Christian the same as the difference between an Arab and a Muslim? Why or Why not? Then, teachers could pass out maps for students to color in that include the Arab world (comprised of North Africa and the Middle East, and easily found in a quick Google search), and countries that have a majority of Muslims throughout the world. Students could color in Arab countries a particular color and predominantly Muslim countries a particular color to see the difference between the two. These tools would provide helpful visual tools in understanding that Arabs belong to a specific geographic region whereas Muslims are found across the globe.

Demonstrate that Many Muslim are U.S. Citizens or American-Born. Muslims are not new additions to the United States—they have been an integral part of its founding. It can be useful to recall with students that the United States is a nation founded by immigrants, and that Muslims have immigrated to the Americas legally for many generations. There are varying accounts of when the first Muslims came to the Americas. According to Haque (2004), and journalist Abdus Sattar Ghazali (2012), Chinese documents contain evidence of the landing of Chinese Muslim sailors on what is today the American west coast. History books record the first Muslim arrival in 1312, when the King of Mali, Mansa (King) Abu Bakr, travelled from Mali to the Americas with a fleet of 2,000 ships. Though the fleet was never heard from again, there is evidence of their arrival in North and South America. In Arizona, for example, an inscription written in Mandikan, a Malian language, was found (Nyang, 1999). Though these first arrivals are all speculative, there are many other accounts of early arrivals to the United States.

European Muslims and Muslim slaves were other early arrivals to the United States. The Moors, who were Muslim, ruled Spain and Portugal during the ninth and tenth centuries. The Moors traveled to the Americas and Africa two centuries prior to Columbus. Moors forced to leave Spain during Isabel and Ferdinand's reign in 1492 migrated to the Carolinas and Florida. It is believed that these early migrants were uneducated and were forced to convert to Christianity (Nyang, 1999). In the 1700s, slave ships sailed from West Africa to the United States carrying African Muslims. In fact, 20% of slaves brought to the Americas from Africa arrived as Muslims, though the religion was brutally suppressed, according to Peter Manseau (2015), a contributor to *The New York Times*. Many of these Muslims were forced to come to the United States against their own free will. However, beginning in the late nineteenth century, many Muslims chose to immigrate to a place they, and many others, considered a land of opportunity.

There have been three major waves of Arab and Muslim immigration in the United States. The first wave of Arab immigration to the United States occurred between 1875 and 1924, according to associate dean for faculty and academic affairs at Harvard Divinity School, Jane I. Smith (2000). An over-whelming majority of the immigrants came from the Ottoman province, now currently the countries of Syria, Lebanon, Israel, and Palestine. However, according to Naff (1993), during this wave of immigration, only 5–10% of Arab immigrants were Muslims. This first wave ended in 1924 with the Johnson-Reed Quota Act. This piece of legislation included a document called the Asian Exclusion Act that, true to its name, totally banned the immigration of Asians or Arabs. According to the U.S. Department of State's Office of the Historian, "... the most basic purpose of the 1924 Immigration Act was to preserve the ideal of U.S. homogeneity." In other words, there were to many non-white individuals being let into the country, and the U.S. wanted to stop that. However, like many others who came during the same time, the Arabs and Muslims who took their chances and moved to the United States believed that in this place anyone could pull themselves up by their boot-straps, regardless of their religion of the color of their skin.

These immigrants came to work, and even though the first wave ended abruptly, there were more waves of immigration to come. Many immigrants of this first wave were "attracted to the great booming Midwestern factories of steel, tin automobiles, and trains in cities such as Pittsburgh, New Castle, Detroit, and Michigan City" (Naff, 1993, p. 97). The second wave of immi-gration between 1940 and 1960 ushered in far more Muslim than Christian Arabs. Whereas 90% of first wave Arab immigrants professed Christianity, only 40% did so in the second (Orfalea, 2006, p. 153). Second-wave immi-gration remained limited due to the restrictive policies set in place at the end of the first wave. However, due to such conflicts as the 1948 Arab-Israeli war, and popular revolutions in countries like Syria, Egypt, and Iraq, many Muslims and Arabs of the educated and elite class fled to countries like the United States. This problem continues to occur, leading to what many refer to as a Middle Eastern brain-drain (Orfalea, 2006, p. 182). Not only eco-nomic opportunity, but political struggles, encouraged many well-established and educated Muslims to immigrate to the United States during this time. With the dawn of the 1960s and a rise in social consciousness, as evidenced through the Civil Rights movement, immigration policies became less restrictive based on race.

The third wave of Arabs and Muslims came after 1965, ushered in with the end of the Asian Exclusion Act, and the opening of immigration and naturalization that obliterated the quota system. This allowed a mixture of skilled and unskilled migrants to the United States. Additionally, the Green Card Lottery system established under the Immigration Act of 1990 offered visas to people from all over the world, allowing the migration of Muslims seeking better lives for their families. Among them were many poor, uneducated, and socially disadvantaged Muslims. For example, among them there were many Muslims fleeing civil wars, and refugees from countries such as Iraq, Lebanon, Somalia, and Palestine. There were also those seeking political asylum from autocratic regimes such as Algeria, Libya, and Tunisia. These individuals all became legal citizens of the United States, and their contributions have shaped our country, just as much as the opportunity to live in the U.S. has shaped them.

This history can be very powerful to share with students in the U.S., as most every student has a recent immigration story in their family ancestry. Teachers can ask students if they have immigrant parents, grandparents, great-grandparents? Ask students to define what it means to be an American, and if Muslims born in America fit this description. Ask students what percentage of Muslim Americans they believe are born in the United States. Then share with them that 37% of Muslim Americans are U.S. born, according to a study by The Pew Research Center in 2011. Ask students what percentage of Muslim Americans they think are U.S. citizens. Then, let them know that 90% are official citizens (Sirin & Fine, 2008). How might this change their perspective of treatment of Muslim Americans through the Patriot Act? Explaining to students the history of Muslim immigration to the United States is an important element of demonstrating that many Muslims are rightful U.S. citizens, too.

Demonstrate that Muslims Contribute Positively to Society. Seeing Muslims in a positive light, as opposed to a more negative one propagated more often by the media, students will begin to see Muslims from a different angle. Teachers can use many tools to teach students about prominent Muslims. These can include people such as the following: (a) the Egyptian American scientist Ahmed Zawail, who won the 1999 Nobel prize for chemistry and became known as the father of femtochemistry (a branch of chemistry that studies extremely fast chemical reactions); (b) Leila Ahmed, an Egyptian

American and well known feminist scholar who won the University of Lou-isville Grawemeyer Award in 2013 for her work related to the "veiling" of Muslim women in the United States; (c) Tawakol Abdel Salam Karman, a Yemeni journalist and co-recipient of the 2011 Nobel Peace Prize; (d) Ingrid Mattson, a professor of Islamic Studies and a well-known Muslim religious leader; (e) celebrity Muslim Americans, such as Ice Cube and Dr. Mehmet Oz, who are active contributors to American culture; (f) and social activists, such as Malcolm X, who demonstrate the role Islam has played in the Civil Rights movement. Teachers can also, or alternately, ask students to go out and find their own examples and report back to the class. In this scenario, ask students to bring examples of this individual's work for a kind of show-and-tell. Learn-ing about Muslims who have contributed positively to society expands the lopsided dialectic.

Demonstrate the Diversity of and within Muslim Societies. Muslims are socially, culturally, economically, and politically diverse. Culturally speaking, there are Muslims across the globe who speak various languages, eat different kinds of foods, and dress in different ways. Muslims speak many different lan-guages (such as Arabic, English, Hindi, and Urdu), and come from many dif-ferent countries. Teachers can share an article called "10 Countries with the Largest Muslim Population in the World" from *Malaysian Digest* (2015) with students. This article was written based on research conducted by the Pew Research Center in 2011, and provides a distilled and easier to read account of Muslim populations across the globe. Teachers can ask students to find images on-line of Muslims from these different countries, specifically looking at com-mon form of dress, food, homes, and general way of life. Teachers can ask stu-dents to dig deeper by comparing images of common form of dress for Muslim women in Saudi Arabia and those who are from Egypt. Teachers can also show different recipes, for example comparing foods from Pakistan and Indonesia. Listening to diverse music genres can also help students gain appreciation for the beauty and complexity within different cultures. Teachers can share music from Amr Diab, famous Egyptian singer, and Cheb Mami, a famous Algerian singer. These activities and more demonstrate to students how unique Muslim individuals are within this global religion.

This diversity is also evident within the United States. Islam is the most racially diverse religion in the United States, according to a Gallup Poll (Younis, 2009), with 28% Caucasian, 35% African American, 18% Asian, and a small but growing Hispanic population. Around 37% of Muslim Americans are U.S. born, however, more than 63% are either first or second generation immigrants with one or both parents born in foreign countries, and around 22% are either third or fourth generation, according to a survey conducted by The PEW Research Center in 2011. Muslim Americans come from at least 77 countries; the largest group is from Arab ancestry representing 26% of all Muslim Americans followed by South Asians who represent 16% of all U.S. Muslims. The rest are from sub-Saharan Africa, Europe, and elsewhere. The majority of Muslim Americans of all racial identities are Sunni while only an estimated 20% of Muslim Americans are Shiites (Haddad, Smith, & Moore, 2006). American Muslims are extremely diverse. However, this conversation about the difference between Sunni and Shiite deserves more attention, since their understanding and application of Islam differs greatly.

The most well-known distinction between Muslim religious belief is between Sunni and Shi'a Muslims. According to Sirin & Fine (2008), around 83% of Muslim's belong to one of four Sunni sects (Maliki, Shafi'I, Hanafi, and Hanbali), and a significantly smaller group belongs to one of three Shi'a sects (Jaffari, Ismailliyah, Alawite). Sunnis and Shi'as have battled since the death of Mohammed, even fighting wars that ended the lives of his grandchildren. Even though Sunni and Shi'as believe in the fundamental principles of Islam (that there is one God, Allah, and Mohammed is his prophet), Sunnis are more traditionalists in following the word of the Qur'an, and Shi'as rely more heavily on imams, or religious scholars, to interpret the Qur'an in a modern context (Sirin & Fine, 2008). Just as Christianity has many different sects, so, too, does Islam. There are also many different degrees of religiosity within Islam, just as within Christianity many individuals relate in varying ways to their faith. A great example of this is showing a video called "Laughs for Muslims" posted on *The Washington Post*. This 8-minute video about a comedy troupe called "The Muslims Are Coming!" is about the efforts of four American Muslims traveling the United States to discuss their faith. To return to the discussion of American Muslims, part of the reason for this great diversity has to do with conversions to the religion.

Many Americans over the years have converted to Islam. The estimated number of annual conversions is 25,000 with the ratio of women to men at 4:1. The first Americans to be attracted to Islam were African Americans who formed several organizations affiliated with Islam, the most well-known of which is the Nation of Islam founded in the 1940s (Haddad et al., 2006; Smith, 2000). To learn more about Blacks involved in Islam, teachers can share a 3 minute video through the PBS called Muslim Diversity (n.d.). While the video touches on important and informative topics, at one point the narrator mentions how Islam is a new religion in the United States. Ask students if they agree or disagree with this comment, and why? Another great resource is an article in the Washington Post called "Son's Muslim Faith Divides One Black Family," in which author, Lonnaei O'Neal Parker (2011), describes the experience of a young black man converting to Islam from Christianity. Finally, to understand the historic significance of The Nation of Islam on the Black community in the United States, it is especially useful for teachers to draw upon speeches given by Malcom X such as his famous speech after returning from Mecca (2011). Teachers can also excerpt sections of The Autobiography of Malcom X, by Alex Haley (1992). Teachers can ask students: (a) Why was Islam attractive to many Black leaders, such as Malcom X? (b) How are the struggles faced by Muslims and the struggles faced by Blacks similar and different?, (c) What challenges might Black Muslims face within culturally Arab communities in the United States, and why?

But Black Americans are not the only Americans to convert to Islam. In the 1960s, many American women in particular were attracted to Sufism, a mystical branch of Islam. There continue to be many American converts to Sufism today. Teachers can share this article, "Sufi Sect of Islam Draws 'Spiritual Vagabonds' in New York," posted in The New York Times (2016) that describes growing Sufism in the iconic American city. There are a growing number of Latino Muslim organizations in the United States, such as the Alianza Islámica, founded in 1975 by a group of Puerto Rican Islamic converts. Just as many individuals become Christian, Islam attracts many new converts every year, increasing the diversity of its followers.

Teachers can share this information with students in many ways. The most straightforward would be through a lecture format. Teachers could also create a jeopardy game in which students ask for "American Muslims for $300!" and so forth. This may be more engaging for students. Another critical element of discussing the diversity of Muslims is reinforcing over and over again that not all Muslims are terrorists.

Demonstrate that Islam does Not Teach Terrorism and Not All Muslims are Terrorists. Islam does not teach Muslims to be terrorists, and teachers should really stress this point in their classrooms. Share Christian, Muslim, and Judaic passages on peace, love and tolerance. Ask students to attribute the passages to one religion or the other. Demonstrate the similarities between the three religions and their fundamental beliefs. For example, teachers can compare passages on peace, love, and tolerance from the Old and New Testament of the Bible, and the Qu'ran as follows:

- "Humanity is but a single Brotherhood: So make peace with your brethren" (Qu'ran, 49:10).
- "We have appointed a law and a practice for every one of you. Had God willed, He would have made you a single community, but He wanted to test you regarding what has come to you. So compete with each other in doing good. Every one of you will return to God and He will inform you regarding the things about which you differed" (Qu'ran, Surat al-Ma'ida, 48).
- "And walk not the earth with conceit and arrogance" (Qu'ran, al-Isra, 17:37)."But the fruit of the Spirit is love, joy, peace, patience, kindness, goodness, faithfulness" (Gal., 5:22).
- "But the wisdom from above is first pure, then peaceable, gentle, open to reason, full of mercy and good fruits, impartial and sincere" (the Bible, James, 3:17).
- "Be of the persecuted, rather than the persecutor." (Talmud, Bava Kama, 93a)
- "The wolf will live with the lamb, the leopard will lie down with the goat, the calf and the lion and the yearling together; and a little child will lead them. The cow will feed with the bear, their young will lie down together, and the lion will eat straw like the ox. The infant will play near the hole of the cobra, and the young child put his hand into the viper's nest. They will neither harm nor destroy on all my holy mountain, for the earth will be full of the knowledge of the Lord as the waters cover the sea" (Jewish Messianism, Isaiah, 11:6–9).

Teachers can also demonstrate how religious leaders from non-Muslim groups acknowledge the difference between the faith and violence. Pope Francis is a wonderful example. Teachers can have students read an article on National Public Radio called "Pope Francis says it is wrong to identify Islam with violence." In this article, Pope Francis says that the real cause of terrorism is caused by the idolatry of wealth. Ask students: (a) Do you believe this is true, why or why not?, (b) What role might greed play in the development of terrorism?, (c) What are some other instances in which lack of money or financial desperation indirectly or directly leads to violence? Understanding other causes of terrorism—besides religion—can help students disassociate the two. Then students can read a short article from National Public Radio entitled "Should the Phrase 'Islamic Extremism' Be Used? It's Debatable." In this article, the author, Jessica Taylor, writes about the challenges of describing terrorist groups such as ISIS/ISIL as Islamic. Teachers can ask students: (a) Is it fair to call these groups Islamic—why or why not?, (b) In what ways do these groups represent the true nature of their religion?, (c) What can political leaders in the United States do to refer to these groups in a fair way? These questions can call attention to how certain terrorist organizations are quickly and easily associated with religion. Additionally, helping students understand that followers of many religions have acted in violent ways will allow students to see that violence does not come from any one particular religion.

Students must learn that many violent individuals or groups have come from religions besides Islam. Ask students—do you believe Protestants are responsible for the rise of pedophilia in the Catholic Church? In other words, should all Christians be held accountable? Similarly, do you believe all Muslims should be held accountable for the fall of the World Trade Center? These kinds of questions help students to begin to deconstruct religion from its adherents.

Other Great Resources. There are many other wonderful resources teachers can find on-line with a quick Google search. For example, *Teaching Against Islamophobia* by Joe L. Kincheloe, Shirley R. Steinberg, and Christopher D. Stonebanks (2010) is a great resource. Also, read this *New York Times* interview with students called "Growing Up in a Time of Fear: Confronting Stereotypes about Muslims and Countering Xenophobia," which also has lesson plans and a reading guide (Gonchar & Schulten, 2015). These resources, and more, are available to teachers quickly and easily.

Media Analysis

A key component to CDP is media analysis, through which teachers must teach the history of the media in politics, the impact of neoliberalism on the integrity of the media, and the diversity of media sources. Most of the teachers and students I interviewed saw mainstream media as an impediment to learning unbiased information about Muslims and the War on Terror. One teacher I interviewed, Cain, even described the media as "an intellectual ghetto." Challenging Islamophobia and improving tolerance towards Muslims requires deconstructing media rhetoric and its underlying ideology. The following section will provide suggestions for addressing this with students.

Compare Media Coverage of Previous Wars with Current Wars. Studying how previous wars were presented and discussed in different forms of media can help students recognize how the media has evolved, or not evolved, over time. George, for example, noticed significant differences between the media coverage of the Vietnam War and the War on Terror. Show students clips from 13-episode PBS series called *Vietnam: A Television History* (1983). It can be found on YouTube, available to watch for free. PBS also has some excellent History, Civics, Geography, and Culture lesson plans on its website in relation to the war, with tie-ins to the War in Iraq. When studying the changes in how media sources present different wars, it is important to also discuss the changing socio-economic structure of media corporations, as well.

Study Media Deregulation. Over the past century, how different media sources are organized has shifted significantly, and this greatly impacts the way the news is covered. Teachers can have students study the history of the deregulation of media in the United States. Teachers can start by showing some helpful videos, such as the six-minute clip by Abby Media Roots uploaded to YouTube on December 6, 2009 (Martin, 2009). Discuss the rise of the Telecommunications Act of 1996. Prior to the signing of this act by President Bill Clinton, companies could only own 40 radio stations. Now the ownership is unlimited. Teachers can ask students: (a) What are the pros and cons of limiting this ownership?, (b) What were the impacts of ending these limitations with the signing of the Telecommunications Act of 1996?, (c) Do you think that the media should serve the role of a business or should it be a public good? To understand the history of the 1996 Act, have students compare the Communications Act of 1934 and the Telecommunications Act of 1996. Ask students: (a) How do these two pieces of legislation differ in their approach to regulating media? Students can conduct research and present them to the class. Students can also have a jury trial in which each side presents their case and evaluates which Act better preserved the integrity of the press. Prior to engaging in this activity, it would be important for teachers and students to develop a list of elements of journalism that they value, and why. To develop this list, teachers can ask students: (a) Why do we need a free press?, (b) What stories that you think are important might not be covered in a fair way if we did not have a free press?, (c) What makes the media "free"? These questions are important to ask in a national context, but can also be interesting and informative when discussed in light of how other countries maintain the structure of their media.

Teachers can discuss the general, international trends of media consolidation. Teachers can ask students to evaluate how the rest of the world perceives the consolidation of the media. For example, in nations described as authoritarian by many NGOs and research institutions across the globe, consolidated media (whether by a dictatorial or capitalist regime) is often synonymous with excessive state control. How do you think the United States fits this bill, given that within America recent media mergers have led to only 6 major media corporations?

The 6 major media corporations, or "The Big Six," include: Comcast, The Walt Disney Company, News Corporation, Time Warner, Viacom, and CBS Corporation. Have students divide into six groups, each group investigating which media outlets each of "The Big Six" own. For example, those in the News Corporation will find they own Fox News and National Geographic, among others. These conversations will put U.S. media trends in a global context. Teachers can also focus on what many individuals consider "conservative" news outlets and compare them to more "progressive" news outlets.

The organizational and funding structures for media outlets that are perceived to be more "conservative" and those that are perceived to be more "progressive" are often quite different, and this does have an impact on the kinds of stories these agencies report. Teachers can ask students to analyze the ideology of conservative news media outlets, such as Fox News. First, students and teacher can come together and define what the term "ideology" means. Next, teachers can have students participate in a picture language activity, in which the teacher prints out a series of pictures of headlines about the same topic that read stereotypically "conservative" or "progressive." Teachers can ask students to silently work as a team to group the headlines into one of two piles based on whether or not the students believe they are conservative or progressive media sources. Then teachers can look at articles on Student News Daily, a non-profit current events website for high school students. There are articles posted with Student News Daily commentary, which also include questions that teachers can use to incorporate discussion in their classrooms. For identifying media bias, the website provides the following types of media bias to look out for: (a) omission, (b) selection of sources, (c) story selection, (d) placement, (e) labeling, and (f) spin. Omission is described as leaving out other sides of the story. Selection of sources is described as including more sources which support one particular view over another. Story selection is defined as a pattern of highlighting stories that support one particular perspective. Placement refers to the physical location of the story either within a newspaper, or during a television show. Labeling can be tagging one person or idea with extreme labels and tagging another person with different or opposite views with either much lighter or no labels. Spin occurs when the story seems to only have one interpretation and can be evidenced through the tone of the author. For example, Fox News was often described by students and teachers as racist and a "joke." Ask students: (a) This is a strong statement. Do they agree, why or why not?, (b) Are there specific examples of biased reporting that students can find? Have them go out and find examples on their own, through on-line searches. National Public Radio and The New York Times have been described as "liberal brainwashing." Ask students if they agree with this, why or why not? Then, have students investigate the founder of Fox News, chairman, and CEO of News Corporation, Rupert Murdoch, and his business and political affiliations. Ask students to investigate their funding structure. How might this funding structure impact the corporations' ability to tell the news? Then have students investigate National Public Radio (NPR). Ask students: (a) What is the funding structure of NPR and their affiliate member stations?, (b) How is this different from Fox?, and (c) How might this impact NPR's programming? For all of these topics, teachers may also ask students how might these events (political affiliations of CEOs, media consolidation, etc.) influence how certain media sources present current events related to Muslims? Studying media deregulation, and how it currently relates to present-day funding structures, will help students recognize the very real influences on media—chiefly, money.

Expose Students to Diverse Media Sources. To help students recognize and understand media propaganda, encourage students to read sources that diametrically oppose. For example, how do Al-Jazeera and Fox News discuss the War on Terror? How does the language used by each media source compare to language used by political progressives or conservatives? Another great resource is a magazine called *The Week*. In this weekly subscription magazine, journalists compare what major media sources are saying about current events. This may help students to understand how politicians and the media position themselves in an argument, and why. Additionally, the magazine has an educational program with weekly lesson guides for teachers. Diverse media sources will help students see the expanded dialectic about Muslims, 9/11, and a variety of other topics.

How does the Media Talk about Torture? Understanding what torture is, and then how diverse media sources talk about it, will help students recognize potential bias in the media. Ask students to analyze controversial issues and events in relation to the media's discussion on torture. For example, NPR banned the use of the word "torture" in 2009 and instead began to use the Bush administration's euphemism, "enhanced interrogation techniques." Alicia Shepard, NPR Ombudsman, explained the decision by stating:

No matter how many distinguished groups—the International Red Cross, the U.N. High Commissioners—say waterboarding is torture, there are responsible people who say it is not. Former President Bush, former Vice President Cheney, their staff and their supporters obviously believed that waterboarding terrorism suspects was necessary to protect the nation's security. One can disagree strongly with those beliefs and their actions. But they are due some respect for their views, which are shared by a portion of the American public. So it is not an open-and-shut case that everyone believes waterboarding to be torture. (Shepard, 2013, para. 10)

Glen Greenwald, a prominent journalist and lawyer, criticized this decision by NPR and other media outlets, calling it a method of corruption enablement. He wrote the following:

This active media complicity in concealing that our Government created a systematic torture regime, by refusing ever to say so, is one of the principal reasons it was allowed to happen for so long. The steadfast, ongoing refusal of our leading media institutions to refer to what the Bush administration did as "torture"—even in the face of more than 100 detainee deaths; the use of that term by a leading Bush official to describe what was done at Guantanamo; and the fact that media outlets frequently use the word "torture" to describe exactly the same methods when used by other countries—reveals much about how the modern journalist thinks. (Greenwald, 2009, para. 4)

Ask students to research and analyze both perspectives: (a) What do they think the role of the media should be in this case?, (b) How did the media later on report Obama's efforts to end these kind of interrogation techniques with Executive Order 13491—Ensuring Lawful Interrogations?, (c) What do they think of the state of torture within the U.S. legal system today, with Guantanamo Bay still remaining open? Demonstrating to students how each media source discusses these controversial topics helps them to make up their own minds in an informed way.

Of course, these economic drivers have much to do with the rise of neoliberal economic policies. Once students understand the breadth of ownership of these News Corporations, ask students how this ownership structure is reflective or not of neoliberal influence? Have students read "Global Media, Neoliberalism, and Imperialism" by Robert McChesney (2001). Then ask them to answer the following questions: What is neoliberalism? What is imperialism? What is the global media system? Then place students in small groups and let them share their responses. Give students poster papers and markers to write their responses. Hang students' posters and compare each group's answers. Ask students to reflect on the following follow-up questions: What is the connection between neoliberalism, imperialism, and the global media? See what students answer on this broad question. If you do not get responses that create a dialogue ask more specific questions such as: (a) How does neo-liberalism influence the deregulation of the global media?, (b) In what ways does neoliberalism and the deregulation of the market influence imperialism?, (c) What is the role of the global media system in influencing neoliberalism and imperialism?, (d) What, if any, connections exist between neoliberalism, imperialism, global media system, and the War on Terror? Have students' research examples to provide evidence for their analysis.

Of course, the media is a reflection of the culture, and it is clear through the analysis presented in this book that American culture is one greatly influenced by Islamophobia and neoliberalism. To this end, it may be useful to have students crunch some numbers and conduct a cost-benefit analysis (CBA) of sorts to determine how certain players in the War on Terror end up.

Economic Analysis

Money makes the world go 'round, as they say. Therefore, evaluating the winners and losers in the War on Terror will shed some light on ulterior motives for engaging in the ongoing War on Terror. It may also shed some light on how destitute young men and women perhaps feel there is no other choice but to fight, even if the world will consider them a terrorist. Again, this in no way excuses or justifies killing innocent victims, but can help students understand the psychological motives of people who are willing to blow themselves up to make a point.

Economic Analysis of the War on Terror: Who Wins? If even Pope Francis says one of the causes of terrorism is excessive greed, perhaps there is something to investigate there. George discussed the economic drivers of war with his students. You, too, can ask your students to learn how the War on Terror has impacted the U.S. and the global economy. A useful and vetted resource for this is Brown University's Cost of War project. They have a section on Corporate Power and Profiteering in which they criticize the "revolving door" between the large defense contractors and government, such as between Halliburton and the Bush administration. Defense contractors also helped to provide arms to the Iraqi government, leading to two major challenges— increased debt for Iraq, and the leaking of arms to organizations such as ISIS/ ISIL. Countless articles recount the many atrocities committed by these companies. One example is that of Kellogg Brown & Root (KBR), a former

Halliburton subsidiary. Having secured almost $41 billion in war contracts, the company has paid over $129 million in fines and settlements for issues including sexual assault, overcharging, racial discrimination, wrongful death, and human trafficking (Greenwald & Crowe, 2012). There are also documentaries, such as *Iraq for Sale: War Profiteers*, available free on-line. These resources will open students' eyes to the economic drivers for promoting the War on Terror.

Boom and Bust: How Wars Create Profit in the U.S. Teachers can make copies of the Imperialism Chapter 7 to share with students, especially the sections that discuss how the U.S. economy is tied to war. Ask students, (a) Do they think it is morally right for the U.S. economy to be tied so closely with war—why or why not?, (b) What are some other ways that different national economies create profits for themselves—ask students to do research on this, (c) What can the students do to draw attention to this, or to express their concern about these issues? Teachers can bring up nation-states like Bhutan, which, instead of evaluating Gross Domestic Product (GDP) on an annual basis to determine the strength of their economy, have devised what they call Gross National Happiness. Gross Domestic Product tallies up the total value of products and services generated within a country. Gross National Happiness measures the progress of sustainable economy and social development, while also ensuring that the environment and local culture are protected. Ask students: (a) Which method for determining national well-being sounds better to them, and why?, (b) What are the pros and cons of each?, (c) If they could devise their own method of determining national well-being, what would it be, and why?

Understanding the modern-day economy is key to unveiling reality, although it can be frustrating and saddening for students. These sorts of deep questions will prepare students, however, to not only inherit the world we have created for them, but also to build a new world that is even better than the one we left in their trust. As students' eyes open up to the world around them, they will be ready to question everything. One thing that is absolutely critical to question, as students become ready, are sources of information that may have always seemed objective and truthful to them—textbooks.

Textual Analysis

A key component to CDP is textual analysis, through which teachers and students must learn that textbooks are subjective, not objective and become able to expose the selective tradition in textbooks. As demonstrated through Chapter 5, teachers and students must constantly scrutinize what and how textbook authors write. Only through dissecting preconceived notions, and exploring where they may come from, can students truly discern their own opinions of a particular historical event. History depends upon who is telling it, and students must know that.

Expose Students to Diverse Educational Resources. Using many textbooks will help students sense the similarities and differences among them, and lead to their questioning as to why these differences and similarities may exist. In order to rupture the hegemonic curriculum presented in the textbooks, George selected excerpts from various resources. Linda recommended specifically Howard Zinn's *A People's History of the United States* (1980), and Sandy Tolan's *The Lemon Tree* (2007). I also recommend excerpting chapters from Naomi Klein's *Shock Doctrine* (2007). Articles from a variety of news sources will also demonstrate to students the various frameworks used by journalists, and how these frameworks reflect the political leaning of the resource itself. Students will begin to ask themselves: why did the author write this as he or she did? This leads me to my next point.

Encourage Students to See Textbook Authors as People, not All-knowing Authorities. Teachers must encourage students to research the people who write their textbooks. What things can students learn about the authors' beliefs based on other personal and professional information they find on-line? How might this impact the kind of worldview these authors support in their textbooks? Seeing textbook authors and people, too, will help students recognize that no thought or idea can exist outside of the person who wrote it or spoke it—thus, everything must be evaluated based on who the individual is, or what the organization stands for.

Research and Critically Analyze Textbooks and their Publishing Companies. Organizations and publishing companies, too, have political leanings that will influence the content of their textbooks. Encourage students to research the funding structures of the textbook publishing companies. Ask them to research what kinds of reviews the textbooks receive on-line. What are the opinions of other teachers, authors, and readers? I encourage teachers to follow one of George's strategies, which was asking students to write a letter to textbook companies providing a critique of these books and asking them to improve certain sections to reflect more diverse opinion.

This book itself is a wonderful resource for textual analysis. Have students read scanned excerpts of high school textbooks and analysis sections, and ask them to analyze both the textbook and my own analysis: (a) What similarities and differences do the students notice within and across textbooks?, (b) Are there any similarities between the textbooks I analyzed, and the ones your students read in class?, (c) What is their analysis of my opinion, knowing what they do about my social and political position on these topics? These questions and more will help students reflect on outside influences on textbooks.

Finally, another important topic to inspect with students is the role of California and Texas in shaping national textbook standards. Since these states boast the largest number of public school age students, California and Texas school boards enjoy the most clout with textbook publishing companies. The Texas school board is known for demanding textbooks that are patriotic and religious, for example, casting doubt on the theory of evolution. California textbooks are known for demanding greater social representation of minority groups, and are opposed to overt representations of fast food because it is unhealthy (Ravitch, 2014). Have students form small groups and research either the California or Texas school board textbook selection system. Do they think that the fact that Texas is a conservative state, and California a progressive one, that the two states balance each other out? Is there a better way that they can imagine managing the textbook publication system? Understanding the political climate in which textbooks are created is another important step in developing a critical awareness of how history and society are described in school.

Engage in Critical Dialogue of What Terrorism Is, and Who Gets to Define It. The very use of the term terrorism is a complicated one, especially within textbooks. Ask students to consider the use of the word terrorism in the textbooks I analyzed in the Chapter 5, and when and how it is applied. For example, not all textbooks referred to the bombing of the Federal Building in Oklahoma City by Timothy McVeigh as an act of terrorism. Ask students—should this constitute a terrorist act, as some of the textbooks claimed? Why or why not? Do students similarly agree that school shootings, such as at Columbine, constitute a terrorist act as some of the textbooks claimed? What about other mass shootings, such as the Charleston Church Shooting perpetrated by a white Christian supremacist? (Gladstone, 2015). Why or why not? Ask students how they define terrorism, and if they agree with the books' definitions. These exercises will help students reflect on what subtle or hidden meanings are embedded within words, and how those meanings are reproduced and circulated through textbooks.

Engage in Dialogue about the Term Fundamentalism. Another term that students can investigate is fundamentalism. I have used this technique in Muslim

American student focus groups, and have found that students feel that the definition of fundamentalism itself seems anti-Muslim. To evaluate your own textbooks, ask students to look up and share the definition of fundamentalism or fundamentalist in their textbook: (a) Where else have they have heard this term?, (b) What sorts of images and thoughts come to mind when they hear this term?, (c) How do they see the use of this word relating to Muslims?, (d) To Jews?, (e) To Christians?, (f) In the War on Terror? Deconstructing words helps students uproot biases within textbooks, and themselves. Another way students can uproot biases is through evaluating textbooks for "card stacking."

Check for "Card Stacking." When playing poker with a friend who keeps an ace up their sleeve, there is no way you can win. Similarly, when textbook authors "stack the deck" against certain groups of people, it is near to impossible for people to develop a positive image of them. George mentioned that he often points out where books "stack the deck." In these instances, the book purports to be fair-minded and objective, yet the examples and language used holds inherent bias. He pointed this out in one of his textbook's descriptions of Palestinians and Israelis. Ask students to look at definitions and quotes in the comparisons of two groups or sides of a story (especially if one of those groups is an ally of the United States, and the other is not). Through seeing patterns in where and how the game might be stacked, students will recognize elements of the lopsided dialectic.

Textual analysis often demonstrates that history books are biased. To develop new understanding of history and reality requires historical analysis of past national and global events and their connection to contemporary historical context.

Historical Analysis

A key component to CDP is historical analysis through which future teachers must learn about the roots of Islamophobia, controversies surrounding U.S. foreign and domestic policy, and deeply understand the theoretical foundations of the United States. Almost all of the teachers I interviewed pointed to the importance of the past in understanding the present. George spoke often about the historical cords leading up to an event. Bill and Cain taught students through Constitutional precedent. Linda and Patrick hoped that through analysis of the past that students would learn to improve the future. The following section will provide strategies for helping students gain greater awareness of how the past impacts the present in terms of the War on Terror.

Analyze Historical Representations of Muslims, Arabs, and Middle Easterners. The old adage that a picture is worth a thousand words certainly holds true in this context. Ask students to evaluate the predominant images of Muslim Americans, or Muslims, in their social studies textbooks. Another great jumping-off point is Linda Steet's seminal work, *Veils and Daggers: A Century of National Geographic's Representation of the Arab World* (2000), in which she discusses the underlying assumptions about Muslim women apparent in how they were portrayed by National Geographic. How might this rendering of Arab and Muslim women carry over into today? Are there any common themes and images? Understanding not only modern images, but historical ones, will help students recognize patterns of treatment of certain groups of people, and how this might effect the lopsided dialectic in present-day. Seeing how the past influences the present in terms of 9/11 is also a useful exercise.

Conduct an Historical Analysis of 9/11. There were many reasons why terrorists did the unthinkable during the early morning hours of September 11, 2001, and not all of them had to do with hating U.S. freedom. It is critical that students recognize that very few situations are causes by one influence. Students could use the textbook excerpts analyzed in this study to dig deeper into sparsely mentioned reasons for 9/11. After reading excerpts of chapters, can students challenge the simplistic explanation given by President Bush and the principal at George's school "that they did this because they hate our freedom" and think of various causations to 9/11 in addition to the ones provided on the surface level? Have students discuss their findings. Why were these issues mentioned with less frequency? Do students believe this changes the way they or others may view the conflict? Should more detail be provided on these other sources of conflict? Why or why not? Have students gather information from alternative resources about what happened on 9/11 then have them reinterpret what happened on 9/11 based on the evidence gathered. This historical analysis will enrich students' perceptions of the world around them, and the fact that there are rarely simple or straightforward answers to complex situations. Another way to rethink history is by flipping the script.

Rewrite History by Flipping the Script. If history was recounted through various perspectives, it might help us all have a greater sense of empathy for those who lived it first-hand. This is especially true for marginalized people, since history is composed of stories written by the winners (Said, 2003). Have students watch the movie, *Robinson Crusoe*, from 1997 and directed by Rod Hardy and George T. Miller. See *Longbourn* by Jo Baker (2014), a retelling of Pride and Prejudice from the servant's point of view. The story is narrated by the character, Crusoe. As an activity, student teachers can "flip the script" by narrating the story from the perspective of another character, Freddi, instead of Crusoe. In groups, ask students to draw a story-board on poster papers and share their stories. Ask students to reflect on how changing the narrator of the story changes the contents of the story itself. Then have them discuss the connection between how narrations of history perspectives influence their stories and that if history were written by another narrator with a different perspective the story would have been different. Have students apply such concepts to rewrite the story of 9/11. In small groups, give students poster papers and markers and ask: Come up with alternative narratives for the event of 9/11. Some examples of perspectives are from a Muslim American man who was in the twin towers and was killed, or a seventeen year old who lived in the Bronx. The more specific the character, the easier it will be for the student to develop a story-board. Flipping the script can help students develop greater empathy, and train them to consider silenced voices when they learn about current events. This can also be useful when looking back U.S. foreign policy.

Analyze and Discuss Controversial U.S. Foreign Policy from the Past. This helps students question the idea of American Exceptionalism, teaching them that the United States' international policing is not always welcome. A starting point for analysis could be the involvement of the CIA in toppling various left-leaning democratically elected leaders in the 1950s–1970s. Couched under a fear of communism, there were many economic reasons for these covert operations. Have students analyze the successful overthrow of Iranian Prime Minister Mohammad Mosaddegh; the CIA-backed coup on Guatemalan President Jacobo Árbenz; and US funding the slaying of Chilean President Salvador Allende. Ask students to analyze the overlap of political and economic motivations for these coups. Naomi Klein's *The Shock Doctrine* (2007) is an excellent resource for this. While some may say it is "un-patriotic" to evaluate past wrongdoings, is it not through revisiting our mistakes that one becomes better? If the United States did not second-guess slavery, would we still have plantations today? The bedrock of a strong democracy is not only the ability, but also the necessity, for constructive criticism. It is through these efforts that teachers can train students to understand both the good and bad that has happened within the boundaries of their own nation-state, and decide for themselves what they would like the future legacy to become.

Review and Dialogue about Previous Human and Civil Rights Abuses. Reflecting on skeletons in the closet when it comes to treatment of people either within the U.S., or citizens of other countries, is also important. Bill and Cain suggested "comparing Muslim and Arab American experiences to Japanese Americans in camps, to the Civil War, the violations of civil liberties and civil surveillance as well." In regards to the Japanese American internment camps, teachers could first anti-Japanese propaganda they find through a Google image search. Ask students: What kinds of stereotypes do you think these images represent? Then teachers can show students videos posted on the National Park Service Website about Wartime Propaganda Films (n.d.). There is also a 14 minutes video available on YouTube called *Manzanar: "Never Again"* (2009) that tells the story of the Japanese internment camps. Ask students: (a) What is the role of the National Park Service?, (b) Why do you think this bureau of the U.S. government believe it is important to recall these stories? Ask students: (a) What were the impacts on Japanese American people interned during WWII?, (b) How do these two examples relate to how Muslim American people are treated now?, (c) Do you think the measures taken by the state were and are warranted in these cases?, (d) Are there any cases in particular in which the U.S. Government prevented a terrorist or internal attack through these methods?, (e) Are there any cases in particular in which the detention or poor treatment of a Japanese or Muslim/Arab American resulted in severe violation of human rights? The National Park Service has lately increased federal funding support for these cultural and historical monuments—there are many resources to be found at the National Park Service website. Using these materials demonstrates to students that it is, in fact, a national value to remember these past injustices, to honor those who suffered unfairly, and hopefully bring a sense of accountability going forward. Some students may be surprised that the Japanese were once an enemy of the United States since the country is currently an ally. It would be useful for teachers to talk about these previous human rights abuses in light of the shifting allegiances that are a part of most nation-states' foreign policy.

Investigate Who has been an "Enemy" or "Ally" in the United States' Past and Present. The enemy is constantly changing. This will help students understand the political and economic motivations for the war, and encourage greater critical probing of the reliance on a religious or cultural framework as an explanation. For example, students could compare the War on Terror to the Cold War. How does the fear of Islam compare to the fear of communism? How were the Russians represented during the Cold War, and how do those images compare to representations of Muslims now? How are Russians represented today in comparison to during the Cold War? Are they considered allies of the United States in the present time? Teachers can have students read the article "Is Islamophobia the new McCarthyism?" by journalist Andrew Bace-vich (2012) featured in *Mother Jones*. It may also be useful for teachers to do a Google image search for anti-Muslim propaganda and anti-Communism propaganda, and then ask students what the similarities and differences are between these images. This will help students to recognize propaganda tactics and patterns, and help them make up their own minds about what level of concern they should have about Islam. In the following two sections, I will provide suggestions of how teachers can encourage a greater historical under-standing of our current economic system.

History of Neoliberalism and Violent Conflict. To understand the present situation, teachers can have students study the rise of neoliberalist poli-cies, beginning with Milton Friedman's reaction against Keynesian thought. Study with students the rise of the so-called developmentalist economies in countries such as Chile, Argentina, Uruguay, and parts of Brazil during the 1950s–1970s. These countries believed they could escape poverty through an inward focusing industry, rather than the exportation of natural resources. These countries also advocated a nationalization of key industries, such as oil and minerals, so that many of these proceeds remained part of a public trust within the government. Decisions to nationalize natural resources and limit foreign investment were not popular among the business elite in the United States, and soon accusations that these countries were, in fact, Communist soon abounded (Klein, 2007). Discuss this history with your students, and study the toppling of democratically elected governments who were opposed to laissez-faire markets such as the overthrow of Mossadegh in Iran, Guzmán in Guatemala, and Allende in Chile. When analyzed economically, what do you see in common among these separate events? What role did the CIA and US government play in the establishment of new economic policies, and the creation of dictatorships? The violent and oppressive history of these current economic policies may lead students to questioning the United States contin-ued faith in them, and prompt them to inquiry about the role of imperialism in the current U.S. government.

History of Imperialism and a Greater Understanding of How it Works. Again, while it may seem un-patriotic to some, constructive criticism, even about the most controversial of topics, can only lead to positive change for all. This is true especially when it comes to the conversation about imperialism, which may be a trigger issue for some students, and perhaps also their parents. Teach-ers can divide the students in small groups and ask them to imagine they are a nation planning an imperial conquest over another. Teachers can prompt the students by asking them: What are some of the strategies their imperial nation would follow to achieve victory against the natives of the occupied nation? In other words, ask students to make a list of what they would do to take over a country. Have student read Kay Givens McGowan's (2010) article "Weeping on the Lost Matriarchy," and reflect on the similarities between the students' strategies and British settlement in their colonization of Southeastern Native American societies. Make connections between past and contemporary imperialism by asking students: (a) Could the War on Terror be considered imperialism—why or why not?, (b) What are some commonalities between the War on Terror and Colonization of Southeastern Native American societies? While these questions are controversial, analyzing the history of imperialism in the United States will see that to be an American means inheriting a legacy that is not 100% perfect. This also holds true, certainly, when it comes to historical white supremacy.

History of Christian and White Supremacist Terrorism. The United States was built on racism leveraged against (a) Blacks, (b) Native Americans, (c) Jews, (d) Irish, (e) Japanese—really, anyone who was non-white. It is an ugly truth, but one that Americans must not forget, lest we stray toward that direction again. Teachers can ask students to study incidents of violence perpetrated by white supremacist groups, such as the Ku Klux Klan (KKK). For example, the KKK killed over 3,000 free blacks between 1865 and 1877 (Grimes, 2008, para. 7). Ask the students; do they consider these terrorist attacks? Another recent incident of white supremacist violence was the June 17, 2015 Charleston shooting in which then 21-year-old Dylann Roof killed nine black people attending church. The United States' Department of Justice investigated whether the shooting should be classified as a hate crime, or an act of domestic terrorism, ultimately deciding upon the former (Craven, 2015). What do you think? Patrick gave his students examples of other Christian so-called terrorist groups, such as the Irish Republican Army (IRA). Teachers could ask students to conduct research on the IRA, and what sorts of methods they used. Ask students: (a) What were the goals of the IRA?, (b) How would you compare the IRA to other terrorist organizations?, (c) How are they similar and different?, (d) Conduct historical analysis on how the British media and newspapers portrayed the IRA, and (e) Compare your findings with how the American media typically portrays Muslim terrorists. Linda brought up the example of fundamentalist Christians killing an abortion doctor. There are actually many cases of bombings and shootings directed at abortion providers, such as the bombing of a clinic by Eric Robert Rudolph in January 29, 1998 (Mattingly

& Schuster, 2005). Another example is the death of Dr. Barnett Slepian who was shot to death in his home on October 23, 1998 (Yardley & Rohde, 1998). Another Christian terrorist anti-abortion organization, called Army of God, sanctions violence against any pro-Choice people or organizations. There are many more examples of attempted murders, assaults, and kidnappings by fundamentalist Christians angry about abortion. Bring some examples to class and ask students if they consider these terrorist attacks. Bringing these examples to students' attention will remind them that the treatment of black, brown, yellow, and red individuals has often been extremely violent at the hands of white individuals, especially in the United States. However, it is not enough to analyze the events themselves—though we have already discussed the media, it is important for teachers to also ask their students to consider how the media presents these attacks by Christian fundamentalists.

Specifically, it is important for teachers to ask students to reflect on whether or not certain sources of media have a pattern of treating violence at the hands of White Christians differently than violence at the hands of Muslims, or Blacks, or any other non-White, non-Christian individual. Teachers can ask students to analyze how the media responded to these Christian fundamentalist attacks. Have them look at more conservative media sources, such as Fox News, and more progressive media sources, such as NPR. For example, after the death of another abortion provider, Dr. Tiller, right wing Anne Coulter said on a Fox News interview on June 22, 2009, "I don't like to think of it as a murder. It was terminating Tiller in the 203rd trimester." What kind of message might this send to viewers, and how might this impact the evolution of the history of the understanding and classification of terrorism? The perpetuation of white supremacy hate crimes is just important to reflect upon as the methods by which they tend to be reported. In addition to studying violence at the hands of white supremacists, it is also important for teachers to ask their students to study acts of gross violence at the hands of the United States government, specifically politically-motivated torture.

The History of Torture. Politically-motivated torture has been sanctioned by the United States in varying degrees since the beginning of the War on Terror, and it is important for students to (a) understand what kinds of torture is used, (b) what the international community thinks about it, (c) and what the Constitution says about these sorts of egregious and inhumane acts. Cain and Bill also taught students about how politically-motivated torture conflicts with human rights. In order to understand the implications of torture, students could learn more about the history of modern physical and psychological techniques, such as electroshock and waterboarding. Some suggestions for jumping-off points are:

- 1949: Geneva Conventions and the discussion of treatment of prisoners of war, including agreements preventing the use of torture methods (Pictet, 1960)
- 1950s: CIA-funded psychological torture experiments at McGill University with Dr. Donald Ewen Cameron (Klein, 2007)
- 1960–1980: CIA-supported coups of democratically elected governments in the Southern Cone (Chile, Uruguay, Argentina, Brazil) and the widespread use of torture, taught to South American dictators by CIA agents (Klein, 2007)
- 1963: CIA torture training manual published, called KUBARK Counterintelligence Interrogation (Klein, 2007)
- 1940–July, 2016: US Amy School of the Americas, re-named the Western Hemisphere Institute for Security Cooperation. A training ground for Central and South American dictators. Torture was among some of the lessons learned (Karlin, 2012)
- 1984: United Nations Convention against Torture, signed by many countries, including the United States in 1988 (Cumming-Bruce, 2014)
- U.S. Code Chapter 113C on Torture (Legal Information Institute, 2002) can describe exactly how the United States defines torture and what rules and regulations prevent it from happening
- 2006: Hamdan versus Rumsfeld Supreme Court Case in which the Supreme Court decided that the Bush administration's attempt to set up its own war tribunals to try terrorism suspects could not proceed because its structures and procedures violated the Uniform Code of Military Justice and the four Geneva Conventions signed in 1949 (McBride, 2006)
- Ask students—what is happening in Guantánamo Bay now? What do they think should happen, based on their historical analysis?

The War on Terror is not something that we have the luxury of looking back upon and evaluating at a distance. There are real and current implications, such as the financial costs for some and the financial gain for others, and the rise of terrorist organization such as Islamic State of Iraq and Syria (ISIS). It is important for teachers to think about how lesson plans about history may be transferable to current events, so that students can weave analysis of past events with current ones, and become better prepared to handle the challenges they will inherit. The following suggestions present some ideas about how teachers can encourage students to connect the past to the present and consider their own opinions about the potential direction of the future.

The Rise of ISIS/ISIL. Understanding how the rise of this militant group is connected with the past is an important step in greater understanding of the present. The rise of the Islamic State in Iraq and Syria (ISIS) or the Islamic State in Iraq and the Levant (ISIL) are one and the same. The group began by splintering off of al Qaeda. Their goal is to create an Islamic state. There are many theories as to how ISIS/ISIL arose. Noam Chomsky, an American intellectual who spent the bulk of his career at the Massachusetts Institute of Technology (MIT), believes that the rise of ISIS/ISIL is directly related to the War on Terror and state-sanctioned violence wielded against civilians in Iraq and Afghanistan. For more on his opinions, share with students his interview with Portuguese National TV on May 2015 (Mateus, 2015). The interview is precisely 27:26, but the question asked by the interviewer at 21:38 is a good starting point. The question was, more or less, "Where is the root of terrorism?" Chomsky's response touches on the double meaning of words used in political discourse, which he divides into (a) the literal meaning, and (b) the political meaning. He says we use the word "terrorism" to mean "there terrorism against us, but not our terrorism against them." The greatest terrorist campaign, in his opinion, is President Obama's use of drones. In Chomsky's opinion, ISIS is an outgrowth of the U.S. invasion of Iraq, as well as the U.S.'s allegiance with one of the most conservative Islamic states—Saudi Arabia. How do students react to listening to Chomsky's opinion? Ask students to share their feelings and opinions. The United States may share some accountability in the rise of this militant group, a fact that will likely be very eye-opening for many students. This begs the question: if violent militant groups who oppose the United States are on the rise, is the United States actually winning in the fight against terrorism?

War on Terror: Are We Winning? How to define a "win" is challenging in this situation. Ask your students, has the United States accomplished its mission in curbing terrorism worldwide? Ask students to brainstorm other methods for minimizing terrorism. After studying these topics, students will be primed to voice their own opinions on what steps the United States could take in order to improve the situation.

Historical analysis helps to interpret the past and to identify patterns. However, history is meaningless unless connected to the present. One way to examine how history impacts the present is through conducting analysis of the legal documents that were and are the bedrock of how our society functions in the present. Legal analysis helps to explore how historical documents, such as the US Constitution, are applied today.

Legal Analysis

An integral element to CDP is legal analysis through which future teachers must study the function of law as a form of public pedagogy, assessing the applications and violations of the United States Constitution and legal system. There are many ways in which teachers can help their students understand the legal implications and ramifications of the War on Terror and 9/11. Deep study of these fundamental elements of the United States democracy will also serve students well in their future as active participants in American democracy. A good first step is for teachers to have their students study some of the most important texts: the U.S. Constitution and the Bill of Rights.

Teach students to Study the War on Terror and Patriot Act through the U.S. Constitution and Bill of Rights. Both of these documents are critical for understanding the U.S. democracy. Bill and Cain taught their students historical and contemporary government, providing a strong base in the foundational documents and inherent values, which govern American policy. This allowed for greater understanding of how certain actions either defied or preserved Constitutional and Civil Rights. Studying the Constitution is also very important for Muslim American students so they may defend themselves using the law when their rights are violated (Abowitz & Harnish, 2006). Teachers may either enroll their classroom in the We the People Program, purchase textbooks recommended by their committees, or download free lesson plans available on-line. Just like history, laws are documents that could become reinterpreted and applied in multiple ways. That is why when Bill and Cain's students conducted an historical analysis of Supreme Court rulings. They found the rulings differed even though they were based on the U.S. Constitution. Engaging students and teachers in legal analysis provides them with practical understanding of holes in the laws and their interpretations and applications. While studying these documents is important, there are many more.

Another opportunity for legal analysis is by having students or future teachers reading and analyzing important legal documents, such as the Declaration of Independence, The United States Constitution, and The 27 Amendments found on U.S. Citizenship and Immigration Services website. Have students summarize the entire Declaration in one paragraph. Compare their summaries in small groups and discuss differences in their interpretations of the Declaration. Then, have students read Naomi Wolf's "Freedom is intended as a challenge" in her book *Give Me Liberty: A Handbook for American Revolutionaries* (2008). In the last paragraph, Wolf wrote: "So real patriotism means understanding that the Declaration of Independence charges us categorically and always as Americans to rise up in person against threats to liberty" (p. 21) Have students compare their interpretations of the action the Declaration calls for to that of Wolf's. As a class, discuss what is meant by "real patriotism" and what the Declaration of Independence might call on us to do in our contemporary social, political, and historical context. Teachers could follow up this conversation by having students or future teachers watch "A Declaration of Interdependence: A crowdsourced Short Film" by Tiffany Shlain (2011). Then ask students: (a) Compare your interpretation of The Declaration of Independence with Wolf's and the version in this film, (b) How do they differ in content and tone?, (c) Do you think this is an appropriate or inappropriate update of the document?, (d) How do you think those involved in the original document would view this version, and why?, (e) What are the differences between the words independence and interdependence? Next, of course, teachers can bring up one of the most important documents to the U.S.—the Constitution.

Studying the Constitution may seem boring initially to students, but its practical applications in every-day life are undeniable. One tactic is to encourage students to compare amendments of the Constitution to how those amendments are managed in day-to-day life. For example, students could watch the comedy show "The Democracy Handbook" with the Egyptian satirist Bassem Youssef (n.d.) in which he compares the US democracy to dictatorships in the Middle East. For example, have students watch the two episodes "The Right to Buy Guns" and "The New Hate Economy" (in which some gun shops do not sell guns to Muslims). Then, let students compare the democratic system of the U.S. to systems in the Middle East. Ask students: Is the right to buy guns the right of all people? Why or why not? I recommend watching all Bassem Youssef's series about different aspects of democracy such as: immigration, presidential campaign and elections, voting, freedom of speech, forming militia at war with the US government, and the separation of church and state. Then develop questions based on Bloom's taxonomy to lead the dialogue about democracy in the United States. In 1879, Thomas Jefferson wrote letters to James Madison stating: "Every constitution, then, and every law, naturally expires at the end of 19 years. If it be enforced longer, it is an act of force, and not of right." The last Amendment of the constitution was ratified in May,

1992—that is 24 years; five more than Jefferson recommended. In small groups have students evaluate the United States Constitution and provide suggestions to amend the constitution. How can we add the voices of people whose input was originally excluded from the Constitution such as women and people of color? Revisiting these critical documents can serve as the background for a deeper conversation on the current state of the U.S. democracy.

Teachers can also encourage students to reflect deeply on the role and status of democracy itself. For example, students could read the *Deep State: The Fall of the Constitution and The Rise of a Shadow Government* (2016) by former GOP congressional analyst Mike Lofgren and evaluate his argument about a hidden government that rules the United States behind the scene day in and day out regardless of who gets elected as president. Ask students for their reactions and feelings then respond to the following questions: Is democracy applicable or is it a utopia? Can students come up with an alternative system other than democracy? Conducting legal analysis and seeing its application in history and everyday life provides insight for those who have the ability to reflect upon it. The ability to reflect is one that can be developed over time, and allows individuals the flexibility of mind to be able to think critically.

Foster Reflection and Personal Connection to Current Events Related to Muslims

A key component to CDP is reflection and a personal connection to history through which future teachers must be able to express their experiences and connect emotionally to history in order to diminish the sense of alienation that many experience to the current events unfolding around them. One of greatest challenges for teachers is handling students' dispositions, particularly when they take dialogues personally or disrespect others' opinions. Freire (1970) believed that students' prior knowledge should be part of the curriculum, and that teachers should encourage a connection between history and the student's personal lives. Consequently, teachers must work with students' dispositions and prior knowledge. A first step to get students thinking about these current events is to ask them how they—or their families—were personally affected.

Personal Narratives of How 9/11 Affected the Student. An important step in helping students reflect in a personal way is through asking them how they individually experienced these events. Teachers could ask students how 9/11 and the War on Terror affected their personal lives. If students did not experience 9/11 firsthand, have them interview a family member or friend of their choice about the topic. Another way to personally connect is to speak with an individual who experienced the War first-hand.

Speak with Veterans, and Learn about Veterans' Issues. Testimony from soldiers is often hard to hear, but it is an important step in students' understanding on a personal level the reality of war. Students could read testimony from soldiers, interview veterans, or investigate the work of organizations such as Veterans for Peace. George suggested discussing the impact of the War on Terror on returning soldiers' lives and suicide rate. Students could speak with people that have experience on veteran suicide hotlines. A specific example to share with students is that of Jacob George, a returned Afghani war veteran who spoke out against the wars and wrote music in support of peace. Jacob took his life in September 2014. You can learn more about his story on *DemocracyNow*, published on September 29, 2014 (Goodman, 2014). Teachers can ask students: (a) How are soldiers impacted by what they did?, (b) How does this affect your opinion of the war itself? These stories may trigger some strong feelings among students, so it is important for teachers to be sensitive to this. There may also be strong feelings elicited when speaking about the impact on innocent people killed in the war, too.

Analysis of the Impact on Iraqis and Afghanis. Though many U.S. soldiers have died, and experience severe Post-Traumatic Stress Disorder (PTSD), there were many innocent Afghanis or Iraqis killed who did not choose to participate in war. According to Brown University's Cost of War project (2015), the number of U.S. combat fatalities in Iraq and Afghanistan passed 6,800 at the beginning of 2015. Prior to introducing these numbers, ask students to estimate these numbers on their own. Approximately 210,000 Afghanis, Iraqis, and Pakistanis have died as a direct result of the war. There is an enormous difference between U.S. military personnel deaths, and the number of innocent civilian deaths in Afghanistan, Iraq, and Pakistan. In terms of the impacts on Iraq, teachers can share with students The Iraq Body Count (IBC) project, which has one of the most detailed and best researched accountings of civilian violent deaths. Based in the U.K., they are often cited by *The Guardian* and other major U.K. press. The Iraq Body Count documents 146,181–266,591 civilian deaths since the 2003 invasion of Iraq. Brown University's Cost of War project also estimates the number to be around 165,000 civilian deaths as a direct result of the U.S. invasion. When compared to the American and U.K. combat service members killed in Iraq, the difference in fatalities is very, very stark. As of January 2015, more than 26,000 Afghani citizens have been reported dead as a direct result of the war (Crawford, 2015). The Independent, a U.K.-based magazine, produced a stunning graphic image (Bartlett, 2014) comparing the number of U.K. service members who have died in the Afghani war (at the time of the article, 435, according to the U.K. Ministry of Defense), and the number of Afghani civilians who had died at the time of the article's release (at the time of the article, around 21,000). The graphic has images of the U.K. service people in the top left corner of a rectangle, taking up about 1/45th of the rectangle's space. The rest of the rectangle is black, and represents the 21,000 Afghani civilian deaths. This image, and these stories, are powerful to share with students. It is also powerful to share with students how the shape of the cities in these countries was deeply changed.

Another impact of the war on Afghani and Iraqi soil is the destruction of infrastructure. One egregious example is the October 3, 2015 bombing by U.S. forces of a Doctors without Borders hospital where 12 staff members and at least 10 patients, including children, died. People across the world consider this a grave violation of International Humanitarian Law. Students could also connect with relief agencies associated with helping Afghan refugees such as Mahboba's Promise, easily found on-line. Destruction of culture is another impact of the War in Iraq, including ransacking and bombing of museums and holy sites with ancient and sacred elements of cultural heritage. For example, the National Museum in Iraq, which held precious relics from the Mesopotamian Civilization, was sacked during and after the 2003 invasion of Iraq. Many criticized the United States for not helping to prevent this cultural destruction. Another example is the destruction of political culture. When the United States occupied Iraq, they promised to quickly hand over the reign to democratically elected officials. Instead, the United States removed the existing Constitution, left untouched by Saddam Hussein, and created a new one; privatized most state-owned companies including the national oil wells, leaving many Iraqis who worked in the private sector without jobs; and imported multinational goods and services which could have been provided by Iraqis (Klein, 2007). How do you compare this information with the response provided by Ralph Peters, a retired U.S. Army officer, in USA Today in 2006?

> They [the Iraqis] preferred to indulge in old hatreds, confessional violence, ethnic bigotry and a culture of corruption. It appears that the cynics were right: Arab societies can't support democracy as we know it. And people get the government they deserve. For us, Iraq's impending failure is an embarrassment. For the Iraqis—and other Arabs— it's a disaster the dimensions of which they do not yet comprehend. They're gleeful at the prospect of America's humiliation. But it's their tragedy, not ours. (para. 7)

Teachers can ask students: (a) Has a store, restaurant, or museum that you really loved ever get destroyed, or have to move away?, (b) If so, how did that make you feel?, (c) How do you think this feeling might compare to what people felt when their entire cities were destroyed?, (d) Write a fictional story about an individual who loses everything due to war. Though facing these realities can be difficult, students will build a sense of empathy because of it. Finally, it is also critical that teachers have space to reflect personally on these stories.

Incorporate Teacher Reflection. As I interviewed teachers, it seemed that the actual interview process itself was a useful reflective practice. Since I have included my interview question list with the appendix of this book, teachers may use this as a guide to reflect more on how they do teach about the War on Terror and Muslims, and how they may change their pedagogies to become more critical moving forward.

Conclusion

This chapter provides lesson plans to teach current events such as 9/11 and the War on Terror using critical dialectical pedagogy (CDP) within the broader state standards benchmarks. It is particularly useful for teachers to do so through greater knowledge of Muslims, media analysis, economic analysis, textual analysis, historical analysis, legal analysis, and deep self-reflection. Through these methods, teachers can rebuild the lopsided dialectic of 9/11 and the War on Terror, and create a safe space in which students truly consider and unveil reality.

I consider this book part of a team effort towards a practical application in the field of critical pedagogy. The field of critical pedagogy has grown in so many positive and impactful ways since its birth, yet it has much more growth to come in order to truly address in actionable ways the injustices of our time. It will be necessary for teachers like you to both challenge yourself to change for the better and also push this field and these ideas to become the best they can be. The following chapter addresses some of the limitations of critical dialectical pedagogy and vision for future research that would help expand the theoretical and methodological aspects of it.

References

Abowitz, K. K., & Harnish, J. (2006). Contemporary discourses of citizenship. *Review of Educational Research, 76,* 653–690.

Bacevich, A. (2012, September 25). Is Islamophobia the new McCarthyism. *Mother Jones*. Retrieved October 12, 2016 from http://www.motherjones.com/politics/2012/09/jerry-boykin-islam-andrew-bacevich

Baker, J. (2014). *Longbourn*. New York, NY: Vintage Books.

Bartlett, E. (2014). How many Afghan civilians have died in 13 years of war? *The Independent*. Retrieved September 29, 2016 from http://i100.independent.co.uk/article/how-many-afghan-civilians-have-died-in-13-years-of-war--lkcwu0y6Le

Brosnan, P. (Actor), Hardy, R., & Miller, G. T. (Director). (1997). *Robinson Crusoe* [Motion picture].

Craven, J. (2015, July 23). Dylann roof wasn't charged with terrorism because he's White. *The Huffington Post*. Retrieved September 29, 2016 from http://www.huffingtonpost.com/entry/dylann-roof-terrorism_55b107c9e4b07af29d57a5fc

Crawford, N. (2015, March). Costs of war. *Watson Institute of International and Public Affairs, Brown University*. Retrieved September 29, 2016 from http://watson.brown.edu/costsofwar/

Cumming-Bruce, N. (2014, December 11). Torture fight set back by U.S. failure to prosecute, U.N. says. *The New York Times*. Retrieved September 29, 2016 from http://www.nytimes.com/2014/12/12/world/juan-mendez-calls-for-cia-torture-prosecutions.html

Freire, P. (1970). *Pedagogy of the oppressed*. New York, NY: Herder & Herder.

Ghazali, A. S. (2012, January 1). *Chronology of Islam in America*. Retrieved September 29, 2016 from http://www.amchronology.ghazali.net/AM_Chro_2012_edition.pdf

Gladstone, R. (2015, June 18). Many ask, why not call Church shooting terrorism? *The New York Times*. Retrieved September 29, 2016 from http://www.nytimes.com/2015/06/19/us/charleston-shooting-terrorism-or-hate-crime.html?_r=1

Gonchar, M., & Schulten, K. (2015, December 17). Growing up in a time of fear: Confronting stereotypes about Muslims and countering Xenophobia. *The New York Times*. Retrieved September 29, 2016 from http://learning.blogs.nytimes.com/2015/12/17/growing-up-in-a-time-of-fear-confronting-stereotypes-about-muslims-and-countering-xenophobia/

Goodman, H. A. (2014, September 17). 4,486 American soldiers have died in Iraq. President Obama is continuing a pointless and deadly Quagmire. *The Huffington Post*. Retrieved September 29, 2016 from http://www.huffingtonpost.com/h-a-goodman/4486-american-soldiers-ha_b_5834592.html

Greenwald, G. (2009, June 6). The NYT's nice, new euphemism for torture. *Salon*. Retrieved September 29, 2016 from http://www.salon.com/2009/06/06/nyt_5/

Greenwald, R., & Crowe, D. (2012, February 14). No success in Iraq—Unless you're a war profiteer. *The Huffington Post*. Retrieved September 29, 2016 from http://www.huffingtonpost.com/robert-greenwald-and-derrick-crowe/no-success-in-iraq--unles_b_1151171.html

Grimes, W. (2008, January 30). A long surrender: The Guerrilla war after the civil war. *The New York Times*. Retrieved September 29, 2016 from http://www.nytimes.com/2008/01/30/books/30grimes.html?_r=0

Haddad, Y., Smith, J., & Moore, K. (2006).*Women in America: The challenge of Islamic identity today*. Oxford: Oxford University Press.

Haque, A. (2004). Islamophobia in North America: Confronting the menace. In B. Van Driel (Ed.), *Islamophobia in educational settings* (pp. 1–19). London: Trentham House.

Karlin, M. (2012, June 10). The school of the Americas, the CIA and the US-condoned cancer of torture continue to spread in Latin America, including Mexico. *Truthout*. Retrieved September 29, 2016 from http://www.truth-out.org/news/item/9685-the-school-of-the-americas-the-cia-and-the-us-condoned-cancer-of-torture-continues-to-spread-in-latin-america-including-mexico

Kincheloe, J. L., Steinberg, S., & Stonebanks, C. D. (Eds.). (2010). *Teaching against Islamophobia*. New York, NY: Peter Lang Publishing.

Klein, N. (2007). *The shock doctrine: The rise of disaster capitalism*. New York, NY: Henry Holt & Company.

Laughs for Islam. (2011, December 28). *The Washington Post*. Retrieved October 14, 2016 from http://www.washingtonpost.com/wp-srv/special/nation/laughs-for-islam/

Lofgren, M. (2016). *The deep state: The fall of the constitution and the rise of a shadow government*. New York, NY: Penguin Books.

Malcom X, & Haley, A. (1992). *The autobiography of Malcolm X: As told to Alex Haley*. New York, NY: Ballantine Books.

Malcolm X's Famous Speech After Returning from Mecca. (2011, December 12). *HonestyIsKey*. Retrieved October 14, 2016 from https://www.youtube.com/watch?v=tuHYZdf-ad0

Manseau, P. (2015, February 9). The Muslims of early America. *The New York Times*. Retrieved from http://www.nytimes.com/2015/02/09/opinion/the-founding-muslims.html?smid=fb-nytimes&smtyp=cur&bicmp=AD&bicmlukp=WT.mc_id&bicmst=1409232722000&bicmet=1419773522000&_r=2

Martin, A. (Producer). (2009, December 16). *Media deregulation*. Retrieved from https://www.youtube.com/watch?v=4_f7s2p1dS0

Mateus, A. (Interviewer), & Chomsky, N. (Interviewee). (2015, May). *Noam Chomsky—Interview with Portuguese National TV*. Retrieved September 29, 2016 from https://www.youtube.com/watch?v=oGmJAQtRHGk

Mattingly, D., & Schuster, H. (2005, April 19). Rudolph reveals motives. *CNN Law Center*. Retrieved September 29, 2016 from http://www.cnn.com/2005/LAW/04/13/eric.rudolph/

McBride, A. (2006). Hamdan v. Rumsfeld: Supreme Court History Landmark Cases. *PBS*. Retrieved September 29, 2016 from http://www.pbs.org/wnet/supremecourt/future/landmark_hamdan.html

McChesney, R. (2001, March). Global media, neoliberalism, and imperialism. *Monthly Review: An Independent Socialist Magazine*. Retrieved September 29, 2016 from http://monthlyreview.org/2001/03/01/global-media-neoliberalism-and-imperialism/

McGowan, K. G. (2010). Weeping for the lost matriarchy. In B. A. Man (Ed.), *Daughters of Mother Earth: The wisdom of native American Women* (pp. 53–68). Westport, CT: Praeger.

Muslim Americans: No Signs of Growth in Alienation or Support for Extremism Mainstream and Moderate Attitudes. (2011, August 30). *Pew Research Center: U.S. Politics & Policy*. Retrieved October 14, 2016 from http://www.people-press.org/2011/08/30/muslim-americans-no-signs-of-growth-in-alienation-or-support-for-extremism/

Muslim Diversity. (n.d.). *Detroit Public TV: PBS Learning Media*. Retrieved October 14, 2016 from http://dptv.pbslearningmedia.org/resource/islam08.socst.world.glob.muslimdiv/muslim-diversity/

Naff, A. (1993). *Becoming American: The early Arab immigrant experience*. Carbondale, IL: Southern Illinois University.

Never Again. (2009, August 27). *The National Parks/Manzanar & PBS*. Retrieved October 14, 2016 from https://www.youtube.com/watch?v=XgmY2P-xT_Y

Nyang, S. S. (1999). *Islam in the United States of America*. Chicago, IL: Kazi Publications.

O'Neal Parker, L. (2011, November 5). Son's Muslim faith divides one Black family. *The Washington Post*. Retrieved October 14, 2016 from https://www.washingtonpost.com/local/sons-muslim-faith-divides-one-black-family/2011/10/28/gIQATW7KqM_story.html

Orfalea, G. (2006). *The Arab Americans: A history*. Northampton: Olive Branch Press.

Pennington, R. (2008, November 26). Arabs and Islam: Are all Arabs Muslims? *Muslim Voices*. Retrieved October 14, 2016 from http://muslimvoices.org/all-arabs-muslim/

Pictet, J. S. (1960). The Geneva Conventions of 12 August 1949. Commentary. *Military Legal Resource*. Retrieved October 14, 2016 from http://www.loc.gov/rr/frd/Military_Law/Geneva_conventions-1949.html

Ravitch, D. (2014, March 28). Public education: Who are the corporate reformers? *Moyers and Company*. Retrieved from http://billmoyers.com/2014/03/28/public-education-who-are-the-corporate-reformers/

Said, E. (2003). *Culture and imperialism*. New York, NY: Vintage Books.

Shepard, A. C. (2013, March 4). Your voices have been heard. *National Public Radio*. Retrieved September 29, 2016 from http://www.npr.org/sections/ombudsman/2009/06/torture_round_two.html

Shlain, T. (2011). *A declaration of interdependence: A crowdsourced short film*. Retrieved September 29, 2016 from https://www.youtube.com/watch?v=fzZ1Gl5UfE0

Sirin, S., & Fine, M. (2008). *Muslim American youth: Understanding hyphenated identities through multiple methods*. New York, NY: New York University Press.

Smith, J. (2000). *Islam in America*. Cambridge: Cambridge University Press.

Sobri, D. (2015, May 26). 10 countries with the largest Muslim population in the world. *Malaysian Digest*. Retrieved October 14, 2016 from http://www.malaysiandigest.com/features/555150-10-countries-with-the-largest-muslim-population-in-the-world.html

Social Studies Standards Grades 9-12 (2009, June). In *New Mexico Public Education Department*. Retrieved September 4, 2017, from http://www.ped.state.nm.us/standards/Social%20Studies/Social%20Studies%209-12.pdf

Steet, L. (2000). *Veils and daggers: A century of the National Geographic's representations of the Arab world*. Philadelphia, PA: Temple University Press.

Suliman, A. (2016, September 23). Sufi sect of Islam draws 'spiritual vagabonds' in New York. *The New York Times*. Retrieved October 14, 2016 from http://www.nytimes.com/2016/09/25/nyregion/sufi-islam-new-york-converts.html?_r=2

The Democracy Handbook with Bassem Youssef. (n.d.). *Fusion*. Retrieved September 29, 2016 from https://www.youtube.com/watch?v=aDGBYbiIzKg&list=PLxd0bZ1RXEzuPCekFpssGpsyUdNSNFLNX

The Future Global Muslim Population. (2011). *Pew Research Center: Forum on Religion*. Retrieved October 14, 2016 from http://www.pewforum.org/files/2011/01/FutureGlobal-MuslimPopulation-WebPDF-Feb10.pdf

Tolan, S. (2007). *The lemon tree: An Arab, a Jew, and the heart of the Middle East* (reprint ed.). New York, NY: Bloomsbury USA.

U.S. Code Chapter 113C on Torture. (2002). *Legal Information Institute.* Retrieved October 14, 2016 from https://www.law.cornell.edu/uscode/text/18/part-I/chapter-113C

Vietnam: A Television History. (1983, October 4). *WGBH, PBS.* Retrieved October 14, 2016 from https://www.youtube.com/watch?v=TqKi-SyRA7I

Wartime Propaganda Films. (n.d.). *National Park Service.* Retrieved October 14, 2016 from https://www.nps.gov/tule/learn/photosmultimedia/wra-documentaries.htm

What You need to Know about Arabs vs. Muslims. (2012, March 23). *ADDtv Channel.* Retrieved October 14, 2016 from https://www.youtube.com/watch?v=tdZuzdh2DZI

Wolf, N. (2008). *My library my history books on Google Play give me liberty: A handbook for American revolutionaries.* New York, NY: Simon & Schuster.

Yardley, J., & Rohde, D. (1998, October 25). Abortion doctor in buffalo slain; Sniper attack fits violent pattern. *The New York Times.* Retrieved September 29, 2016 from http://www.nytimes.com/1998/10/25/nyregion/abortion-doctor-in-buffalo-slain-sniper-attack-fits-violent-pattern.html?pagewanted=all

Younis, M. (2009, March 2). Muslim Americans exemplify diversity, potential. *Gallup.* Retrieved from http://www.gallup.com/poll/116260/Muslim-Americans-Exemplify-Diversity-Potential.aspx

Zinn, H. (1980). *A people's history of the United States.* New York, NY: HarperCollins.

· 1 0 ·

DIALECTICS AND THE FUTURE
OF DEMOCRACY

Next Steps

The fact that 9/11 and the War on Terror occurred so recently and are still ongoing, paired with the emotional trauma associated with the event and the aftermath might scare many teachers away from educating their students on the topics. Nevertheless, teaching about these controversial events is critical in understanding resultant policies and contemporary sociopolitical context as well as developing learners' intellectual skills and democratic values. Teachers might feel confused on what to teach due to a lopsided dialectic about 9/11 and the War on Terror due to a public pedagogy that dehumanizes and silences Muslims, while covertly pushes the agendas of neoliberal imperialism in the local and global society. They might even feel discouraged to teach about the topics due to power structures that dictate the curriculum and penalize intellectual freedom. In such an environment, it may often seem easier to follow the path of least resistance and teach using a banking model of education that fosters the fear, resists dialogue, educates only for success on state exams, and maintains the status quo.

It is also extremely hard to teach critically or imagine that schools can transform society or mend democracy given the fact that to do so not only requires swimming upstream, but also necessitates an interrogation of the school system itself, and schools' role in reproducing inequality in society. But what is more ethical? To teach knowing that the end result serves a system of oppression that threatens the democratic foundation of society, or to teach for social change towards justice and inclusion? And if it is the more ethical choice, than how can researchers, administrators, and educators in the field of critical pedagogy support teachers on the ground in making the right choice?

Imagine if all teachers take up the call to action of this book. The outcome might be a rational and accepting environment, humanization of Muslims, and restoration of democracy in society. There could be change in the way society sees all marginalized populations, in fact. Perhaps changes in the way current events are perceived—not as what is hot on the news, but as social issues that concern everyone. If there was a drive to dig beneath the surface, the news media would likely supply this demand. The way the media handled current events coverage might even change, to become more inclusive and dialectical, in response to student-citizens who required and demanded it. And imagine the impact of such an education on students. How self-assured, compassionate, and intelligent they must be to demand these kinds of changes. How well-rounded, opinionated, yet flexible of mind they might be. The wisdom they might gain and always return to, having been trained to listen to all voices before making judgments, their hunger to learn all sides to the story. How might these students, in a critical mass, impact their communities? What if instead of division and hatred, there was mutual caring and respect? What if instead of focusing on blame, communities concentrated on improving society? What if love reigned, instead of hate?

This is not a shot in the dark, nor is it a foolish mental exercise. Making these changes are possible, and these changes often begin in the hands of one, caring teacher. However, teachers need support in this process. They need theories and methodologies to serve as a launching pad for their own creative juices. This is the purpose of this book—to help teachers accomplish what may seem impossible.

I add my effort to Freire, critical pedagogues, and other scholars and educators who believe teachers can work within their classrooms to challenge societal injustice and achieve humanization to all. I developed Critical Dialectical Pedagogy (CDP) that focuses on exposing the system of inequality through dialectics of a current event. By showing the missing parts of the lopsided dialectic of 9/11 and the War on Terror, I am hoping that teachers might understand that to formulate an opinion about a current event, all parts of an event and all voices and perspectives must be included. Then teachers might realize that they have to think logically about the given information before they engage their students in a dialectical dialogue about all the findings. Through deep analysis of reality, teachers could rectify the lopsided dialectics in their classroom, help students to critically think about given information, and develop an inclusive classroom. By involving all students, including Muslims, in dialogues and activities regarding social matters, a teacher is likely to humanize all.

Since I consider this book part of a team effort towards a practical application in the field of critical pedagogy, I have included here my future vision of the next steps to push this field and these ideas to become the best they can be.

Paulo Freire's work is philosophical, and therefore provides the advantage of imaging and reinventing his work in many ways. For teachers, it might feel challenging to translate his philosophy into classroom application. Therefore, my original intention in writing this book was to create a practical application of Paulo Freire's theories—one that educators could see and use as a teaching manual. So I began by breaking down his main points into categories and developed questions based on which I assessed the pedagogies of teachers interviewed in the book. However, through this process, I noticed a few instances in which the theory and practice of Freire's critical pedagogy were not enough, particularly when considering dialogue, as well as the more specific goal of unveiling reality about a current event such as 9/11 and the War on Terror. That is why I added the dialectics aspect to critical pedagogy, as well as the tailored focus on current events such a 9/11 and the War on Terror. As a Professor, currently teaching diversity courses in higher education, I imagined how I could transform his ideas into applicable classroom activities. That is why I added classroom suggestions to accompany the theory since I did not want to ask teachers to do the impossible. I wanted to make it possible for you, and them, to re-evaluate the narrative about Muslims and the War on Terror.

Although CDP stands on the shoulders of giants—such as Freire, without whose ideas my own would be impossible—my theory also has holes and areas for improvement. There is room for growth within CDP, and it will be made all the better with ideas, suggestions, and empirical research. Here are some areas in which I believe CDP may grow and evolve.

Evaluating CDP in the Classroom

CDP relies on teachers' willingness to be objective; to consider themselves as outsiders of the current event, neither oppressor nor oppressed. But, what if a teacher is affected by a current event? For example, what if the teacher is a Muslim, or what if the teacher had a relative impacted by a terrorist attack? How could they apply CDP in such case? It would be useful to conduct a future study to explore how influences in teachers' lives might affect their ability to utilize CDP in the classroom and effectively teach in a dialectical manner about current events such as 9/11 and the War on Terror. Similarly, when teachers do have strong feelings or personal involvement in a particular current event, it would be useful to learn what specific strategies are helpful for teachers to be able to balance sharing their personal experiences with students while giving students the space to formulate their own opinions without pushing them to think in a particular way.

CDP as Applied to Other Current Events and Political Movements

CDP is a tool that is specifically designed for teachers hoping to rectify the lopsided dialectic about 9/11, the War on Terror, and Muslims. However, its underlying theories and methodologies can be adapted to teaching about other current events, and other oppressed peoples. As such, I see two potential avenues for further research. The first is to apply CDP to the study of political movements such as Black Lives Matter or the stand against the Dakota Access Pipeline by the Standing Rock Sioux Tribe in Native American land. The second is a comparative analysis between current events related to 9/11 and the War on Terror, juxtaposed with the War on Drugs. There are opportunities for comparisons between treatment and representation of Muslim Americans in comparison with African Americans, who are more likely to be incarcerated due to drug-related offenses than any other racial or ethnic category. This comparison might provide more clarity of both current events.

CDP and Its Impact on Society

I see CDP as a big project that starts with teachers in their classroom and ends up branching out into society to change it for the better. Therefore, an important next-step in furthering the goals of CDP are including individuals and institutions at various levels of power to work together towards enhancing the dialectic, and, thus, democracy. An obvious first step might be the evolution of this theory for school administrators. How can we train them to be more critical, knowledgeable, and supportive of critical thinking? Another obvious example is education policymakers—how might the theory and methodology evolve to incorporate them? This, of course, could extend into various other sectors of society—the financial sector, media, etc. How can CDP help teachers work with other people in society towards repairing democracy?

CDP and Its Impact on Muslim American Youth

The book discussed the effect of the lopsided dialectic on Muslim American youth struggling with questions of faith and citizenship, and an oppressive classroom environment. Future projects, however, might explore how a transition from a lopsided to a complete dialectic impacts Muslim American youth. For example, how does rectifying the lopsided dialectic through CDP mitigate Muslim American youths' questions of faith, or improve their sense of citizenship and belonging? This book has evaluated the results of an uncritical, banking pedagogical model. To convince other teachers, administrators, and professors of education of the usefulness this method, it will be important in the future to evaluate its efficacy. However, a closer read on the problems (specifically, the impact of culture, media, and textbooks on Muslim American students) could provide more fuel for the fire in terms of convincing educators of the need for change. My study only brushed the surface on investigating this issue. Understandably that investigating these issues is extremely hard. Nevertheless, I believe it might be done. Future projects might explore these issue in depth. For example, asking Muslim American students specifically how textbooks may have contributed to their relationship to their faith, identity, and sense of citizenship and belonging?

CDP and Its Impact on Diverse Muslim Populations

While I included a diverse array of Muslim American youth in the study, the sample size does not represent a large enough sample for each category. For example, although my study involved both Arabs and non-Arabs, males and females, Shia's and Sunni's, etc., the sample size for each category was too small to draw any conclusions about how males and females may have reacted to and integrated negative representations of their culture and faith. It would be useful for future research studies to either evaluate a larger sample size of various categories to draw statistically significant conclusions about specific Muslim (and Arab) populations, or to focus the study on one particular, segmented population. Nonetheless, by examining the roles of various types of Muslim diversity, this study was able to answer questions other studies could not. Specifically, this study gives a detailed picture of Islamophobia and imperialism that affects all types of Muslims.

CDP and Triangulation of Data

One of the strengths of the research conducted for this book are the inclusion of textual analysis, cultural/media analysis, student analysis, and teacher analysis. Having all of these elements in conversation with each other paints a more complete picture for the reader. However, there are ways to bring this triangulation of research into even closer relief. For example, it would be useful to interview teachers, *their* students, and analyze *their* textbooks. In my study, the teachers were not the educators of the students' interviewed, and so while it is possible to demonstrate correlations between teaching and student experiences, it is not the same as demonstrating the relationship between a particular teacher and student. On the subject of textbooks, not all my teacher participants used the textbooks I chose to analyze. However, selecting to examine the recently adopted textbooks by the New Mexico Department of Education ensured that the context analyzed is also what multiple generations of students and teachers will use in their classrooms, likely until 2017. Such timeliness makes the study relevant and hopefully will play a role in influencing textbook authors and producers to become more conscious about the contents of these textbooks and how they affect Muslim American students' lives. However, analyzing the specific textbooks that interviewed teachers use might give greater insight into their pedagogy. This is an opportunity for future researchers in this field.

Even though the teachers' pedagogies of 9/11 and the War on Terror cannot be generalized, their perspectives give us an idea of how these topics are taught, the challenges that accompany teaching these issues, and some curricular and pedagogical recommendations for how to teach them. My hope is that the research will inform teachers' curriculum and material choices and presentations so that misrepresentations are mitigated.

Conclusion

Teaching about 9/11 and the War on Terror in critical ways might be considered swimming backstream and therefore might result in backlash. What might scare teachers even more is not knowing the content of the events or even how to teach it in a way that does not anger everyone. The lopsided dialectic that favors the agenda of neoliberalism and silences Muslims has clouded the truth about 9/11 and the War on Terror making it stressful for teachers to fathom what happened or what to teach. Facing such stress might defer teachers from pursuing teaching about these events altogether and instead focus on students' success on state exams. Unfortunately, this way students would become ignorant about the real world and would only learn to obey authorities and accommodated to a system that maintains the status quo. Understanding such dilemma prompted me to write this book in which I outline a theory I call Critical Dialectical Pedagogy (CDP) that branched from Critical Pedagogy to provide the knowledge about the topics as well as how to teach it. This way teachers will have a jumpstart on teaching these topics. Still, CDP is imperfect and there is room for growth. Future research is needed in evaluating the effectiveness of CDP in the classroom particularly when a teacher is involved in the current event they teach about. Applying CDP to teach about other current events and political movements than 9/11 and the War on terror, the impact of CDP in society through the work of teachers with individuals and institutions at various levels of power towards enhancing the dialectic, and, thus, democracy. I also see growth in research that investigates the impact of CDP on Muslim American youth in general and on specific Muslim populations, finally enhancing the triangulation of data in a future study that interview teachers, their students, and analyze their textbooks would provide a more complete picture for the reader.

· 1 1 ·

PUTTING THE PUZZLE PIECES TOGETHER

When they see divergent voices and they get different information, they start making up their own minds. Often times, they are in conflict with what they hear at home or on TV, versus the research that is being done that shows them another reality. Over the years I have seen students that get angry, but that are very hungry to find out what the truth is. It seems once a student starts developing a taste for what is really happening, then it is kind of like the doors of perception start opening. It is very powerful. They get hungry for more information. They wanna know what is going on, they don't care for Fox News or CBS. They wanna know really what the facts are and what it means to them.

—Bill & Cain [teachers], personal communication (May 29, 2010)

Bill and Cain experienced first-hand the impact of exposing students to diverse perspectives. By researching opposing views on a topic, the students start developing their opinions after initially being confused or angry due to finding new information that shakes the stability of a core unidimensional perspective that students had absorbed through ideas at home or on the TV. Bill and Cain drew a conclusion that when students become exposed to multiple perspectives on an issue, they feel that there is not one truth presented by public pedagogy through mainstream media outlets such as Fox News or CBS. Instead, they understand that they can access the truth by researching alternative views on a subject. By collecting enough evidence and examining how convincing the data are, they start identifying the truth. Once students develop such habits of searching for the truth, they will not become satisfied with only one explanation or a single perspective. If all teachers engaged their students in research and collecting evidence to find the truth about a topic, schools would equip students with the knowledge that would help them imagine and plan a better future. In this case, education would indeed become a cornerstone in transforming society for the better.

The Problem: Teachers Are Not Teaching Critically about 9/11 and the War on Terror

The terrorist attacks of September 11, 2001 caused more than the destruction of the World Trade Center, and the killing of 2,996 innocent people, it also caused lasting pain and grief of an entire nation and led to sweeping changes in social system and policies. It was an event that has spawned various complex issues that may be hard to understand. Nevertheless, teaching about 9/11 and the War on Terror is extremely important.

In a time where education is increasingly shaped by the ethics of the market, and saturated in a culture of fear, teachers are scared or ill-equipped to teach critical and democratic education. Notions of solidarity and respect run the risk of being lost. However, in the face of fear, confusion, and ignorance, teachers are our nation's best chance at cultivating the opposite. Through facing the facts head-on and encouraging students to question everything, teachers can indeed cultivate love, understanding, and knowledge. It is only through strengthening these qualities among our youth that the United States can truly address the root of the War on Terror, and begin to see all of humanity as one. The time has come that teachers see their role in helping students search for the truth about current events in order to unravel reality.

The War on Terror and 9/11 are current events that define the socio-historical context of contemporary United States. The attacks on the World Trade Center happened more than a decade ago, yet the United States still has troops deployed in Afghanistan, Iraq and other Muslim countries. Many Americans' lives have been impacted because of the event and the War. Because of these lasting impacts, people have strong opinions about the topics and teachers therefore might be hesitant to teach about them.

However, teaching about current events such as 9/11 and the War on Terror is urgent. Students must be able to make sense of the world in which they live.

Teaching about controversial current events also provide rich opportunities for teachers and students to develop skills such as critical thinking and democratic ideals. Unfortunately, there are societal pressures from individuals and institutions in power that encourage, or perhaps even enforce, that teachers teach in certain ways or avoid teaching about certain topics. Teachers must ask themselves in these instances—what is school for? Certainly it is important for students to learn skills and abilities that will prepare them for professional life, but shouldn't they also be equipped to build a better society?

The War on Terror has increased the acceptance and power of today's neoliberal society and all sectors have been impacted, including the educational system. Schools are now geared to train students to serve the continuation and expansion of neoliberalism which now exists on a global scale and serves the interests and increases the wealth of a handful of elites on the expense of the masses. Neoliberalism exists in a culture of terrorism in which fear, silence, discrimination, and loss of freedom are the new modes of existing. Schools serve the interests of neoliberalism by encouraging or allowing heightened security, non-dialogical pedagogy, blind patriotism, and intolerance. Acceptance of these radical changes is made easier through a selective tradition represented by a hegemonic curriculum, as well as a public pedagogy spread by the media. Embracing neoliberal ideologies and policies contributes to the minimization of intellectual curiosity, breeds intolerance, and corrodes democracy.

According to many philosophers of education and teachers, critical pedagogy is one of the best methods for teaching students about the War on Terror, and about any subject matter, in that it encourages the development of critical thinking skills. Critical pedagogy is a philosophy of education that emerged to liberate learners, so that they may exercise free will. The ability to think for oneself is urgent, especially in a day and age when very strong opinions about the War on Terror are espoused left and right. Many of the strong opinions tend to be anti-Muslim. For many students, and teachers, it is hard to know what to think, and many feel pressured to choose a particular side. Critical pedagogy theorists recognize that education is political. They recognize that this anti-Muslim sentiment is a temporary situation that can be changed by a deep understanding of reality. They give teachers the tools to change the world through the application of this ground-breaking theory.

Through presenting two oppositional models of education; banking and problem-posing, Paulo Freire's goal in *Pedagogy of the Oppressed* was to demonstrate that there was only one path that teachers should choose—problem-posing. Freire contrasted banking education with a problem-posing educational approach by highlighting the instructional methods used in each approach and the impact of the outcome of such educational approach on students and society. A banking model's one sided, hierarchical, and non-dialogical approach results in indoctrination of students with dominant ideology and a fatalistic acceptance of oppression as inevitable. On the other hand, a problem-posing education that investigates reality, eliminates hierarchy, embraces dialogue, and empowers students to reflect upon and transform the world.

In order to help teachers support open-mindedness and social justice for all, it was important to evaluate how teachers teach about controversial current events such as 9/11 and the War on Terror. The interviews of the five teachers from New Mexico help illuminate common struggles, and provide a rich and informative method for reflection for teachers and critical pedagogues reading the book in the hopes of developing better strategies to combat xenophobia and bias. As a former teacher, I know how important it is to reflect on one's teaching, and also how little time there is for it. Reading about the stories and experiences of the teachers interviewed is an important step in the direction of understanding what it means to be a critical pedagogue, and how to get there. Teachers were evaluated based on a rubric developed based on Freire's critical pedagogy in *Pedagogy of the Oppressed* that specifically focused on assessing five issues: whether the teacher unveils reality, upholds dialogue, eliminates hierarchy, encourages praxis, unveils reality, demonstrates to students that they can become agents of change, and works towards liberation. What is important to recall about these analyses is not which teachers was problem-posing or banking, but rather what each individual teacher was doing in order to improve. These teachers are the ones that understand what is at stake—the intellectual freedom and the silencing of an entire, marginalized population.

The Result: Muslim American Students Experience Discrimination and Question Their Identities

After 9/11, combining terms such as "Muslim" and "terrorist" and repeating them in society generalized all Muslims and categorized them as terrorists. Stigmatization of all Muslims as if they were one homogenous group who is an enemy of the United States supports binary thinking of good versus bad; in which Muslims are seen as evil in comparison to the United States which is good. It also separates Muslims from America, making it impossible for anyone to fathom the religious and the nationalistic identities going together or becoming compatible. In such an environment, heightened by a patriotic drive, fighting against Muslims, in lieu of fighting terrorism, is inevitable and is even heroic. This lopsided dialectic of 9/11 and the War on Terror results in fear of Muslims, and leads to a cycle of hatred, disrespect, and discrimination against them. I interviewed nine diverse Muslim American students, who shared shocking stories of violence and disrespect leveraged against them in and out of school. The more stereotypically "Muslim" they looked, the worse the discrimination became. Many of them felt that their schools and teachers had failed them. Many of them did not feel capable or comfortable with calling themselves "American," even though they were card-carrying citizens. Many of them were shocked and psychologically traumatized by the blatant ignorance and intolerance they experienced every single day at school.

These students and citizens deserve more. They deserve teachers who will stand up for critical education, discipline, and basic human rights for all living beings. They need a critical education of 9/11 and the War on Terror so that they would stop blaming Muslims for the attacks of 9/11. Nevertheless, all of the Muslim students felt that their teachers did not do enough to educate peers about the controversial events. Teachers must understand the dire effects on Muslims and other marginalized populations when they do not teach critically about current events. On the other hand, allowing students to voice their experiences, and teaching against a lopsided dialectic of 9/11 and the War on Terror, will help stop discrimination against Muslims and will help Muslim students regain their humanization in order to develop a positive sense of self. Indeed, when a teacher uses a problem-posing education, encourages dialogue and embraces diversity, this will affirm the humanity and identity of all students including Muslims, will foster tolerance, and will strengthen democratic society, and students' cognitive development.

Cause #1: Biased Textbooks and Curriculums

Breaking the cycle of intolerance takes more than understanding who Muslims are. Indeed, teachers are surrounded by a lopsided dialectic and it is hard to imagine what a holistic dialectic of 9/11 and the War on Terror might look like when the state's curriculum and textbooks include bias and misinformation. Many teachers observe that the textbooks they used demonstrated bias such as American exceptionalism, while at the same time portraying people of color such as African Americans, Native Americans, and Muslims in bad light as if they have no right to nationalistic goals, freeloaders on the American economy, or hurdles to be jumped on the race towards progress.

The textbooks industry is a complex and massive one greatly influenced by conservative states, such as Texas. These conservative views impact the way textbooks discuss controversial current events, such as the War on Terror and 9/11. Despite these strong influences, the information presented in textbooks is often considered absolute truth.

Many scholars argued that textbooks contents are not just to convey knowledge, but through a selective tradition, a textbook asserts the knowledge of elites on the expense of others, inculcate a particular national identity, and advances a certain political agenda. I examined these issues by analyzing seven U.S. History 11th Grade textbooks adopted by and in contract with the New Mexico Department of Education from 2011–2017. Textbooks often conflated Arab/Muslim/Middle Eastern identity as one, thus ignoring geographical, political, and cultural differences among them. All textbooks enforced an "us" versus "them" ideology that contrasts American identity defined by heroism, democracy, and liberation of women with an Arab/Muslim/Middle Eastern identity defined as violent cowardly, undemocratic, and oppressive to women. Textbooks pushed for patriotism and an exaggerated American exceptionalism and failed (a) to provide logical connections between 9/11, terrorism, and weapons of mass destruction, (b) present the true impact of the War on Terror on the people of Iraq or Afghanistan, (c) acknowledge the role that the United States played in the rise of terrorism world-wide, or (d) encourage critical thinking among the students reading the book. The missing and skewed information strengthen the growing lopsided dialectic about 9/11 and the War on Terror. Teachers must counter this selective tradition by questioning these resources, and encouraging students to think critically about these issues.

Cause #2: Islamophobia in the Culture

However, it is not only textbooks which influence the ability of teachers to teach critically about controversial current events. Another challenge is a form of "public pedagogy" that seeps into almost every home—the media. The media's representations and views of Muslims as backwards, oppressive, terrorists is similar to the selective tradition and hegemonic curriculum evident in the textbooks. Movies, television, video games, and the news all present the same message of Muslims—get rid of these violent, undesirable others. This image is reinforced through a comparison that the viewer would make when seeing how other religions such as Christianity, Buddhism, and Judaism are represented. Thus, the media's representations of Muslims enforce Islamophobia and reproduce the lopsided dialectic about 9/11 and the War on Terror. Consequently, it becomes easy to pass laws that take away American freedoms, swallow fundamental values, and discriminate against Muslims. The fact that Muslim students' social experiences resembled their educational ones shows the mobility between school and society and also proves the importance of teachers work in rectifying the lopsided dialectic to bring justice to Muslims.

Failing to teach against Islamophobia will likely result in an intolerance classroom environment, will further dehumanize Muslims, and will grow an already strong lopsided dialectic. Growing Islamophobia in the media and American imperialist culture contribute to the lopsided dialectic in the classroom about 9/11 and the War on Terror through bolstering stereotypes, ignorance, and fear, while minimizing or disregarding other aspects of the dialectic such as historical, political, or economic factors. For instance, Post-9/11, Islamophobia helps a neoliberalist imperialist project in Muslim land. While the media exaggerates the terrifying Muslim image, Islamophobia heightens, and by not discussing imperialism, the public is only left believing that Muslims are a big problem that needs to be dealt with instead of seeing how they are portrayed as a problem to justify occupation of their lands, and astounding financial gains for war profiteers. A war for democracy is a disguised war to serve the interests of a few elites. Unfortunately, by highlighting Islamophobia and hiding neoliberalism and its imperialist projects, the public is tricked into allowing a few elites to pursue their violence against the oppressed disposable global populations for their own economic profit. That is why teachers' role is very important to educate Americans about the reality of social, political, and historical complexities of 9/11 and the War on Terror. Understanding the complexity of the topics will help Americans make informed and rational decisions that are consistent with their democratic values.

The Solution: Critical Dialectical Pedagogy

The best method to address the causes of the lopsided dialectic of 9/11, as well as prevent the resulting alienation of innocent Muslims, is to train teachers in the art of Critical Dialectical Pedagogy (CDP).

CDP is comprised of a modified version of Freire's critical pedagogy. For instance CDP shies away from binary thinking and embraces dialectical pedagogy that celebrates diversity and complexity through examining all logical perspectives on a current event to unravel reality. In addition to the theory, CDP includes a methodological aspect that is comprised of a web of teaching methods and lessons used by other critical pedagogues to develop critical thinking skills among their students.

CDP is a theory that recognizes that most teachers fall along a spectrum between problem-posing and banking, and that teachers, as they work towards improving their skills and abilities, pass through stages of intellectual and technical development. Therefore, CDP re-theorizes critical pedagogy in a way that is more geared towards practical ways of helping teachers improve their pedagogies to rectify the lopsided dialectic of current events such as 9/11 and the War on Terror.

CDP helps teachers develop three aspects of their teaching; 1) the art of dialectics, 2) critical thinking and pedagogy skills, and 3) lesson plans that incorporate CDP while also meeting state standards. The critical thinking and pedagogy skills are based off of Freire's understanding of problem-posing pedagogues, but include more space for self-reflection for the teacher, as well as a more central role to Freire's idea of dialogue, re-imagined as dialectics. Dialectics is the central part to CDP, and it is defined as the science and art of investigating the truth about a current event through viewing the situation through multiple angles. Mastering these skills will allow teachers to use the lesson plans provided in the book in an effective way, as well as give teachers the background knowledge and confidence to build their own lesson plans. Through these efforts, it is my hope and belief that teachers will be able to rectify the lopsided dialectic about 9/11, the War on Terror, and innocent Muslims.

Where to Go from Here?

Being part of a whole, this book represents only a fraction of the great field of critical pedagogy and there is so much growth needed in order to address and counter socio-cultural, educational, and political injustices of our time and mend social democracy. I have identified areas that could become developed in future projects. For instance, evaluating the applicability and effectiveness of CDP in the classroom specifically when a teacher is traumatized by the current events they are teaching about. It would be important to see how CDP could be applied to unveil reality of other current events and political movements by directly studying them or by juxtaposing them with other current events. As well, investigating the impact of CDP on society and expanding the work of teachers beyond the school borders to mend democracy. Further, the book focused on the impact of a lopsided dialectic on Muslim youth, a reverse project that investigates the impact of a holistic dialectic on Muslim youth identities, citizenship and sense of belonging would be great in shedding light on the direct impact of CDP in the classroom. Future studies that enlarges the sample size and focus on a specific Muslim population would be important to better understand the challenges and necessities of this particular population and adapt CDP to address such needs. One of the strengths of this book is that the conclusions are drawn from a triangulation of empirical data, but this triangulation could provide a more holistic picture by interviewing the teachers of the students and analyzing the textbooks the teachers use. Also, enlarging the sample size of the teachers to examine diversity on how they teach these topics would bring nuance ideas that would help expand CDP.

Teaching to think critically, for tolerance, and acceptance certainly means teaching against powerful socio-political and economic forces. Choosing this route means walking a path full of big rocks, however, teaching against such policies is critical if we would ever dream about restoring democracy. The lopsided dialectic of 9/11 and the War on Terror is dominant, pervasive, and determined to maintain the status quo. Therefore teaching against this lopsided dialectic is like swimming against the current. This will not be easy and may involve conflicts with those in power because it rocks the boat and challenges the stability of status quo. However, teachers are uniquely positioned to open the minds and hearts of their students. It is my hope that this book will be one helping hand along the way to encouraging greater love and respect in the world for all.

Thank you for reading this book and taking action!

INDEX

Studies in Criticality

General Editor
Shirley R. Steinberg

Counterpoints publishes the most compelling and imaginative books being written in education today. Grounded on the theoretical advances in criticalism, feminism, and postmodernism in the last two decades of the twentieth century, Counterpoints engages the meaning of these innovations in various forms of educational expression. Committed to the proposition that theoretical literature should be accessible to a variety of audiences, the series insists that its authors avoid esoteric and jargonistic languages that transform educational scholarship into an elite discourse for the initiated. Scholarly work matters only to the degree it affects consciousness and practice at multiple sites. Counterpoints' editorial policy is based on these principles and the ability of scholars to break new ground, to open new conversations, to go where educators have never gone before.

For additional information about this series or for the submission of manuscripts, please contact:

Shirley R. Steinberg
c/o Peter Lang Publishing, Inc.
29 Broadway, 18th floor
New York, New York 10006

To order other books in this series, please contact our Customer Service Department:

(800) 770-LANG (within the U.S.)
(212) 647-7706 (outside the U.S.)
(212) 647-7707 FAX

Or browse online by series:
www.peterlang.com